T0149220

The
Great Highway of
LIFE

The Great Highway of LIFE

Navigating the Bible through Metaphysics

Carole Lunde

iUniverse

THE GREAT HIGHWAY OF LIFE
NAVIGATING THE BIBLE THROUGH METAPHYSICS

iUniverse books may be ordered through booksellers or by contacting:

iUniverse
1663 Liberty Drive
Bloomington, IN 47403
www.iuniverse.com
1-800-Authors (1-800-288-4677)

ISBN: 978-1-4917-9552-1 (sc)
ISBN: 978-1-4917-9553-8 (e)

Print information available on the last page.

iUniverse rev. date: 04/21/2016

There is a deeper story about the psychological and spiritual pathway that all human beings take step by step in the sure development toward its ultimate true nature as Christ in us, our glory.

By Rev. Carole M. Lunde

Other Publications by the Author

Deborah, Judge Prophetess and Seer
The Woman Born to be God's Military Leader

You Are in The Bible
Metaphysical Bible Interpretation for Your Life

Stories from Martha's House
The Biblical Gathering Place for Friends and Strangers

The Divine Design,
How to Spiritually Interpret Your Life

CONTENTS

ACKNOWLEDGMENTS

I would like to acknowledge the students who, over my years in ministry, attended my Bible classes, especially those students in the church in Lincoln, Nebraska, who shared the path of forming this book with me for three years.

Also I am immeasurably grateful to my friend and editor, Steve Sanders, who patiently read every word, commenting on the content, finding my typos and generally helping me step back and look at the work through his eyes.

PREFACE

Did you awaken one day to your spiritual nature and wonder how you got there? The flower grows from a seed in the physical ground, pushes up toward the sunlight, growing a stem and leaves that reach for the light, and suddenly it blooms! It is a beautiful bloom that is nothing like the stem, leaves, seed and ground it came from. A friend asked if the flower is as surprised when it blooms as we are when we suddenly step into the light of our spirituality.

Would you like to explore your own development, mirrored to you by the deeper meaning of the Bible events and stories? The Bible gives us a clear pathway, a highway, not a confusing tangle of byways that lead nowhere. This is what Isaiah was telling us in Chapter 40:3.

"In the wilderness prepare the way of the Lord, make straight in the desert a highway for our God. Every valley shall be lifted up, and every mountain and hill made low; the uneven ground shall become level, and the rough places plain. And the glory of the Lord shall be revealed and all flesh shall see it together, for the mouth of the Lord has spoken."

Navigating the Bible through metaphysics leads you book by book, chapter by chapter, and sometimes verse by verse on that highway of psychological development, from infancy to the gates of spirituality that open into the Gospels. There Jesus leads us forward with the example of his life and teachings showing us the kingdom of heaven. The Apostle Paul sees the Christ nature in each of us and endeavors to live it every day. Then we reach the book of Revelation. We trod the final steps to the New Jerusalem, the Christ consciousness, where we shed all earthly limitation and are totally prepared for God to return us to our true home.

INTRODUCTION

Life is not simple. The Bible is not simple. In trying to make sense of the Bible, there are many "easy read" versions. They are evidence that people really do want to understand its contents. I am one of those people. Using the easy-read paraphrased versions, while enjoyable, still gives me the impression that I am looking at someone else's life experience, but not really my own. My questions are not so much about morality and how I should behave, but how was my whole being knit together from the beginning. Just as a baby's nervous system is not complete at birth, so our psychological system is in its infancy as well.

In my exploration, I chose a scholarly version, The New Oxford Annotated Bible, Revised Standard Version, which is one of the most accurate renditions using the oldest known manuscripts. Accuracy was the goal of the editors and the vast army of scholars working for them. There are copious footnotes to help explain obscurities and add to our knowledge of biblical times. There is helpful cross-referencing to note where else in the Bible certain things are repeated.

My task has not been to change the Bible text but to take a heightened approach to it, bringing to light a wider understanding of our own development as human beings. I am sure many have looked back upon their earlier experiences and asked, "Why did I do that? What was I thinking?" We were in a former stage of development, so our thinking corresponded to that stage. Research tells us that the adolescent brain is not configured the same as the adult brain. Teenagers will have different reasoning patterns at that time than they will have as their brain reconfigures into the adult. Is this in the Bible? Most assuredly. How do we find it? Allow me to show you!

Beginning with the Hebrew Testament and looking at it through the eyes of a metaphysician, we can see the early stages of the psychological human as it begins its journey from infancy. If you are a parent you know the minute you forbid something to your child, that is the first thing the child will reach for. The child reaches beyond the limit to experience things for him or herself, often burning fingers or being hit when pulling objects off a table.

This is not very different from the story of Adam and Eve. They were in a state of infancy and when God said "Do not eat of this fruit," that was the first thing they reached for. We launch ourselves into the world of experience for better or worse, and try not to repeat the worse ones. Once we start on this journey of development and discovery, we can never go back. As the story goes there was a guard set at the gate to the garden so humanity could not return to the infant state for eternity. Was it a fall or a rising to the challenge of co-creatorship with God?

This book is the result of years of classes I have taught, volumes of research, and the participation of intrepid students who were willing to go through the Bible with me verse-by-verse, chapter-by-chapter, and book-by-book. Teachers will begin by interpreting a few well-known stories, a good start for learning to understand the metaphysical discipline. But to get the whole picture of humanity through all its development, my students and I started at the beginning and faithfully worked our way through the whole Bible, from Genesis to Revelation.

CHAPTER ONE

A short Overview

I grew up in mainstream Christianity in a denomination that is somewhat liberal. I learned the more positive Christian teachings about the Bible, but nothing that explained life beyond the commandments, don't steal, don't kill, don't lie, and be a good person. My early thinking was dominated by ignorance and fear of the Bible, worry about sin, and anxiety of not understanding what my own life was to be about.

When I found Unity's metaphysical interpretation of the Bible, I simply could not get enough of it. It lifted all the fear, guilt, anxiety, misery and ignorance I had been carrying around all my life. The study of metaphysics and subsequently metaphysical interpretation of the Bible had my full attention. It was the first teaching that really opened the Bible for me and provided something deeper for my understanding of life.

Metaphysical Bible interpretation means to see beyond the story and writings to find deeper meaning. Learning to see more deeply through metaphysical teachings is essential to living a spiritual life. Seeing more deeply into the mirror of the Bible helps us see our own interior in helpful and fascinating ways.

Some authors use the words metaphysical and spiritual interchangeably. They both mean above the physical. I will mostly use the word metaphysical throughout this text.

Metaphysical interpretation is always beautiful, positive, and helpful. It touches the soul. When the soul is touched we are softened and our lives become lovelier in ways we can hardly describe. Our prayers become prayers of thanks breathed quietly in the privacy of our own perception of the divine.

We metaphysically interpret the Bible writings because we are created as spiritual beings indwelling a physical body, producing a lifetime. We interpret because we are the curiosity of God discovering who we are. We are far more than our finite intellectual mind can comprehend. There are evolving dimensions of ourselves we have yet to discover. They are alluded to in the Bible text if we know how to look for them. In searching we discover that we do have eyes to see and ears to hear if we will develop them.

Academic Metaphysics

The term metaphysics originally referred to the writings of Aristotle that came after his writings on physics, and were brought forth by Andronicus of Rhodes about three centuries after Aristotle's death.

Traditionally, metaphysics refers to the branch of philosophy that attempts to understand the fundamental nature of all reality, whether visible or invisible. It seeks a description so basic, so essentially simple, and so all-inclusive that it applies to everything in life, divine and human.

Jesus was a metaphysician interpreting the Hebrew Scriptures to the disciples on the road to Emmaus. He showed them the deeper meaning concerning his ministry. If we look to Jesus' examples, we understand that he valued interpretation. Therefore we also should value this pathway to deeper understanding.

Great Metaphysicians

To call one's self a metaphysician indicates a devoted interest in attempting to discover what underlies everything. Some metaphysicians focus on prosperity and some on healing, depending upon the need at the time. They use the power of spiritual principle to bring forth the perfect pattern of the Creator to bear upon all their experiences.

Mary Baker Eddy, who founded Christian Science, focused on healing. More recently Reverend Louise Hay, a Religious Science minister, also focused her work on healing.

Napoleon Hill's book, "Think and Grow Rich," is focused on prosperity and success.

Annie Rix Militz' book "Riches and Honor" focuses on prosperity and spirituality.

Charles Fillmore, co-founder of Unity, found all these areas spoken of in the Bible as he studied it from a metaphysical point of view. His famous work, "The Metaphysical Bible Dictionary," is a great starting point for Bible interpretation. It contains all the proper names in the Bible and their Hebrew or Greek meaning. The meaning of these names and the context in which the character is found are the keys that begin to reveal the message we are seeking.

The Bible is studied on several levels. Many books are written about the Bible as history, literature, poetry, morality, laws, religion, and the study of God. Unity is the teaching organization that combines metaphysics and the Bible as a way to study our human experience and our relationship to God.

There are some independent authors who also combine them. Dr. Daniel R. Condron of the School of Metaphysics published the book "The Universal Language of Mind, The Book of Matthew" interpreted. He thought the Book of Matthew would be the best expression of the symbolism, since Matthew was written to convince the Jews that Jesus was their long awaited messiah. So it stood to reason the symbolism drawn from Jewish writings would be most abundant in the Gospel of Matthew.

The metaphysical work of the Jews is expressed in the Kabbalah. Some of Unity's metaphysical interpretations are influenced by Kabalistic writings. The Bible was written as a mirror for us to look into, to have deeper understanding of who we are. The Bible reveals how our being is knit together as a whole and not just bits and pieces. The books are arranged in the order of our development with details and images to help us understand. The Hebrew Testament was written as saga to explain what God had done for his people. The sagas of Moses, Abraham, and Jacob are the three basic developmental cycles of humanity.

The first cycle, the Moses story, is about the psychological aspect of our being, drawn out of the darkness of the purely physical, symbolized by Egypt. Still representing the physical consciousness Moses went to the mountain, a high place in thought, to receive stone tablets of rudimentary laws for creating a society and a nation.

The second cycle, the Abraham story, is about our willingness to leave a comfortable but limited state of mind and follow God's leading. When God instructed Abraham to go and settle in Canaan, he disobeyed. He went on into Egypt, the physical realm because he did not recognize the potential of the Promised Land. Abraham represents the first fragile development of faith. When we lose our faith we cannot move forward. We revert to an earlier stage of development.

The third cycle, the story of Jacob, is about the first organizational budding of the Hebrew civilization. He had twelve sons and their names were given to the twelve tribes of Israel. This was the first attempt in the long process of creating a nation.

The New Testament Gospels

Except for the name Saul, who later became known as Paul, all the proper names of the New Testament people are not found in the Hebrew Testament. The names in the gospels have spiritual meanings. The names in the Hebrew Testament have psychological meanings. The name Jesus is Joshua in the Hebrew Testament, indicating the beginning of Christ awareness, but still rooted in the physical.

Jesus the Christ is about the divine within us. He demonstrated the power of God in physical expression. *"The things I do you will do and even greater will you do…you are in me and I am in you." (John 14:12)* Although the Gospels contain many stories of Jesus and his disciples, nothing in the Gospels is about physical living. It is all about spiritual living and how we develop as spiritual beings.

Jesus constantly interfaced with God Mind. He was an example of how to use God Mind instead of the psychological or ego mind. He pointed us toward God within him, and not his own personal being. His mind, body, and affairs were subject to his spiritual nature at all times.

The Letters

The apostle Paul was a mystic with an explosive and passionate nature. We first experience him as a policeman of the Sadducees, sent to arrest and imprison the followers of Jesus and in some cases murder them. He had a spiritual experience of the risen Christ on the road to Damascus, and became an apostle to Christ Jesus. He realized that the Christ pattern was in all people, as well as in Jesus.

Paul lived at the same time as Jesus, but it seems they never met. The Epistles or letters, written soon after Jesus' death, are the earliest writings concerning Jesus. Some of the epistles were written by Paul and some by various scribes. The deepest spiritual understanding is revealed in his words in *Colossians 1:27*, *"Christ in you, your hope of glory…grow up into the head of Christ…we are the body of Christ, if there is a physical body, then there is a spiritual body,"* and many more indications of our divine nature.

The Four Books

The book of John is considered the most spiritually revealing of the four Gospels. But the writer's emphasis is that Jesus was the only Son of God, the only Christ, God incarnate. The writer of Matthew wanted to convince the Jews that Jesus was their long awaited messiah. The book of Luke, who was known as the beloved physician, was written for the gentiles. The book of Mark is thought to be the earliest gospel written. Matthew and Luke copied stories from Mark for their own gospels and added stories of their own. Some stories are identical in the four gospels and some are found in only one gospel book.

All of these writers were teachers expressing their own views and their own understanding. Each had a mission to accomplish, to spread the word of Truth. The Gospels were written 80 to 120 years after the death of Jesus.

But a metaphysical interpretation of these teachings takes them out of the realm of time and personal perception into the realm of the Universal. Regardless of the editing and redacting over the centuries, the deeper meaning remains untouched.

Aten

The older biblical movies were so fascinating because they each had a metaphysical message at some point. The movie "The Egyptian" was about the Pharaoh, Akhenaten, who believed there was only one god, the sun. Some postulate that Moses was a disciple of Aten, bringing the concept of one true god from Egypt to create the Hebrew religion. This teaching was carried into the land of Canaan and it later became known as Judaism.

CHAPTER TWO

Creation Stories

The writings in the scriptures do not always run in logical sequences. There are additions, scribal glosses, and contradictory telling of stories and events. Metaphysical interpretation enables us to look more deeply at why the contradictions are there. Nothing is there by accident, but is most likely mirroring the contradictions in our own thinking.

For instance First and Second Chronicles are a rewrite of First and Second Kings. Often for that reason a Bible teacher may skip Chronicles because it is a cleaned up or idealized version of King David's life. Many of the details of David's wild and unsavory activities told in Kings are left out of Chronicles. There comes a time when our own experiences need a rewrite. We need to find a more positive way of looking at our past. Often people are not aware that such a thing is possible. The facts of the past are unchangeable, but they can be reframed. This is done by forgiving and releasing the negative feelings that are stored in subconscious mind. If we do not reframe the memories by neutralizing the feelings, they re-emerge throughout our lives to torture us again and again.

Adam, Eve, Cain, Abel, and Seth are the first family in the Hebrew Testament. There are similar stories in other cultures to explain the beginning of humanity. This story is an anchor for the human mind. It gives us a place to start in explaining our existence. Whether or not these people actually lived is not relevant. They symbolize the early elements that formed our being.

In Genesis 3:20 Eve is called *"the mother of all living."* The name Eve means life, living, *"Feeling without which nothing lives. She is the mother principle of God in expression. Back of the female feeling nature is the pure essence of God."*

The name *"Adam means red, firm, representing the first movement of mind in its contact with life and substance. Thought and feeling are the primal elements of human existence. They represent the forces of Being Itself."*

"Man is Spirit, absolute and unconditioned; but man forms an Adamic consciousness into which the Creator breathes the breath of life; this in its perfect expression, is the Son of man, an expression of the God's divine idea for humankind. The Holy Spirit as humanity chooses a consciousness of form and gives it life and character."

All definitions quoted in this text are from the *Metaphysical Bible Dictionary* by Unity School of Christianity. The definitions in *Gaskill's Dictionary of all Myths and Scriptures* are similar and are occasionally used.

The metaphysical understanding of these symbols is important to understanding the continuing story of humanity from Adam to Christ, beginning in the Hebrew Testament and continuing on into the Christian Testament to Revelation. As we move along through these writings, the pattern of development in humanity from the physical/psychological into the spiritual will become clearer. The seeming chaos of the writings will become a highway made straight in the desert of our developing thinking.

Two Creation Stories

Chapters one and two in Genesis are both creation stories. The first chapter is the mystical story of creation. The second chapter is the physical creation story.

Genesis 1 reads, *"In the beginning God created the heavens and the earth. The earth was without form and void, and darkness was upon the face of the deep; and the Spirit of God was moving over the face of the waters."*

There are several variations of the beginning story and the first chapter is the work of the priestly writers. They set down these very ancient oral teachings into a Hebrew context and manuscript. Later on we will encounter the priestly writers again as they add the temple records into the text at various points. The temple records recorded the wealth of the tribes and families. They numbered the family members, genealogies, sheep, goats, cattle, servants, land and vineyards.

God created light first before the sun and moon. Some critics think God made a mistake. But the light represents understanding. For example people dive into a project before they really understand what is needed. It is like walking into a dark room without first turning on a light. There may be many things to trip over or holes to fall into. Before we take a step forward it is wise to ask in prayer for light and understanding

The text continues in Genesis 1:5, *"And there was evening and there was morning."* The Jewish day began at sundown. A day when creating begins in the evening, develops through the darkness or night, and emerges into expression, its dawn. During the night when our conscious minds are quiet, the mysterious creation is at work. Creation works in the darkness like a child growing in the womb. It starts with a rhythm or beat and the heart then forms around the beat.

The firmament mentioned is a puzzling part of the story. The waters were separated, some above and some below the firmament, and the firmament God called heaven. There may be a mix of mythologies here because it isn't clear what was meant if read literally. But when we ask for light or understanding, it means we must then clear a firmament in mind. It is likened to a garden where you prepare the soil by clearing out the weeds and stones. The weeds and stones of the mind are doubts and fears. When we completely eliminate these we are in a heavenly state of mind.

On the third day the dry land appeared. This is where the ideas of our imagination begin to grow in the prepared soil of the mind. Vegetation or roots appear and begin bearing fruit. *"And God saw it was good."* Up to this time, all our work is done in the mind. Nothing has manifested in material form as yet.

On the fourth day the lights appeared in the heavens, the sun, stars, and moon. They are far distant from our physical lives. They represent

God at work on our idea. This is the time when it seems that nothing is happening. God is not answering our prayers. But in fact God is energizing the form of our idea with the power to bring it forth into our life experience.

On the fifth day living creatures came forth. Our idea begins to manifest in forms. Man is given dominion at this point. We can look over our creation coming into form and decide if it is what we really wanted. Is it turning out the way we hoped? If not we can go back to day three in the process, re-imagine our idea, and wait for God to empower it and bring it forth again. When we first begin this process, we may not be very skilled at choosing what is for our highest good. But we are never stuck with our first choice. We can choose again. We can always reset the image and watch it come forth as many times as it takes to manifest exactly what we desire.

A lady passed a castle every day on her way to work. Every night she dreamed of it being hers. It turned out that she was a very distant relative of the original owner. When he died and all the relatives were dead as well, she inherited that very castle. Soon she had to give up her dream castle because she did not have the funds on her meager wages to support it, repair it, and pay the taxes on such a huge edifice. We have to look around at our situation in life, ask for light and understanding, before we embark upon something that is far outside the realm of practicality for our present situation in life. We need to build our consciousness to support our dream. First we build the prosperity consciousness to manifest the finances and other essential elements of support.

You are here to be a co-creator with God and have unlimited chances to learn what that means. With practice you become proficient at using this wonderful process of creation to manifest your world as you desire it to be. You are here to learn. How do we know this is our purpose? In royal theology, as in Egypt, the king was believed to be the image of God. According to Genesis 1:26, we are created *"in the image and likeness of God."* Being in this image of God sets humanity up as the creator and ruler of his or her own kingdom of being.

On the seventh day, God's work was finished and God rested. From then on God's work became ours to continue. We are to take this power given to us and create our life experiences. Any time we need guidance, answers or ideas, we turn within to this power or God Mind and focus it by our thinking to bear upon our lives.

In Genesis 1, God began to be called Lord God. According to scholars, writers who added the word "Lord" to God knew the people wouldn't understand a distant invisible God, so they referred to the deity as Lord God. People knew about landlords or overlords, and could relate to a Lord God that conjured up a physical image in their minds. This also solidified the idea in religion of God as male. There was no corresponding Lady God mentioned.

However Genesis 1:26 reads, *"Let us make man in our image, after our likeness..."* So now we have a plural reference to God. In many cultures, male gods had female counterparts who were equals. It made sense to early cultures that it took male and female to produce offspring. Even though God is neither male nor female, but Creative Principle, people tend to make God after their own image and likeness instead of the other way around.

In Genesis 2:24 we have another anomaly. *"Therefore a man leaves his father and his mother and cleaves to his wife..."* As far as we know Adam and Eve did not have an earthly mother and father. Already a writer has inserted a cultural instruction for humanity in the beginning of the story. This is most likely a scribal gloss or addition, an attempt by a writer to insert a religious tenet into the script. The "one flesh" idea in this verse might have signaled equality of the sexes, but clearly it has been ignored in favor of existing moral, cultural, or religious rules of the time.

The blame game started in the garden when Adam blamed Eve for giving him the forbidden fruit and Eve blamed the serpent for enticing her. Since then the church has blamed women for all the evil in the world. Thanks to the literal interpretation of this story the church teaches that everyone is born in original sin. Humanity was not originated in sin or evil, but in God. Original sin does not refer to sexual procreation, but to the fall in consciousness from the spiritual to the physical. Genesis 1:27 reads, *"Male and female he created them. And God blessed them."* We were created in blessing, as also set forth by Matthew Fox in his book *"Original Blessing."*

Adam and Eve tasted of the fruit of the knowledge of good and evil, life and death. In other words they became aware of opposites, God and not God. Cain and Abel, sons of Adam and Eve, represented the first experience of mental thought when they were born into the physical realm. Then they experienced other opposites such as innocence and guilt, love and hate, and from opposites sprang anger and jealousy. Cain became jealous of *"Abel the innocent"* and killed him.

Cain was the first-born that represents the physical nature. Abel was the second born representing the mental. Throughout the Hebrew Testament, the nature of the first-born always represents the physical and the second born the mental. This is consistently revealed by the Hebrew meanings of their names. In the early development of humanity, the physical always seeks to overcome the mental. In our youth our emotions and physical drives very often overtake rational thinking.

Death had not been introduced as yet. Did Cain know that Abel would die? Did he expect him to jump right back up and continue on? Good questions. This is the story of our innocence. We came into this world not knowing much of anything and made errors without knowing about consequences. The consequences of Cain's action are spelled out in Genesis 4:11, *"Now you are cursed from the ground which has opened its mouth to receive your brother's blood from your hand."* Cain was clearly distraught when he now realized that in killing his brother, he also was subject to death. When we judge another, we become subject to the same judgment because it comes from within us and we have unleashed the same upon ourselves.

At this point there was only the physical nature, the angry son to carry on, so Seth was born. His name means *"the compensator."* He represents the balancing power of good. Humanity was still caught in the duality, but life could now go forward. Metaphysically when we have wandered away from God, nearly to become extinct, a great compensating reaction sets in and we are led back to a saner level where our development can continue. We have a powerful destiny that is not to be denied by our errors. The ideal nature, represented by Seth, causes us to realize the futility of destructive human efforts and recognize the force for good within us.

We are not the products of original sin, but of original blessing. The cards are stacked in our favor, so to speak. When Abel was killed the good came back even stronger. We become stronger by overcoming our errors. We begin to recognize the error thinking that brings unhappy experiences. We can turn that thinking to the positive quickly before the result of the error thought can manifest and destroy our progress.

Once we solidly understand these underpinnings of our human origins and development, we are on our way to greater awareness of what our life experiences reflect back to us. We can choose positive creative thoughts that manifest good in our lives, and actually begin to make the kingdom of heaven our experience now.

Genesis 2:25 states, *"And the man and his wife were both naked, and were not ashamed."* In the Garden of Eden, humanity was still in spirit, without material bodies. In Genesis 3, the serpent, which represents the ego mind, strives to influence human reason. It tells Eve that she will not die, but will know good and evil and be like God. So they ate the forbidden fruit. *"Then their eyes were opened and they knew they were naked..."* Ego mind brings shame, fear, anxiety and hatred. Fear leads to a guilty attempt to hide from God. This has been the condition of unenlightened humanity through the ages.

In Genesis 3:11 God said to Eve, *"Who told you that you were naked? Did you eat of the tree of which I commanded you not to eat?"* In the anxiety already at work in their minds they feared God and hid. Adam blamed Eve for giving him the fruit and Eve blamed the serpent for telling her it was good to eat of this tree. The tree was beautiful and alluring, as is the material world. It draws humanity down into physical awareness where ego mind causes us to hate ourselves and fear God.

CHAPTER THREE

Two Beginnings

Genesis attempts to explain how the earth was populated. We have no way of knowing how years were counted. Many prominent people were reported to live up to 930 years, the age of Adam and Methuselah.

In Genesis 5:3, *"And Adam lived an hundred and thirty years and became the father of a son in his own likeness, after his image; and named him Seth."* From the Metaphysical Bible Dictionary, Seth represents *"the compensator, the one who draws us back from the edge of the abyss and leads us back to sanity."* Seth lived nine hundred and twelve years."

In Genesis 5:4, *"And the days of Adam after he became the father of Seth were eight hundred years: and he had other sons and daughters."* When Cain killed Abel the cycle would be cut short. This indicates that the cycle was then continued after the birth of Seth the compensator. *"And all the days that Adam lived were nine hundred and thirty years and he died."* This was the completion of the Adam cycle. Cycles will be discussed further on in this text.

According to the Metaphysical Bible Dictionary, age represents *"a cycle or a dispensation."* From the *American Heritage Dictionary*, *"In theology a dispensation indicates a divine ordering of worldly affairs."* To interpret the length of their lives literally is to base our thinking on the false concept of time as a reality. Time is a human construct and varies in different people's perceptions. In joy an hour can seem to fly by quickly or in agony drag slowly on.

Jesus was aware of cycles and ages. In Matthew 24:3, *"As he sat on the Mount of Olives his disciples came to him privately, saying, "Tell us when will this be, and what will be the sign of your coming and of the close of the age?"* Thus the ages of these early people are signaling the completion of an early area of development within humanity.

If we look into the Hebrew translation and the value of numbers, we can understand more. The number forty symbolizes completeness. There were forty days and forty nights of the flood. Moses spent forty days and forty nights on the mountain. King David reigned forty years. Jesus spent forty days in the wilderness. The numbers 40, or 4000, or 40,000 are used all through the Bible text signaling a completion of some segment or stage of development.

From *The Dictionary of All Myths and Scriptures by Gaskill* on page 290, *"The number forty is expressive of a period of probation or trial. The Israelites wandered forty years, Elijah was in hiding forty days, and the flood was forty days. Forty is symbolic of transitory conditions of the soul moving through a process."*

In Genesis 4:26, *"And to Seth also was born a son; and he called his name Enosh. At that time men began to call upon the name of the Lord."* This early in human development here is a glimmer of a higher power.

Enosh means *"miserable mortal man. Humanity comes to the end of its physical resources and sees the nothingness of all its efforts in the outer apart from Spirit. So humanity begins to call upon the name of Jehovah. This is the beginning of recognition of the source of all good."* Metaphysical Bible Dictionary

At this point the begats or the genealogies begin. First it repeats Genesis 1:27 *"So God created man in his own image, in the image of God created he him; male and female created he them."* Eve is mentioned twice in Genesis, and Eve is not mentioned anymore except in 2 Corinthians and 1 Timothy when the writers quoted Genesis.

Genesis Chapter 5:1, *"This is the book of the generations of Adam. When God created man, he made him in the likeness of God. Male and female he created them and he blessed them, and named them Man when they were created."*

Here the creation of male and female is called Adam. *"Together they are the primal elemental forces of Being itself."* Metaphysical Bible Dictionary

This ends the dualism of Adam and Eve as separate, and begins the androgynous oneness of Being. They are not two separate beings. Mankind, in its dualistic thinking, does not understand this but sorts by physical maleness and femaleness. This human judgment characterizes these differences as strong and weak, intellectual and emotional, worthy and not worthy, more and less.

In Genesis 2:24 a fragment appears, *"Therefore a man leaves his father and mother and cleaves to his wife and they become one flesh."* Not one flesh but one in Spirit. The writer or redactor inserted his own beliefs that led to this error in understanding.

From Wikipedia, *"Redaction is a form of editing in which multiple source texts are combined (redacted) and altered slightly to make a single document. Often this is a method of collecting a series of writings on a similar theme and creating a definitive and coherent work. "To redact" later came to be used in the sense of selecting from or adapting (as by obscuring or removing sensitive information) a document prior to publication or release."*

Redactors had power to insert their own beliefs, slant a meaning, and omit selected items. The spiritual message cannot be tampered with in this manner, because redactors of the Bible were not aware of spiritual interpretation, but more interested in political biases and theological tenets.

In Genesis 6:4 is another story fragment from a different writing. *"The Nephilim were on the earth in those days; and also afterward, when the sons of God came in to the daughters of men, and they bore children to them. These were the mighty men of old, the men of renown."*

This could be a fragment of a lost document. Nephilim were a giant people once thought to be *"mighty men of old."* In Number 13:33 where Joshua and Caleb first spied out the land of Canaan, is a mention of Nephilim, giant sons of Anak. Some thought they might be from the gods. Goliath was thought to be a throwback to these early people. But Goliath was slow and stupid, not at all like a god. There are many such story fragments from earlier civilizations mixed in with the Hebrew Scriptures.

The story of Noah is superficially similar to the Babylonian Gilgamesh Epic. Gilgamesh was ordered to build a boat, sealing it with pitch. The dimensions were about 450 x 75 x 45 feet. *(From footnotes p. 8 of the Oxford Annotated RSV)*

There is a mixture of writings in Genesis 6 where the Noah story stops and a fragment begins. The first eight verses are written in the distinct style of the Ephraim or the southern writer. Genesis 6:9 again takes up the story of Noah in the style of the Judah or northern writer, a continuation of Chapter 5. A more detailed explanation of the three major strands of writing, the Ephraim, the Judah or Yahwist, and the Priestly, can be found in the *"Interpreters One Volume Commentary on the Bible," Abingdon Press, 1971.*

The *"begats"* are the genealogies in the Bible. There were many sons and daughters, but the ones named and the meanings of their names are listed below. These tell us of the struggles of humanity at its inception. You can follow the meanings of these names as they depict the ups and downs of early human development:

Seth – Compensator for the loss of Abel
Death was not yet known and humanity needed a buffer for its grievous errors in order to continue its development.

Enosh – Miserable physical man, his works come to nothing
Hard work in the physical and material world does not carry humanity forward in its development.

Cainan – Centralizer, Centering in Spirit.
Humanity looks for a way to progress from within.

Mahalaleel – Mighty Rising, Praise of God
The very beginning of higher thinking, which is not yet spirituality.

Jared – Declining, going down
Progress is not yet sustainable. Humanity does not know how to support its progress.

Enoch – A new state of thought, "walked with God"
Humanity began searching for what will sustain its growth.

Methuselah – Sting of death, death not yet overcome
Death is still the ultimate mystery. It ends everything gained.

Lamech – Inspiration to keep on living, but allows the organism to disintegrate into material attachment.

Humanity falls back into the physical mind, hoping for a purpose in the material world.

The flood story exists in other cultures. It is an archetypal story, *"The original pattern in which all things of the species are represented. The model, the prototype."* (*American Heritage Dictionary*)

Genesis 6:3 reads *"And the Lord said, 'My spirit shall not abide in man forever, for he is flesh...'"* Here God was displeased with man and planned the flood. Man had become contentious, material minded, with no spiritual consciousness. The name Noah means *"At rest with God, tranquility."* Noah was instructed to build the ark to preserve humanity and animals while everything else is washed clean. Then God repopulated the earth with Noah's family and with animals brought into the ark two by two, male and female. This story is a symbol of starting over. The ark represents a consciousness that will contain and sustain the seeds of creation through a period of destruction and new beginning.

In the development, the early growing stages serve only to a certain point and break down. Then there is a new start with the preserved good that will help humanity continue developing. Noah had three sons who represent those aspects that had been preserved. Regardless of the failures and the flood of cleansing, these three elements remained intact.

Shem (spiritual) – Righteous, dignity, shining
Ham (physical) – Inferior, blackened, hot sensuality
Japheth (mental) – Expansive, without limitation

These are the creation stories, the beginnings of humanity, and the first struggles of humanity to develop outside the Garden of Eden. Adam and Eve tasted the fruit of the knowledge of good and evil. A serpent tempted them. This serpent was not a snake. Only later does it become an animal that crawls on its belly. Then the wrathful God showed up, chastised Adam and Eve and the serpent. God punished them by sending them out of the garden to toil and never to return to the ease of the Eden. This is called the fall of man. It attempts to explain our situation of pain and toil. Men were to work in the soil and women were to bear children in pain.

In Genesis 3:22, *"And the Lord God said, 'Behold, the man has become like one of us, knowing good and evil; and now, lest he put forth his hand, and take also of the tree of life, and eat, and live forever.' Therefore the Lord God sent him forth from the Garden of Eden..."*

Here is the puzzling situation. The Lord God is plural and already knew the danger of the knowledge of good and evil. God kept it from Adam and Eve and yet allowed a serpent into the garden to tempt them. Adam and Eve were "naked (innocent)." They were spirit and had no physical bodies. When they ate of the forbidden fruit, they saw that they had bodies, were naked and ashamed.

Falling from purely spiritual beings into physicality is the so-called fall of man into the material world. The way back home to spirit is described in the Hebrew testament, the Gospels, and finally the Book of Revelation. The tree of life in the Garden of Eden reappears in the New Jerusalem, in the Book of Revelation and the overall cycle of human development is complete.

CHAPTER FOUR

Making Sense of the Beginning Stories

In Genesis 8:18 when the families went out of the ark after the flood, *"Noah built an altar and took of every clean animal"* and offered burnt offerings. If Noah had the only surviving animals from the earth on the ark and only two of each, it seems he would have partly destroyed the possibility of re-populating the earth by cooking one or both of several pairs. Genesis goes on to say God smelled the aroma, was pleased, and decided never to curse the earth again. At this point in the story God becomes understood as a carnivore. God resigned himself to man's evil *"from his youth"* for the love of a good steak.

This is not ridicule of the Bible, but rather of the belief that every word is to be taken literally. Very early in the scriptures we can see the problem with this literal level of reading. If we hope to understand what the writer was symbolizing and teaching us about developing consciousness, we must look deeper than the surface story.

Near the end of Genesis 7 and on into Genesis 8 the writings begin to be a mixture of Priestly and Yahwist writers, commonly referred to as the J writers and the P writers. The Elohist or E writers begin in the Genesis 15. Scholars determined these distinctions among the strains of writers by noting the differences in writing style, cultural approach and word usage.

In Genesis 2, Abel was the first tiller of the soil. In Genesis 9:20, *"Noah was the first tiller of the soil."* Symbolically after the flood the beginning story starts over. Many times our most treasured beliefs are wiped out because they are of a lower or erroneous understanding. To continue our life journey we must start over with a more expanded understanding that will carry us forward.

Now, unlike Adam and Eve, Noah and his family were already in physical bodies. Noah's son Ham accidentally stumbled upon his father lying drunk and naked in his tent. His brothers took a sheet and walked backward into the tent to cover their father without looking at him.

This is similar to Adam and Eve's first reaction to their lack of physical identity. Adam and Eve were ashamed so God gave them bodies symbolized by the fig leaf. In the next beginning story, Noah and his families were ashamed of their physical bodies. Looking upon the nakedness of one's father was culturally forbidden.

The message here appears to be that we are spiritual beings inhabiting physical bodies, which are not our natural state. Humanity from then on was ashamed of what they believed was the fall into physicality. The fall of mankind was not about birth through sexual contact but disobedience to its spiritual nature. The belief in original sin indicates humanity did something wrong that caused it to fall into a lower state of being, the physical world.

Ham was the dark son of Noah. However it was Ham's son Canaan, not Ham, whom Noah cursed. This may be the beginning of the saying that the sins of the father fall on the son and succeeding generations. Canaan was the son of Ham, the dark offspring of Noah, dark meaning unenlightened. The son's name Canaan became the eponym for the land and people of Canaan. Much later in the Hebrew Bible the twelve tribes were named after each of Jacob's sons. Their names were also used as eponyms, or the source for the names of the twelve tribes.

Canaan is symbolic of the dark side of humanity that was stuck in the worship of the physical nature. Canaanites worshipped wooden and stone idols and were not evolving in consciousness toward their spiritual nature.

Another genealogy now starts with Noah instead of Adam and Eve. Those named in the genealogy represent descendants who spread out and populated different and distinct areas of Israel. More distant areas include Asia Minor, the Aegean area, Babylonia (Shinar), and Assyria. An interesting difference in the stories is that Adam and Eve are both included in the beginning of their genealogy, but Noah's wife is not included. She is not named in the Bible text. This is the beginning of a lopsided patriarchal consciousness that pervades many cultures. Only the Jewish tradition gave her a Hebrew name, Naamah, which means pleasant.

This is where nations began, all originating with Noah. Tying everyone back to Adam and Eve, as the Mormons are dedicated to doing, now means they have to go through Noah as the second beginning point.

It is written that these families each had their own language. Even though Genesis 10:5 according to the P writer, each nation had their own language, the story of the tower of Babel is inserted in Genesis 11:1, which says *"now the whole earth had one language and few words."* Could this mean they communicated telepathically and were not yet using verbal language? Again this is a mixture of writers, thus the different versions of the development of language.

In Genesis 11 the people of Shinar (Babylonia) spoke one language and they decided to build a tower to reach God. Shinar was in the plain of the Tigris-Euphrates basin containing ziggurats or pyramidal towers. Those towers were believed to be the gateways to heaven and were common in that culture. Babel means gate of God, not a babble of languages. Humanity could not continue developing in error ways because it separated them and caused them not to be able to understand each other. They were scattered to begin anew. The way to God was not by climbing a stone tower, but by lifting their thinking.

Interestingly, this story again speaks of the "gods" (plural) who banished Adam and Eve from the garden so they could not bring back their knowledge of good and evil and become like the gods. This story of the tower of Babel indicates God was displeased that once again the people were trying to reach Him through the physical level and He *"scattered them abroad over all the face of the earth."* This is like an older sibling kicking over your wall of dominoes or scattering your house of cards. This is the destroyer god of the Hebrews so hated by the Marcionites, an early sect of Christianity. They utterly rejected Judaism and everything to do with it, as inferior to Christianity's loving God.

There is another genealogy listed in the story of Abram, who is later to be known as Abraham. The Jews believe Abraham is their historical father. His story is where they believe their history begins. Abraham is also considered to be the father of the Arab Nation. This is the basis of the constant quarrel between Jews and Arabs over Jerusalem. They both claim the sanctity of the rock upon which Abraham nearly sacrificed his son, Isaac, and where Mohammed ascended to heaven. In the early stage of psychological growth, we develop a division between mind and body, mental and physical. The Jews metaphysically represent the mental and the Arabs the physical.

The Hebrew name Abram means, *"expanding of faith."* He represents faith in its early establishment in the human consciousness. Abram was still a long way from exercising steady and reliable faith in God, just as developing humanity is unsteady in its first glimmerings of faith. When God said, *"the land I will show you,"* this represents for us not a change in physical location, but a new level of consciousness. The literal interpretation of this has caused Christians, Jews, and Muslims to remain at odds to this day over who owns the "Holy Land."

At God's call Abram left his home in Ur to adventure into a land that God promised him. His name remained Abram until God made a covenant with him that he would be the father of all nations. In Genesis 17:5 his name became Abraham. The "ah" inserted in his name represents the breath of God. In Genesis 17:15 the same was done for his wife, Sarai. She became Sarah, blessed to be the mother of nations.

Abram did not immediately go to Canaan as God directed, but settled in the home of his father in Haran (Turkey). They dwelt there until the death of his father, Terah. It was some years later that Abram, Lot, and their families continued on into Canaan. By this time there was a famine in Canaan. Abram built altars in Canaan to mark places where he believed God had spoken to him. Then he took his family into Egypt. It is like leaving bookmarks so we can get back to a page that inspired us. Abram did eventually return to one of those altars in Bethel to begin life in Canaan, the Promised Land.

Often when we receive spiritual guidance much time passes before we are ready to follow it. By the time we make up our minds to follow it, the good that was waiting for us has waned and we seek physical sustenance in other places instead. Egypt represents the physical world that is dark and full of dangers. In Egypt Abram faced many problems that he fearfully tried to solve with his intellect. Not once did Abram ask God for help or guidance. When folks are struggling with the physical world, they often forget their spiritual or religious training and revert to the intellect and its lack of wisdom for answers.

The biggest problem facing Abram was Pharaoh and the strange laws of that land. Physical laws without spiritual guidance are demanding and cruel. Abram was warned that if Pharaoh saw Sarai he would take her for his harem. Abram was afraid Pharaoh would kill him if he said she was his wife, so he lied saying Sarai was his sister. He had no proof that he would be killed. He only had fears of the ego mind whispering to him. The choices in the intellect or ego mind are usually bad to worse. We call this being between a rock and a hard place. Abram's lie brought more complications, which lies always do, because now Sarai was indeed taken away from him to Pharaoh's harem.

If Abram and Sarai were to fulfill God's promise and birth a nation, it was becoming clear that this path was going nowhere. So God had to intervene and inflicted plagues on Pharaoh. When Pharaoh learned the truth about Sarai he railed at Abram saying, *"Why did you not tell me she was your wife? You have brought plagues and destruction to my land!"* Abram was now blamed for all the woes in Egypt, and Pharaoh expelled him immediately. The ego mind blames us for everything, but its own bad advice is never blamed.

Abram had prospered materially in Egypt and Pharaoh allowed him to take all the rich gifts he paid to Abram for Sarai, which were considerable. It is true that you can prosper in the physical world using mental, intellectual, and emotional tools. God intervened with the only thing that would make the physical world, Pharaoh, back down. Plagues are the results of the ego's negative thinking. You could say God fought fire with fire. Like Abram we are usually lucky to get out of purely physical thinking with our lives and property still intact.

Abram and his nephew, Lot, were very close. They were like brothers. Lot traveled with Abram and Sarai into Egypt and then back to Canaan. The Hebrew name Lot means *"dark, covered, hidden."* Lot represents the negative or subjective side of faith that has limited ability to expand. This is the hidden part of man's consciousness that is still in the dark.

When their families and herds became too large for the small area of land they shared, the sons and shepherds began to fight over the grazing resources. Abram and Lot decided it was time to part. Abram gave Lot the first choice of land and Lot chose the fertile Jordan valley of Zoar near Sodom. Abram chose the barren mountains of Canaan that God had promised him.

Lot's choice took him to the evil city of Sodom, a place similar to Egypt. Sodom was the purely physical consciousness full of licentiousness and trouble. Lot could see only the exciting city life, the glitter and prosperity. He had no connection with God's promises to Abram. Abram on the other hand knew God was the Source of his wealth, and the appearance of barren desert mountains did not blind him to God's abundance.

In Genesis 14, the kings to the north and east were at war with the kings of the south and the victorious northern kings carried away Lot, his family, and all his riches. The powerful ego thoughts that rule the physical dimension make war against each other constantly coveting each other's riches. Abram, representing expanding consciousness, was not about to let the dark side gather power. He organized an army, and went to rescue Lot and his family. He returned triumphant and immediately placed all the spoils of the war at the feet of Melchizedek, the King of Salem. Salem is the earlier name of Jerusalem.

This is the first mention of a tithe in the Bible. It was not a tax but a gift freely given that all might know God alone prospered Abram. This is the great spiritual principle of prosperity. This principle is practiced through tithing, causing abundance to appear in the experience of the one who tithes. Melchizedek was the priest of God Most High. He blessed Abram. The king of Sodom, the lower consciousness, desired to get in on the blessing by giving his portion to Abram, but Abram refused his gifts. Abram now recognized the higher principle and would no longer look to the material world represented by Egypt and Sodom for prosperity.

As humanity develops understanding, the consciousness turns from the material to the spiritual as the source. The dark forces will always try to be part of the light, offering their gifts of darkness and fear. But they will never be accepted as part of the spiritual realm. Later in the book of Leviticus, the tithes became taxes paid to mortal men, but with Melchizedek they are received of God.

Melchizedek is mentioned again in Psalms 110:4. Melchizedek was a messianic or Christ figure manifesting as Priest of the Most High God, representing a higher order of being. This is the earliest indication of a spiritually evolved order. In Hebrews 7:1 Melchizedek was said to be *"without mother and father or genealogy and has neither beginning of days nor end of life, but resembling the Son of God he continues a priest forever."* He is mentioned in Hebrews 5:5 where it is said of Jesus Christ that he was a priest after the order of Melchizedek.

When the tribes were formed in Judah, only those born of the tribe of Levi could be priests. The appointing of the Levite tribe as the priestly tribe represents the earlier stages of humanity's psychological development, priests by physical birth. In the New Testament, Jesus represents a higher order of priesthood than the Levites. Jesus was spiritually evolved. Levite priests were no longer priests after death, but Jesus as Christ was a priest by the power of indestructible Life that would not die.

Again from Hebrews 7:15, *"This becomes more evident when another priest arises in the likeness of Melchizedek, who has become a priest, not according to a legal requirement concerning bodily descent, but by the power of an indestructible life. For it is witnessed of him (Jesus) 'Thou art a priest forever after the Order of Melchizedek.'"*

CHAPTER FIVE

Abraham, Sarah and Lot

A bram was a herder and a nomad. He traveled from Ur to Haran to Canaan to Egypt and back to Canaan. He appears also as a warrior and leader of forces that defeated the kings of the north. He went from being a herder that feared for his life in Egypt and lied about his wife, to one who gathered troops and went to rescue his nephew and family from the northern kings. Abram matured from being fearful to being fearless. Humanity needs to make this transition from fearful to fearless as it continues to develop in faith.

Abram did not yet have a covenant with God. In the beginning God was showing Abram the Promised Land, but the Covenant that would give it to him was not yet offered. Humanity has the promise of the blessings of faith and spirit, but is still wandering around in a lower state of consciousness and unable as yet to receive it.

Abram built altars as markers in Canaan as he went through it on his way into Egypt. They were small stone altars that marked the place where he had heard God's instructions, but he still did not understand that he must also follow God's lead. He heard but continued on in his own way. We build churches over sacred places and forget what made the place sacred. Folks go to church as a duty or social event, but usually do not delve into the sacred mystery for themselves.

When he came home from defeating five kings, he participated in the deeper spiritual practice of tithing, momentarily recognizing the

Christ figure of Melchizedek. With this development in consciousness, momentary as it was, he became ready for the Covenant.

In Genesis 14:19 there was a shift in his awareness when Abram tithed to Melchizedek. There is no previous mention of tithing or the *"King of Salem."* It was a breakthrough from faith into a glimmering of spiritual practice through the tithing.

In Genesis 15:1 God came to Abram in a vision. *"Fear not, Abram, I am your shield; your reward shall be very great."* But Abram saw only the physical evidence that he and Sarai had no son. He told God that since he had no heir, he would adopt a boy slave who was born in his house to be his heir. By civil law Abram could adopt the boy, Eliezer of Damascus, a slave born in his house.

"Inscriptions from Nuzi in Mesopotamia (middle of the second millennium) show the law there stipulated that a slave could be adopted as the heir in case of childlessness, a practice which is apparently presupposed here." Annotations, p. 17 Oxford RSV.

God assured Abram that his own son would be his heir, not the adopted slave, Eliezer. The name Eliezer is Hebrew meaning, *"God is help."* This meaning indicates a master/slave situation and God was not making a slave of Abram and his heir, or just helping Abram a little as the name suggests. God was lifting up Abram's consciousness to a higher understanding of who he was as a Son of God himself.

We must go beyond begging God for help when things aren't going our way and step into this covenanted partnership with God. Again, *"Fear not, Abram, I am your shield; your reward shall be very great."* Abram had to believe this with no tangible evidence just as we learn to believe in God when no physical evidence is appearing.

Genesis 15:7 describes a blood ceremony that took place so Abram would recognize the unbreakable Covenant. The promise was,

"To your descendants I give this land from the river of Egypt to the great river, the river Euphrates in the land of the Kenites, the Kenizzites, the Kadmonites, the Hittites, the Perizzites, the Rephaim, the Amorites, the Canaanites, the Girgashites, and the Jebusites."

The prophecy was told to Abram of all that would happen to his descendants. It said that they would be in a land that was not their own as slaves for four hundred years. God's judgment would be against Israel's oppressors and the people would come forth with great possessions. Of course Abram would be *"sleeping with the fathers" (dead)* before all of the prophecy actually manifested.

So far, Sarai was not part of this interaction between God and Abram. She too decided to take matters into her own hands according to the laws of the land. Sarai was feeling guilty that she had not produced Abram's promised son, so she turned to a law that said Abram could impregnate a servant, and the child would be born on Sarai's knees and thus become her own son. But a human substitute for spiritual law will not work, as we will see when the story continues.

The name Sarai is Hebrew that means *"bitter, contentious, dominative, and quarrelsome. In Sarai the soul is contending for its rightful place in consciousness... The divine must not be united with the material conditions, but with Spirit."* Metaphysical Bible Dictionary

Abram impregnated Sarai's slave, Hagar. The name Hagar is Hebrew means fugitive, wanderer, and stranger. Hagar represented the ego consciousness that is haughty and resentful. She was hateful toward her mistress and continually turned the child she bore against Sarai. The child's name was Ishmael, a Hebrew name that means, *"whom God understands, personality which must also be redeemed from error and corruption."* Metaphysical Bible Dictionary

Ishmael is further described in Genesis 16:12, *"He shall be a wild ass of a man, his hand against every man and every man's hand against him; and he shall dwell over against all his kinsmen."*

Angry at Hagar's antagonistic and hateful behavior toward her, Sarai demanded that Abram send Hagar and her child away. Abram was most likely tired of the quarrels and told Sarai to do with her slave whatever she wanted, which was Sarai's right. *"And Sarai dealt harshly with Hagar."* Anger, antagonism and hate have only one direction in which to take humanity and that is toward separation and destruction.

In Genesis 17 God spelled out his covenant with Abram again and changed his name to Abraham. The extra "ah" in the name is the breath of God expressed. This extended covenant included all his descendants for generations, the nation of Israel. The physical sign of the covenant was circumcision. This physical marking of circumcision was the designation of those who were of the covenant with God. Some neighboring peoples also practiced circumcision in order to become part of the Jewish Covenant.

Marking a child to designate it as belonging was common. It was also the practice in ancient times to bind the head of a newborn child of royalty so the head would grow in a high cone shape. Thus the child could never be mistaken for a commoner or a commoner for royalty. A crown was specially created to hide the deformity.

"Under the law of Jesus Christ, circumcision is fulfilled in its spiritual meaning – the purification of the individual from the law of sin and death… When one has entered into the spirit of divine law, the symbol is no longer necessary to soul growth." (Metaphysical Bible Dictionary) and from Romans 2:29, *"Circumcision is that of the heart, spiritual and not literal."*

God blessed Sarai that she would bear a son at 90 years old. Sarai's name was then changed to Sarah. *"Abraham fell on his face and laughed at the thought. 'O that Ishmael might live in thy sight!'"*

But Ishmael could not be the spiritual heir of God and live in God's sight from the description, *"his hand against every man and every man's hand against him; and he shall dwell over against all his kinsmen."*

This is a grim characteristic of humanity that will not be the seed of spirituality. God assured Abraham that Ishmael would be the father of twelve princes and be exceedingly prosperous, but His Covenant would be established with Isaac. God chose the name Isaac for Abraham's son. The name Isaac means, *"God laughs, joy, singing, leaping."* The beginning of the awareness of spirit within each one of us brings forth joy, singing, and leaps in consciousness.

Hagar and Ishmael were still with Abraham and Sarah. Ishmael and the entire household were circumcised, Abraham as well, at age 99. They all, negative and positive, had the mark of the Covenant. All aspects of humanity are drawn into a Covenant with God, even though some stray into darker places of development for a time. In the book of Revelation, all is eventually refined in the *"lake of fire"* or refined in the lifting up and purification.

In Genesis 18:1, *"And the Lord appeared to him (Abraham) by the oaks of Mamre, as he sat at the door of his tent in the heat of the day. He lifted up his eyes and behold there were three men who stood in front of him."*

The plain near Hebron is an important location for many patriarchs. The Hebrew Bible uses the words alonei mamre, which means "oaks of Mamre", to refer to a grove of oaks named after Mamreh the Amorite, who dwelt near Hebron (*Genesis 14:13, 24*). Abraham built an altar to the Lord there and it was there that he learned of the capture of his brother's son, Lot *(Genesis 14:13)*. The Lord appeared to Abraham there in a vision *(Genesis 15:1)* and the place where Abraham lived was soon sanctified. The Septuagint refers to *"the oak of Mamre,"* which would imply that one of the oaks was already being venerated as Abraham's altar. Isaac also lived there to the age of 180 years. *(Genesis 35:27)*.

Mamre (Hebrew) refers to the front brain, the seat of conscious thought. *(Metaphysical Bible Dictionary)* All the events we read about in this area are about the development of conscious thought. Humanity becomes conscious of its thinking and reasoning power. Father Pierre Teilhard de Chardin in his book *"The Phenomenon of Man"* called it the advent of complexity consciousness, where humanity first became aware of its surroundings, its thoughts, and ideas to improve its living situation and to create.

Humanity can flourish and prosper in the material world seemingly without God, but that limits it to be merely finite physical beings. The Covenant was about eternity that requires spiritual development. As was said by the Apostle Paul, the physical does not inherit the kingdom, only the spiritual.

We are not sure why Abraham saw three men when it was "the Lord" who spoke to him. It could be a symbol of God in three aspects. The church says *"God in three persons."* The three asked where Sarah was and the Lord said she would bear a child. So were there four? Or was the Lord the voice of the three? Three was a symbolic number indicating the number of creation, and a child was about to be created.

In Genesis 18:15 Sarah also laughed. When the Lord asked her why she laughed, she was afraid and denied laughing. And the Lord argued with her *"No, but you did laugh."* Spirit attempts to gently argue us out of our fears. Now Abraham became part of the Lord's counsel as he spoke with the three about Sodom. Evidently there was some questioning by the three as to whether Abraham should be part of this, but the Lord thought Abraham had to know everything in order to keep the ways of righteousness and justice in this great new nation. We can see by the elevating of Abraham how humanity had progressed in its development:

Adam and Eve – the beginning, creation
Noah – the restart of humanity

Abram - the herder
Abram - the general
Abram - the awareness of spiritual practice – tithing
Abram – the Covenant with God
Abraham – the thinking being
Abraham – the member of God's counsel
Now, Abraham, the contender with God

Abraham started to think about the destruction of Sodom and argued for the preservation of Sodom and Gomorrah. He bargained with God to save Sodom if he could find fifty good men there. God agreed. Then Abraham asked if God would destroy Sodom for a lack of five. God agreed to forty-five, then forty, then thirty, then twenty, and then a mere ten.

At this stage we bargain, beg or hedge, on our spiritual practice. We want to save our pet peeves, temperamental habits, grudges, and other things the ego mind treasures. God already knew the outcome, but as he said earlier, he must let Abraham learn for himself.

We are not punished for our fledgling understandings and God does not force anything upon us. We must learn for ourselves through human experience and reasoning. Ultimately we must find the Truth for ourselves.

In Genesis 19, we see that Lot must have had some good in him. He saw two men (angels) arriving at the gate of Sodom. He offered them hospitality and the advice to leave quickly in the morning. They offered to spend the night in the street and Lot went berserk. He knew the evil of Sodom and what would happen to them. At Lot's insistence they stayed in Lot's house.

But the men of the city came to Lot's door and asked him to send the men out to them. The law was binding upon Lot. If guests had eaten in his house, he must guarantee them protection. So Lot offered his virgin daughters to the men if they would leave the visitors alone. The men of the city broke in the door and reached for the guests, but they were struck blind. The intruders groped on the floor toward the door and crawled out. The guests told Lot that anyone else in the house should leave early in the morning with them because the Lord was about to destroy the city.

If there were husbands-to-be of the daughters, they probably thought Lot was jesting and stayed. Lot took his wife and daughters and fled to Zoar. The town of Zoar was still a town of wickedness, so Lot had not traveled very far from danger. He and his family were admonished not to look back upon Sodom, but Lot's wife looked back longingly at the life she had once lived and was now forced to abandon. It is written that she was turned into a pillar of salt when she looked back.

Around the Dead Sea there are many bizarre formations of salt. They look like pillars due to the seismic activity that sends sprays of water full of salt and minerals into the air. They settle on the rocks and over the years build these formations. Tradition has it that one of these pillars is Lot's wife.

Jesus' similar teaching was, *"No one who puts his hand to the plow and looks back, is fit for the kingdom of God." (Luke 9:62)* Each time we look back longingly to the "good old days" or a time when we were younger and more prosperous, we become frozen in time, like a pillar of salt. We cannot move forward.

Seeing the horrific destruction of Sodom, Lot was afraid to stay in Zoar. His fears sent him to the hills to live in a cave of darkness with his two daughters. His daughters had their own fears, that there would be no men left in the world with whom they could mate. The eldest daughter hatched the plan for the two of them to lay with their father when he was drunk. That way they could both be with child and carry on the race.

The eldest daughter had the idea. The younger one just followed along. The child born of an idea became father of the Moabites, the tribe of Ruth, who married Boaz, and became the ancestral line of Jesus. The child born in darkness without an idea became father of the Ammonites. The Ammonites were eventually eradicated by the Israelites. Nothing was left of that tribe.

Bible teachers often do not want to dwell on this story of what they believe is terrible sin and degradation. But there is a powerful metaphysical principle here. Regardless of how desperate a situation looks and how hopeless, an idea is the way forward. We may not have means or finances, and the predicament we are in may look hopeless, but we can always have an idea. The world may not approve of the eldest daughter's idea, but it became part of the chain of consciousness eventually leading to the birth of Jesus who expressed the Christ nature.

CHAPTER SIX

Rewriting Our Story

Abraham and Lot journeyed together all their lives, but Lot is now gone from the picture. The name, Abraham, means *"father of a multitude"* or father of our thoughts. *"The power to make substance out of ideas."* (Metaphysical Bible Dictionary)

The name Lot represents the negative or physical side of faith, connected to the intellect. When Abraham rescued Lot, he reset the proper place of the physical that was taken out of context by the northern kings. Our physical nature cannot be abandoned but must be kept safe and integrated into the whole of our being for development to continue.

Genesis 20 seems to parallel Genesis 12:13 where in Egypt Abram lied, calling Sarai his sister for fear of Pharaoh. In Genesis 20 the story repeats in a different setting. *"When Abraham and Sarah journeyed toward the Negev and dwelt between Kadesh and Shur"* Abraham again lied, this time to Abimelech, the king of Gerar, saying that Sarah was his sister. The king took Sarah into his harem.

These are essentially the same story told from two different perspectives. A northern writer writes Genesis 12 with inserts from the priestly writer, and a southern writer writes Genesis 20. The writers are making the same teaching point, each in their own setting. It is well known that we each tell of an incident from our own perspective and all perspectives are slightly different. But the teaching is the same. The thing we fear comes upon us and lies do not save us.

This time God comes to Abimelech in a dream and tells him the truth about Sarah. God also keeps Abimelech from sinning by not allowing him to touch her. God calls Abraham a prophet now and threatens Abimelech if he does not return Sarah to Abraham.

This is the classic question that Abimelech asks Abraham, *"What were you thinking?"*

Now we are learning something more about Sarah from Abraham. The writer of Genesis 20 was most likely interested in cleaning up the lie and making it all right for Abraham to say Sarah was his sister. *"She is indeed my sister, the daughter of my father, but not of my mother, and she became my wife."* The location was changed from Egypt to Gerar, and the kings from Pharaoh to Abimelech. Abimelech was a Philistine king, which makes him still an outsider like Pharaoh. Neither was allowed to violate Sarai, now Sarah.

There is a third time the lie was told, and this time by Isaac in Genesis 26:6. He married Rebekah and went to live in the land of Gerar, and for the same reasons passed his wife off as his sister. The story turns out the same as the others, except when the misunderstanding was cleared up, Isaac and Rebekah remained in Gerar to live.

Sarah and Rebekah were beautiful goddess-like women. Sarah means princess and Rebekah means beauty. Abram was a herder and Isaac did nothing noteworthy in his life. Faith is often shaken when the beauty of our lives is threatened by the ego, the dark side, and we try to deal with our fears from a lower state of consciousness, to lie to ourselves. Abraham and Isaac both had forgotten God and reverted to the ego's inferior ways.

There are other rewrites intended to clean up certain stories. The next one would be First and Second Chronicles, which is a rewrite of First and Second Kings, done to idealize the life of King David. In Kings, David was a pretty unsavory character. But Chronicles did not replace Kings in the Hebrew Testament. Both writings were included intact and we can see a sample of idealizing our lives, and the freeing ourselves from the past.

In the Gospels after Peter denied he knew Jesus three times, Jesus later cancelled out the denials by asking Peter three times if he loved him. The three affirmations of love cancelled out the three fearful denials. We have many opportunities to rewrite our lives and recreate our future experiences. We are always creating our future by our present predominant thinking. When we turn our minds from reliving the past, our future changes for the better.

Metaphysically, the rewrite is a form of forgiveness and healing. We can remember a painful incident and neutralize the pain by restructuring our thinking, changing our perception of the story. We rewrite by letting go of blame, realizing that if people knew better they would do better. This is true for us personally as well. This may be hard to take in, but we can only do in any given moment what we know. When we neutralize the emotions that come with blame or shame, the pain ebbs away and we can stop reliving the past in our minds.

Much is made of laughter in Genesis18:15 when Sarah, Abraham, and the Lord have a humorous conversation where Sarah laughed to herself about her lost ability to have a child. When God questions Abraham, *"Why did Sarah laugh?"* she evidently heard the question and said, *"I did not laugh,"* and he (Abraham?) said, *"but you did laugh."* There is no need to fear our own potential and we need to smile at our own doubts, or take them lightly to lessen their negative effect. Laughter is good for body and soul.

In Genesis 21:7 Isaac was born to Sarah and Abraham. *"God has made laughter for me; everyone who hears will laugh over me."* Abraham and Sarah both laugh with joy at the birth of Isaac. His name in the Hebrew means laughter, joy, singing, and leaping. This signals the advent of an entirely new state of consciousness that is joyous, humorous, and celebratory.

There was no possibility of conception in their existing physical circumstances. Abraham was almost 100 years old and Sarah close to that as well. Metaphysically there is no possibility of the conception of the divine in the human physical course of events. The new humanity is a new creature, begotten by the Divine Seed, the Word, the Logos.

The divinity within us does not come through the processes of the human physicality, but from a higher consciousness, Spirit, God Mind. This is a cosmic foretelling of the birth of Jesus by Divine Seed. Humanity must evolve until it becomes Christ, just as Jesus became Christ.

Abraham's first child, Ishmael, represents personality gone wrong. At Isaac's weaning celebration Ishmael was playing with Isaac, which incurred the wrath of Sarah. She didn't want it thought that Ishmael was equal to Isaac. That which is born of personality is never equal to that which is born of spirit.

Hagar looked upon Sarah with distain *(Genesis 16:4),* and taught her son the same. Sarah told Abraham to send Hagar and Ishmael away. Abraham tried to mediate, but Sarah was adamant. Sarah had the power. God reassured Abraham that Ishmael would be taken care of and he would make a nation. So Hagar and Ishmael were turned out into the desert.

Hagar took a wife for Ishmael from the land of Egypt. This is the end of another cycle of human development. Egypt represents the return to the material world where no evolution is possible. Ishmael was not out of the picture completely. He turned up at the death of Abraham to stand beside Isaac as they buried their father at Machpelah. Ishmael's descendants are chronicled in detail. They are thoughts and states of conscious belonging to that in man for which Ishmael stands, the physical.

Machpelah means place of caves, a place symbolic of where Ishmael dwelt in this early years. Abraham, Sarah, Isaac, Rebekah, Leah, and Jacob are all buried there. The fathers and mothers of humanity sink down into subconsciousness to underscore and aid the whole human organism to attain a higher plane of expression. *(Metaphysical Bible Dictionary)*

These are the twelve tribes of Ishmael and they each have a metaphysical meaning. It is important to know that these unevolved aspects of humanity precede the more evolved meanings of the twelve tribes of Jacob. Again the physical is born first and then the mental, later to become spiritual. The Apostle Paul wrote, *"If there is a physical body, there is a spiritual body. The physical comes first and then the spiritual."*

In every instance of siblings in the Bible, the first child's name has a meaning that represents the physical nature and the second, the mental and spiritual. You will see by this listing of the sons of Ishmael how that shows up. In each case life starts with possibility and descends into mournfulness and longing, stuck in the physical. His latter six children represent a rising of consciousness, especially the last child.

Nabioth – Possibility of bringing forth good. First born means heights.
Kedar - Dark, overcast, mournful
Adbeel – Languishing for God, for something higher

Mibsam – Sensing joys and beauties of the spirit, sweet odor, pleasant.
Mishma – Obeying answering, outer sense consciousness
Dumah – Silence, a tomb
Massa – Prophecy, fruitful thoughts of the natural man in the flesh.
Hadad – Might, powerful intellect, power, glory, splendor, rejoicing
Tema – Good fortune, prosperity, good faith
Jetur – Order, solidarity, strength
Napish – Breath of life, refreshed, re-inspired,
Kedemah – Principle, ancient, eternal, inner true being of man.

In later chapters we will find the formation of the twelve tribes of Israel, where the meaning of the names indicates a more intertwining and cohesive picture of man's development. These that are of the ego nature seem to be separate parts, but those of the spirit converge as one.

Ishmael died at 137 years old. The significance of the ages recorded in the Hebrew Testament is still a mystery. Scholars are not sure if in ancient times they counted years symbolically or if these are actual numbers of years as we count them now.

In Genesis 20:2 Abraham lied to Abimelech saying that Sarah was his sister because he feared his life was in danger. The same story is told in Genesis 12:10 only it was Pharaoh he lied to. The reason for two stories in different settings is because they were written by two writers, one from the northern kingdom and one from the southern or Judah. The endings were different. Pharaoh told Abraham to leave and Abimelech told him to stay as long as he wanted.

In Genesis 21:22, Abraham was still sojourning in the land of Abimelech after this incident over Sarah. Abraham was still a herder and was grazing his sheep in the area. There came a dispute over a well of water. Disputes over water were common since water was scarce in that area. Abimelech, Philcol the army commander and Abraham made a pact to be honest with each other. When Abraham reported that someone had seized his well, the other two swore a pact that the well was indeed Abraham's. This first oath between humans was to be truthful and not steal from each other.

Another pact was quite different in tone and intent. From Genesis 31:49, *"the Lord watch between me and thee, while we are absent one from the other."* This is often repeated at the end of a service in the Christian church. But as you will see it is not a benediction but a threat, a line drawn in the sand.

The whole passage reads:

"...for he said, The Lord watch between you and me, when we are absent one from another. If you ill-treat my daughters, or if you take other wives beside my daughters, although no man is with us, remember God is witness between you and me."

In Genesis 31:51 Laban said to Jacob, *"See this heap of stones and behold this pillar, which I have set between you and me. This heap is a witness, and this pillar is a witness, that I will not pass over this heap to you, and that you wall not pass over this heap and this pillar to me for harm."*

Many pacts from then on were made between kings, rulers and others to avert an attack. The ego mind engenders fear and distrust and makes it seem reasonable to require a surety of some kind to be safe, ultimately fueling the fear.

In Genesis 22 is the famous story of the near sacrifice of Isaac. It is thought by scholars that Abraham might have been sojourning and wandered from the Promised Land into Philistine country. To a metaphysician this would represent traveling in a lower state of consciousness. In this lower state Abraham misinterpreted God's message to mean he should make a burnt offering of his son Isaac.

Abraham simply goes about preparing for the sacrifice without question or pause, without thinking this would spell the end of the promise that Abraham's descendants would cover the earth. He did, however, formerly bargain with God to save Sodom and its people. This time he did not bargain even though it was his own son. Ego mind at the physical level has its own agenda, not taking into account anything but retaining its own temporal power over the conscious mind. It would have destroyed Abraham to kill his own son. But an angel stayed his hand and told him to sacrifice a wild ram. It would destroy our own spiritual growth to kill the first glimmering of spiritual thought, because ego mind convinced us of some nonsense.

This event sounds like a vision rather than an actual event. George Lamsa, translator of the Lamsa Bible, observed that Sarah was not mentioned in this story and she would surely have objected. He believes this event was a vision that Abraham spoke of later and interpreted it to others. The people of that time lived in a rich mixture of visions, prophecies, dreams, and interpretations. It is difficult to discern when and if many of these biblical events actually happened. The Bible writers were not concerned with writing history, but saga. They told stories to show what God had done for His people.

In a sense this story of Isaac is a parallel of the Gospels in which God sacrificed his own son on the cross. Much of the Gospels were written from the older Hebrew texts and teachings. For instance the Lord's Prayer and the words of Jesus on the cross were all taken from these Hebrew Testament writings.

In today's world we have abandoned these visions in favor of empirical evidence and material events. Thus people have lost the ability to see beyond appearances into deeper meanings or motifs. Most modern people of today's world do not interpret meanings or discern evolutionary markers.

"Jacob's sons represent the twelve foundational faculties of man. The name of each of these sons, correctly interpreted, reveals the development of its particular faculty in spirit, soul, and body. Their mother, Leah, gave the meaning of their names at their birth." (Metaphysical Bible Dictionary)

Reuben - Vision, understanding
Simeon - Hearing, understanding
Levi – Love is the uniting
Judah – Praise quickens the mind
Dan – Righteous judgment
Napthali – Strength restorative
Gad – Abundance, good fortune
Asher – Happiness through wisdom
Issachar – Brings reward, compensation
Zebulun – Order of habitation
Joseph – Progressive Increase in Character
Benjamin – Active Faith

These meanings are all a function of the psychological level, creating a foundation in human consciousness for the eventual development of human spirituality. The evolution of this foundation will be further represented in the Gospels as we study the twelve disciples called into the service of Spirit by Jesus.

CHAPTER SEVEN

Abraham Attended to Business

Genesis 23 notes that Sarah died at age 127 and Abraham negotiated with Ephron the Hittite for a safe burial place in Hebron for Sarah. The Hittites sold the land to Abraham. They would have given it to him, but he insisted on paying full price to gain legal title to it, four hundred shekels. Abraham believed in the covenant with God that said all the land was already his, but he wisely negotiated an ironclad agreement with the lower material nature for Sarah's burial place. At the human, physical level, he took care of business. Knowing we are created in the image and likeness of God, we know we must still deal with the transient nature of the physical world and insist upon clear "ironclad" dealings with it.

At that time the Hittites had a large empire. The Pharaoh Ramses attacked them, drove them back behind their barriers, but could not defeat them. Ramses went home without a victory. This was serious for him because the people considered the Pharaoh to be a god, and now in defeat Ramses proved he was not a god. The lowly Sea Peoples, the Philistines, came onto the land at some point and scattered the Hittites.

The name Hittite is Hebrew meaning scattered, broken in pieces, terror, and dread. They represent the fragments of doubt and fear that continue to live in the subconscious mind of humanity. They were the ones Joshua was supposed to drive out of the Promised Land later on, but he didn't quite get the job done. His people began to live among the Canaanites and Hittites, worshipped their gods, learned farming from them, and in some cases intermarried. This shows us how deeply rooted fear and negativity are in human consciousness to the point that we become comfortable with them.

The only one who knew how to defeat fear was Jesus the Christ. He did it by turning his mind away from fear and focusing upon God. Jesus always interfaced with God Mind, which contains no fear. Humanity in the Hebrew Testament had not yet developed to the point of embodying the higher consciousness.

In Genesis 24, Abraham had other business to attend to and that was to find a wife for Isaac. He did not want Isaac to marry a Canaanite woman, a corrupting influence who would lead him into idolatry. The name Canaanite means one who exists for material things. Canaan means *"realized nothingness, material existence, inferior."* The Isaac consciousness within us *(Divine Sonship, beginning spiritual consciousness)* must have union with the soul's natural delight in beauty represented by Rebekah. The name is spelled Rebecca in Romans 9:10. *(Metaphysical Bible Dictionary)*

A prominent servant was entrusted with finding a wife for Isaac. He placed his hand under Abraham's thigh, an old form of oath taking, reflecting the view that the fountain of reproduction was sacred to the deity. *(Footnotes p.27 Oxford RSV.)* Thus we get the words testament, testimony and its variations from the oath taking on the testicles. The servant had to know how to recognize the right woman and how to approach her and her father. He brought ten camels laden with various gifts and went to the city of Nahor, home of Abraham's late father, Terah, and his family. The servant carefully laid out a plan and prayed for his success. He told God exactly how he would recognize which woman coming to the well was the right one. The servant assumed God already knew who it was and would reveal her in a way the servant could recognize.

This is the servant's prayer in Genesis 24:12. *"O Lord God of my master, Abraham, grant me success today, I pray thee, and show steadfast love to my master, Abraham. Behold I am standing by the spring of water, and the daughters of the men of the city are coming out to draw water. Let the maiden to whom I shall say, 'Pray let down your jar that I may drink,' and who shall say, 'Drink, and I will water your camels,' let her be the one whom you have appointed for your servant Isaac. By this I shall know that you have shown steadfast love to my master."*

The last sentence is a reminder to God of his promises to Abraham. Reminding God of His promises was often included in great detail in the prayers throughout the Hebrew Testament. It serves us well to be reminded of the Truth of our spiritual path, and remember the strength and direction it has given us as we grow. This story indicates that we need a clear idea of what we want and what form it should take. Often people pray without a clear idea and their answer may be unrecognizable because they aren't specific. Then they assume the prayer is not answered.

Then the servant identified Rebekah by carefully following his plan. He immediately gave her rich gifts and joyfully went to her father bringing ten camels laden with gold and gifts. This probably convinced the father of the servant's identity and mission, but things still had to be done in proper order. He recounted to the father every detail of the story starting with Isaac's birth and the promise of nations. The food set before him probably got cold and the wine warm because he said in Genesis 24:33, *"I will not eat until I have told my errand. He (the father) said, 'Speak on.'"*

Stories were not written down in early times. They were told by tribal storytellers over and over around the evening campfires and passed to succeeding generations in exacting detail. So the servant carried on this tradition and told everything accurately to the last word. In our busy world today we have many time constraints and barely take the time to listen to each other. We limit the number of characters in a text message so the recipient can quickly and sometimes barely grasp the surface detail.

In Genesis 24:64 when all was appropriately carried out, Rebekah agreed to go with the servant to meet his master. She saw Isaac coming across the field and immediately jumped off her camel. It was love at first sight. They ran off to Isaac's tent to consummate the union...but again not before the servant told Isaac all the details of all he had done so Isaac would know everything was accomplished according to law.

The last verse of this story reads, *"So Isaac was comforted after his mother's death."* It is written that Abraham mourned Sarah's death, but this is the first mention of Isaac needing comfort. This was this most likely the redactor turning our attention away from the immediate and passionate coupling of Isaac and Rebekah that had just taken place. He called it comfort instead of lust. Humanity is prone to hedging rather than telling the whole truth. People lie to themselves and others with something they think will be more acceptable and in so doing turn away from knowing their true passions.

In Genesis 25 Abraham was not finished yet. He took another wife, Keturah. Her name means fragrant incense. Incense symbolizes higher aspirations, the process of transformation. She bore him six sons and they are all listed by name. Each name has a Hebrew meaning, and a pattern that reveals the darker side of human development.

Zimran – song, music, positive expression
Jokshan – sly, treacherous, deceitful
Medan – contention, striving, righteousness
Midian – government, striving, dominion
Ishbak – leaving, forsaking, human ambition
Shuah – despair, depressed

Sons of Jokshan were:

Asshurim – guided by the senses, seems invincible
Letushim – sharp, stern, oppressing
Leummim – multitudes of thoughts but dry, lack of spiritual quickening
Sons of Midian were:
Ephah – overcast, obscured
Epher – Quick, light, ethereal
Hanoch – Agony of the soul, arrested
Abida – Father of knowledge, discordant
Eldaah – Whom God has called, he has no descendants

The Bible is known as the book of life because every aspect of human development is revealed if one knows the meanings of the names. They were not given randomly like many names given today. Our children are named after something or someone we like, or one picks a quirky name that pleases the parents at the moment.

Abraham had already given everything in the Covenant to Isaac, so he gave gifts to the sons of his concubines and before he died, sent them away from Isaac to the east, essentially to Arabia. You can see by their names why Abraham sent them away from Isaac. These are not the attributes we want to develop in consciousness. There are glimmerings of something higher, but they do not manifest and essentially go nowhere. There were no descendants.

In Genesis 25:12 are the descendants of Ishmael, which were listed in a previous chapter. These later children of Abraham seem to fit more closely with the Ishmael consciousness. These represent the many facets of humanity, but only one is the chosen for the Covenant and that is the precursor of Christ consciousness, Isaac.

Isaac was forty years old when he married Rebekah and she was barren for a long time. Isaac prayed for her and she became pregnant with twins. These infants struggled within her womb and she asked God what this meant. From Genesis 25:23, *"Two nations are in your womb, and two peoples, born of you shall be divided, the one shall be stronger than the other, the elder shall serve the younger."* These children were Jacob and Esau. Esau was first born, hairy and red faced. When Jacob was born, he had a grip on Esau's heel. Jacob means, *"he supplants." Oxford RSV notes. P.30*

In the Scriptures the first-born always represents the physical nature, and the second born is always the mental/spiritual. This interpretation holds true for all siblings in the Hebrew and New Testaments. The birthright is given to the firstborn, and must be taken over by the second born. The physical realm cannot carry the birthright to a higher plane of consciousness.

Esau became the game hunter. Isaac preferred to stay at home. *"He was a quiet man dwelling in the tents."* Tents, houses, or dwellings represent mind. Esau was body consciousness, and Jacob was mind consciousness. Esau was easily outwitted on an empty stomach. He wanted what Jacob was cooking and Jacob said, *"First sell me your birthright."* Esau said, *"I am about to die, of what use is a birth right to me?"* Jacob said, *"Swear to me first."* So he swore to him, and sold his birthright to Jacob for a bowl of essentially lentil soup.

Again there was a famine in the land and Isaac started south as far as Gerar when God came to him and told him not to go into Egypt. So Isaac lied this time to the men of Gerar about Rebekah, as did Abraham about Sarah. *"Abimelech looked out of a window and saw Isaac fondling Rebekah, and shouted, "She is your wife! How could you say she is your sister?"* When things become difficult, we tend to turn to the material world for resolution, sustenance, and assurance. Egypt and Gerar represent the material world that always requires false thinking and self-deception. God calls us to stay in the realm of mind and spirit and not descend into that material state. God said to Isaac, *"I will be with you"* and again promised that his descendants would become nations, the same promises He made to Abraham.

Isaac was not a herder or nomad. He was a semi-nomad and tiller of the soil. He was extremely successful, so much so that the Philistines were jealous and fearful. They filled all the water wells with dirt to drive Isaac away. When we are successful, others may try to fill our minds with doubts, and speak ill of us. When we are praying for guidance ego mind tries to throw us off the track with scoffing and derisive thoughts.

So Isaac moved out and encamped in the Valley of Gerar, which wasn't too far away. Isaac's people started digging out the wells the Philistines had stopped up. But when they hit water, the herdsmen of Gerar would come and claim the well as theirs. Isaac's people dug out two more wells. The herdsmen claimed the second one but not the third. There was no use trying to drive Isaac away because he could successfully dig more wells than they could claim. The depth of our being is unending and the water of life flows wherever we dig deeply enough to find it.

Isaac moved to Beersheba, pitched his tent there and again they dug a well. The Philistines were frightened by now. Isaac's tribe was very large and his prosperity seemed to have no end. So King Abimelech, his advisor and his general, all came to visit Isaac. They saw that Isaac's God was obviously very powerful and they wanted to make a peace covenant with Isaac so he would not attack them.

They represent that lower consciousness of fear that can only envision attack. In their culture those who were stronger always attacked the weaker. The physical is threatened when the mental demonstrates its power. The ego of the physical realm decides to insure its survival by rushing to make a covenant of peace, but only until the balance of temporal power changes.

While Esau and Jacob were growing up the father's blessing was supposed to go to Esau. We do not know if Isaac knew Esau had already sold his birthright to Jacob, or if it would have made a difference in who got the blessing from Isaac. Isaac was now old and blind, and promised Esau the blessing if Esau would bring him game from the field and prepare his favorite dish. Rebekah was listening. Jacob was the son she loved. Rebekah hatched a plot to deceive Isaac by wrapping Jacob's arms and neck in the skins of kids and dressing him in Esau's rough smelly clothing. Jacob was terrified. He didn't think he could pull it off, but Rebekah convinced him to follow her plan quickly. They had to get this done before Esau returned from hunting. Jacob did pull it off and received the father's blessing just before Esau returned.

In modern day interpretations Rebekah is thought to be wicked and deceptive, but this is a story meant to illustrate that by whatever means the mental/spiritual must carry the birthright and blessing. The future of the nation promised by God was at stake. This is the blessing given by Isaac in Genesis 27:28:

> *"See, the smell of my son is as the smell of a field which the Lord has blessed! May God give you the dew of heaven, and the fatness of the earth, and plenty of grain and wine. Let peoples serve you, and nations bow down to you. Be Lord over your brothers, and may your mother's sons bow down to you. Cursed be everyone who curses you, and blessed be everyone who blesses you!"*

In Genesis 27:35 Esau came in a little later to discover what happened. "He begged his father to bless him too. *'Have you not reserved a blessing for me?'* Isaac answered Esau, *'Your brother came with guile and he has taken away your blessing. Behold I have made him your Lord..'"*

Isaac continued, *"Behold, away from the fatness of the earth shall your dwelling be, and away from the dew of heaven on high. By your sword you shall live and you shall serve your brother; but when you break loose you shall break his yoke from your neck."* Then Esau hated Jacob and planned to kill him after their father's burial.

"When you break loose, you shall break his yoke from your neck" means to us when you break loose from your anger and hatred you will not be enslaved to it. Any time we carry enmity for another we are under the yoke of that negativity until we break loose from it. Only then can we move on with our lives.

Rebekah heard of Esau's plan and urged Jacob to flee to her brother, Laban, in Haran and dwell there until Esau forgot his anger. She asked Isaac to charge Jacob not to marry one of the Hittite women, but to find a wife among the daughters of Laban. Our growth toward spirituality must be guarded and nurtured, and not allowed to fall into destructive patterns of thought.

In Genesis 26:34 is a comment on Esau. *"When Esau was forty years old, he took to wife Judith and Basemath (Hittite women) as his wives and they made life bitter for Isaac and Rebekah."* Seeing their son Esau being drawn into worshipping the pagan gods was an abomination to Isaac and Rebekah. The hope was in Jacob to stay the course of human development.

CHAPTER EIGHT

Jacob, Laban and Rachel

After Jacob deceived this father and brother, he left in haste to Paddan-aram, to the home of his mother's brother, Laban. This is a place in the north of Syria. Paddan means "a broad level plain" and Aram symbolizes the intellect. The name Laban means white, clear, shining, gentle, noble. He lives in Haran meaning "exalted mountain."

Metaphysically, Jacob's fall from grace symbolizes our own fall when we get into a dis-graceful state of mind. We need to leave it with haste and find a reasonable place in our thinking, a broad level plain in mind to sort ourselves out until we again find our place sitting at the feet of exalted ideas and divine aspirations. This was necessary for Jacob, as well as for us, to reconnect with the soul and continue on the divine journey. As the story continued Jacob grew rapidly in understanding and possessions in the land of Laban.

In Genesis 29, Jacob traveled to Haran and was amazed at the abundance before him with a well of water, flocks of sheep, green fields, and shepherds. Filled with excitement he approached the shepherds and asked them who they were. Behold, they were from Haran. He inquired after Laban found that they knew him. One pointed to an approaching flock and said, *"See, Rachel his daughter is coming with the sheep!"*

At that time, a well could not be uncovered until all rightful parties were present. The stone covering the well was so large it took more than one man to lift it. This didn't stop Jacob. He saw Rachel and rushed to open the well for her by himself. In the coming together of these two aspects of our development, the mental and the innocent seeking something higher, there is instant joyous recognition. She represents the soul that is still in a transitory state and will be fruitful only on the higher spiritual plane of ideas.

Laban greeted Jacob enthusiastically. The clear shining presence of spirit welcomes us on our next step higher on the path. This is similar to the story of the Prodigal Son, where the son squandered his inheritance and decided to return home. His father met him on the road with a robe, shoes, and a ring, and gave a celebration honoring his return. In the New Testament, the story tells us of spiritual rather than psychological development. The son is welcomed back to his home to a higher state of mind. Everything that happens in the Hebrew Testament is about the psychological/intellectual development. Everything in the New Testament is about the spiritual development. The stories can be similar, but the levels in consciousness are different.

Did the writers know they were writing about the progress of human development? Yes and no. They taught these stories as segments of development. But the orderly progression through the Bible is the hand of Spirit. It is up to us to perceive the progression, and thus interpret our own life experiences accordingly. In this way, the Bible is the handbook for humanity. It is up to us to use it to grow in awareness and wisdom. Our lives can look like a hodge-podge of experiences until we come up to the high level plain where we can look back and see the perfect ordering of each event that brought us to this place and moment.

Through interpretation, I could see how what I thought was my stumbling, was absolutely necessary for my growth. I didn't need to feel guilty or a failure, but rather feel joy that it all brought me up to where I am. My father said it was a shame that I wasted so much time in my life before I entered ministry. He was not aware of the necessary stages of development in our life experiences. We cannot just jump into a higher state. We must develop into it. When Myrtle Fillmore met someone she would say to him or her, *"So! You have come up to here!"*

Jacob and Rachel's meeting is the second mention of love between a man and a woman. The first was Isaac and Rebekah. Until now love was usually mentioned only in regard to God and a dependence upon God. Love is mentioned most often in the Gospels and Epistles where it is used as a teaching, but not romantic love popularized in our modern world.

Interestingly, Jesus was quoting Leviticus 19:18 when he said, *"Love your neighbor as yourself."* Then he taught the disciples and crowds how to accomplish this as their way of being. He did not come to break the law but to enhance the use of it spiritually.

So here in the early Hebrew Testament we are seeing the first component, personal emotional attachment developing.

Laban wanted to know what Jacob's wages should be but Jacob wanted only to labor the seven years required by Laban for the hand of Rachel. In Genesis 29:16, *"So Jacob served seven years for Rachel, and they seemed to him but a few days because of the love he had for her."*

This is an interesting reference to the collapse of time, or to the unreality of the existence of time. The Course in Miracles, and most any other spiritual teaching, indicates that time does not exist except in the mind of man. It is a human construct. We experience days spinning by or dragging on, depending upon the content of the mind. Joy can make time fly and anticipation can elongate it, even though it is the same number of hours.

Then came what Jacob thought was the great deception. After seven years he was to finally marry his beloved Rachel, but the next morning after the wedding it was Leah in his bed, not Rachel. According to George Lamsa, honeymooning was not known in that culture. After wedding festivities that lasted for several days, everyone had lots of wine and at dark went to bed, sometimes ten people to a room. There were no lights. Jacob assumed it was Rachel in his bed, but Laban had slipped Leah into his bed instead.

It is hard to believe Jacob did not know the custom of marrying off the eldest daughter first. Sometimes being engulfed in emotional bliss, one becomes blind to the realities of living in society. George Lamsa said that Rachel had the pretty eyes, and Leah's eyes weren't so pretty, but she had a more attractive body. Jacob was in love with Rachel simply because she was younger and he had seen her first. Laban did not think he had done wrong. He then offered Rachel if Jacob would work another seven years. The agreement was that Jacob could have Rachel in seven days, but then would work seven more years. Laban was very smart. Jacob was prospering them all and he wanted to keep Jacob around.

Leah always hoped Jacob would love her, but he just did not. It had nothing to do with her eyes, as is commonly thought. Even when Leah gave Jacob ten sons he still did not love her. The name, Leah, means weary, sluggish as opposed to the name, Rachel, which means migrating ewe. The migrating soul is not immediately ready to manifest its gifts. It was many years later when Rachel finally became pregnant and bore Joseph.

Again the first-born sister is Leah whose name has a physical meaning. Rachel is the second born and her name represents movement toward spiritual development. The same is true of Martha and Mary in the Gospels. Martha, the older one, was busy with physical things and Mary, the younger sister, was listening to Jesus' spiritual teachings. It is the same principle of the first and second born that holds true throughout the Bible.

Eventually Jacob desired to be on is own. Laban did not want to lose a good thing in Jacob and in Genesis 30:27 said, *"I have learned by divination that the Lord has blessed me because of you; name your wages and stay."* We are not told what method of divination Laban used. In Genesis 30:30 Jacob cautiously agreed saying, *"The Lord has blessed you wherever I turned. But now when shall I provide for my own household also?".*

Like Abraham, Jacob would not accept money or goods as direct payment. *"You shall not give me anything if you will do this for me…"* He wanted to take all the speckled and spotted sheep, and every black lamb, the same with the goats. This way he could prove to Laban that he had not stolen from him because Laban's flock would be pure white. White wool was more precious. Black wool was considered undesirable because it was thought to represent death.

God gave the increase to Jacob. Jacob took only what God had given, not what Laban wanted to give. Now Laban, still trying to keep Jacob with him, ordered his men to take all the spotted and black sheep and goats and drive them three-days' journey away so Jacob would not have his own flock.

But in Genesis 30:37 Jacob was clever and his action is an essential metaphysical teaching for us today. Jacob took rods or branches from the poplar, almond and plane trees, peeled the bark in strips leaving white streaks, and set them in front of the water troughs where the flocks came to drink. The sheep breed when they come to drink. The flocks bred looking upon the striped rods and brought forth speckled, striped, and spotted young. He laid the rods in front of only the strongest of the flock, not the weakest. So Laban got the white ones as promised, but they were the weakest. Jacob retained the black, spotted, and strongest lambs and became very wealthy.

What we focus upon predominantly in our thinking becomes stronger in our beliefs and manifests in our experience. Thoughts we hold in mind reproduce after their kind in our lives. Teachings about positive thinking come from this understanding of divine law. We must focus our thinking upon what we want for our lives, rather than upon what we do not want. Whether the story about the sheep is actually true makes no difference. It is the Truth teaching that is important. King David said he had God always before his face.

There was great strife between Jacob and Laban's sons. Even Rachel and Leah got involved, accusing Laban of using up their dowry money so that there was no inheritance left for them. They felt sold out by their father and urged Jacob to take them, their families and possessions, and leave. He knew Laban would try again to prevent them from leaving, so while Laban was away shearing sheep Jacob gathered all he had gained and prepared to leave.

While Laban was away, Rachel hid her father's household gods in her personal bundles. In the cultures in the area, people had household gods they prayed to in the form of little statues they hid in the eaves of their homes. They believed the gods brought them good crops, flocks, many children, and protection from enemies. Rachel had grown up with them. They were her gods too. It was unthinkable that she would leave them behind.

Laban caught up to Jacob three days later and he was irate. In Genesis 31:26, *"What have you done, that you have cheated me, and carried away my daughters like captives of the sword? Why did you flee secretly and cheat me, and did not tell me, so that I might have sent you away with mirth and songs, with tambourine and lyre? ...and why did you steal my gods?"*

Jacob had worked so hard to be sure Laban could not accuse him of stealing, and in innocence declared that Laban could search their tents and anyone who stole the gods would not live! Jacob knew he must get back to his home and the One God. It didn't occur to him that Rachel believed in these household gods and would take them. But Rachel, too, was clever. She hid the statues under a camel saddle and sat upon it. When they came into her tent, she apologized to them that she was in the way of women and could not rise. The men of that time would not come near a menstruating woman or demand that she rise from her rags. So the gods were not found and Rachel was safe.

The belief in one god came through Abraham, Isaac, and Jacob, but was not necessarily prevalent among the outlying tribes of Abraham. Laban was in the north where other gods were worshipped. It appeared he had honored all beliefs in his gods and Jacob's father's god.

In Genesis 31:29 Laban said, *"It is in my power to do you harm but the god of your father spoke to me last night saying, take heed that you speak to Jacob neither good nor bad."* In other words don't try to talk him into staying and do not attack him.

Jacob had prospered in Laban's lands just as Abraham had prospered in Egypt. But the intention was always to return to the Promised Land, as it still is today. We may go far afield in our everyday living, prospering in the material world, but the urging is always within us to return to our true home in spirit and to the one God, Creator of all. At last Jacob was returning home not only to God but also to his angered brother, Esau.

CHAPTER NINE

Jacob and Esau

J acob knew he would eventually have to face his brother, Esau. Even after twenty years Esau surely would not have forgiven him and might even attack him and his family. All sorts of fears and nightmare scenarios ran through his mind. It seemed sure there would be punishment at the hands of Esau.

How like Jacob we still are in our experience. He was full of fear and guilt because he and his mother tricked Isaac and stole the birthright. We fear the worst and torture ourselves with imagined events before we meet the thing we fear. Often there is nothing to fear after all.

Jacob went on his way after making this pact with Laban. In Genesis 31:49 the pact was, *"The Lord watch between you and me, while we are absent one from the other. If you ill-treat my daughters or if you take wives beside my daughters, although no man is with us, remember God is witness between you and me."* Then they built a heap of stones past which neither would transgress. This pact is often used in churches as a closing blessing, but it is actually a threat between Jacob and Laban. The meaning is essentially, if you transgress, God will see and punish you. Jacob was still in a state of great fear. As he continued he met God's army of angels. Nothing more is said about their purpose or the effect they had on Jacob. However their appearance seemed to shore up his confidence a little.

We can sense God's army of spiritual thoughts coming to help us, but we go right on focusing on fear and making plans according to our fears. We search for ways to somehow buy off our fears. Jacob sent a messenger to Esau telling him how rich he had become. He thought perhaps to intimidate Esau by recounting his riches so Esau would think better of attacking him.

Jacob didn't expect the messenger to return saying Esau was coming with four hundred men! It was worse than Jacob thought! His fears deepened. When our fears deepen we cannot buy them off or deflect them. We must meet them and work through them until we see their unreality and be no longer afraid.

But Jacob panicked, hurriedly created a plan of defense, and divided his people and flocks into two "companies." His thought was if Esau destroyed one company, the other could escape. In Genesis 32:9 Jacob prayed for deliverance, always fervently reminding God of his promises to the fathers, Abraham and Isaac.

In Genesis 32:13 is a list of gifts Jacob decided to send to Esau through his servant. It consisted of a huge number of livestock as a peace offering. Still fearing, he divided them into two droves. He would stay behind and appear in the third group, after the gifts were given to Esau. That night his fears caused him to move those family members who were with him back across the river for their protection and Jacob stayed alone.

At a place named Peni-el Jacob wrestled with a man all night, and when the man could not prevail against Jacob, he wounded his thigh and put it out of joint. In Genesis 32:26 the man said, *"Let me go for the day is breaking."* But Jacob refused to let him go until the man blessed him. The man said, *"Your name will no longer be Jacob, but Israel, for you have striven with God and with men and have prevailed."*

At this point Jacob's name was changed to Israel, which means *"God rules."* This is what the name Peni-el means. The "el" signifies God. Jacob then declared he had seen God face-to-face and lived. Remember that Moses was told he could not see God and live. So it seems that consciousness has expanded to where "seeing" God is now possible. But Jacob was not advanced enough to maintain this high state of consciousness and the name Israel. He continued to waver and fear, so the name Jacob remained with him.

Esau arrived with his four hundred men. Our biggest fear arrives and is not assuaged by the bribes we offer. Jacob, not feeling too brave, put the maids and their children in the front line to face Esau. The second line of defense was Leah and her children. Jacob, Rachel and Joseph were behind them. Finally Jacob had to go out to meet Esau alone, bowing to the ground seven times. Esau ran to Jacob, hugged and kissed him, and wept.

We can be so frightened and so resistant to our good that we build up in our minds the worst nightmares and then make elaborate preparations to fend them off. Only to find that it was all unnecessary. Esau did not want to kill Jacob or accept the rich gifts that Jacob brought him. In Genesis 33:9 he said, *"I have enough, keep what you have for yourself."*

But Jacob encouraged Esau to accept the gifts because they were from God. It would also signify that Esau had forgiven Jacob. Jacob, after seeing the face of God, then turned and now saw the face of God also in his feared brother, Esau. *"Truly to see your face is like seeing the face of God."(Genesis 33:10)*

Humanity progresses from Moses who was not prepared to see the face of God, to Jacob who sees the face of God and lives, and to Jacob now seeing the face of God in another person, his brother Esau. Human development had come a long way, and still had a long way to go. Jacob said it was like seeing God, but it doesn't say he actually saw God in Esau's face. So this is not quite like Jesus' saying, *"When you have seen me, you have seen the Father."*

Esau wanted Jacob's tribe to follow him, but Jacob made the excuse that he would have to stay behind to care for lambs and small children. Actually he planned to turn and travel another way so as not to be led home by Esau. We are no longer going to be led by the physical or emotional level. We are going to choose our own way home to God, not follow another's path. Jacob settled in a place he called Succoth, meaning temporary dwelling.

The story of Dinah, Leah's daughter, begins in Genesis 34. The name Dinah means judged, avenged. Dinah went to visit the women of Shechem. Shechem was a Canaanite city and carried the name of Hamor's son.

The son Shechem always took what he wanted. When he saw Dinah he took her shamefully and then begged his father to buy this girl for him. Hamor was more than willing and would pay any price. Little did he know how high that price would be.

Hamor was a Hivite and his name means wild ass. His tribe was descendent of Ham, son of Noah. Ham means dark, Hamor means red and wild.

Hamor wanted to trade daughters between the tribes, but Hamor's daughters were Canaanites and Jacob remembered well the admonition of his mother, *"Do not marry a Canaanite."* Jacob did not respond to Hamor's offer until his own sons returned home. Jacob would not take a dowry from Hamor, but requested every male of them be circumcised. *"Then we will give our daughters to you... we will become one people."*

When the sons came home, they were outraged and plotted the destruction of Shechem. *In Genesis 34:14 they said, "We cannot do this thing, give our sister to one who is uncircumcised."* They were not people of the covenant of Israel and Jacob was not about to give his daughter to a wild Hivite. Jacob's sons created a trap but Hamor did not know that. Hamor convinced the men of Shechem to be circumcised because he thought this would give him ownership of all Jacob's property and flocks.

In Genesis 34:25 *"On the third day, when they were sore, two sons of Jacob, Simeon and Levi, Dinah's brothers, took their swords, came upon the city unawares, and killed all the males including Hamor and Shechem... They took Dinah out of Shechem's house and went away."* So evidently Shechem held Dinah at his house hoping to keep her. Then the brothers went back and plundered the whole city.

In Genesis 35 Jacob was again afraid. The rage of his sons was far greater then he knew. He feared all the surrounding tribes would attack him after this unbridled destruction. So, God told him to move to Bethel to live. The name Bethel means house of God. When our anger and rage does great destruction in our consciousness, we need to turn our thoughts immediately to God Mind and the Truth of our being before we suffer the consequences of the anger.

Jacob felt the need to purify his family again and ordered them to give him all idols and household gods. When he was given all the gods and gold earrings, he ordered them to change their garments and purify themselves before going to Bethel. A danger or narrow escape causes us to look at what was going on in our thinking that caused destruction and take steps to rectify or purify our thinking.

God appeared to Jacob again and reiterated, *"Your name is Jacob; no longer shall your name be Jacob, but Israel shall be your name."* All the promises to Abraham and Isaac were now conferred upon Jacob who again became Israel.

In reading through these stories in Genesis it is good to understand that the book is comprised of writings from the southern Ephraim writers and the northern Judah writers with some parts inserted by the priestly writers from temple records. The priestly writers wrote the first chapter of Genesis. The Judah writers wrote the second through the fourth chapters, containing the second creation story. The priestly writers wrote the fifth chapter. The Judah writers wrote the sixth chapter, verses one through eight, and the priestly writers finished that chapter.

From here on the writings are more mixed, sometimes from one sentence to the next. The exact verses each wrote are listed in the *"One Volume Interpreters."* Following their listing of the verses and writers, you would be able to color code your working Bible with colored pencils to see the differences in writing styles. If you color code with colored pencils, you will be able to read one color and it will make sense. And then read the other color and it too will make sense. The editors and redactors of the scriptures did not edit or attempt to bridge the differences. They just shuffled it all in together creating a confusing situation for the reader.

In Genesis 35:16 Rachel had conceived again and was in hard labor. She gave birth to Benjamin and gave him the ominous name of Benoni, meaning son of my sorrow. She died just as she named him. But his father changed the name to Benjamin, meaning son of good fortune. Every sorrowful thought we have should be quickly changed to something joyous and positive. Our future will reflect our thoughts and we have the choice to make the resulting future negative or positive.

Jacob still had problems. His eldest son, Reuben, had laid with Bilhah his father's concubine, which was against their law. Simeon and Levi, who deceived Hamor's people murdered them all. Reuben disobeyed the law. All lost power and prestige, and are not mentioned prominently again. *Oxford RSV Footnotes, p.45.*

We cannot straddle the law, obey it one day and disregard it the next. Any spiritual power one carries is released like the air from a balloon when we break spiritual law. We must work to regain it time and again until we learn not to sacrifice it to our emotional and physical distress.

Jacob and Esau came together to bury Isaac, who died at 180 years old. *"Isaac breathed his last; and he died and was gathered to his people, old and full of days, and his sons Esau and Jacob buried him."* A similar thing was said at the death of Abraham. *"Then Abraham gave up the ghost, and died in a good old age, an old man, and full of years; and was gathered to his people. And his sons Isaac and Ishmael buried him."* (*Genesis 25:8*)

A similar indication of the condition of life before death is in Job 5:26 *"Thou shall come to thy grave in ripe old age, like as a shock of grain comes up to the threshing floor in its season."* Again in 1 Chronicles 23:1 *"So when David was old and full of days, he made Solomon his son king over Israel."* A different translation is "old and satisfied with days." Another writer says, *"Satisfied with life,"* and yet another says *"you will come to your grave full of vigor."*

This is an archetypal commentary on the ideal way of living and approaching death that we come to it satisfied with our days and not feeble but with vigor. In Hebrews 12:1 our great thoughts are called *"a great cloud of witnesses."* In death we are gathered to our people, our great thoughts. Goethe wrote that Faust sat on the shore of Maine reclaiming the land from the sea. We reclaim all the good we created in our lives, just as God drew his creations from the waters and pronounced them *"very good."*

Isaac and Ishmael, former enemies representing the mental and physical, came together at Abraham's death. Jacob and Esau, again former enemies representing the mental and physical, come together in peace at Isaac's death. Life leads us down many paths. The ego mind or physical mind is full of divisions, fears, wars, and grief. Ultimately we leave the limitations and lies of ego mind behind to experience a life full of satisfying days.

In Genesis 36:7, there is an accounting of Esau's household, and then he moved away from Jacob *"for their possessions were too great for them to dwell together."* This echoes Abraham and Lot separating because their possessions were too great for them to dwell together. Physical possessions will weigh on consciousness because they take up physical/psychological space. It is good to lighten our physical load by giving away things that no longer serve a purpose and free ourselves.

Esau's descendants, called the Edomites, were eventually enemies of the Israelites and were conquered by KING David in 2 Samuel 8:13. The rest of Genesis 36 lists the descendants of Esau. An era of the rough physical nature has come to an end in favor of the higher mental nature, which in the Gospels eventually opens the way to the spiritual mind.

The story of Abraham is known as the first cycle of the saga of beginnings. The second cycle is the story of Jacob, and now the third cycle of beginnings is the story of Joseph. Genesis 37 begins with the story of seventeen-year-old Joseph, Rachel's first child with Jacob. He was Jacob's favorite son. Jacob made him a robe with long sleeves. A different translation says a coat of many colors. Either way this was a coat signifying royalty. Only royalty or the very rich had robes with long sleeves and/or dyed with many colors.

Joseph was a brat and a tattler. His brothers were jealous and *"could not speak peaceably to him."* He delighted in bringing bad reports of his brothers to Jacob. He bragged to them about his dreams where they and their households were bowing down to him. Joseph was actually prophesying the truth. He would become royalty and he would rule over them. We must first mature or our prophesying will sound like the bragging of the ego mind. Joseph was not yet mature enough to control the ego mind, which would lead him toward near disaster. The brothers were angry at his behavior. They moved the flocks to a farther pasture. The next time Jacob sent Joseph to find them, they had moved to Dothan, a place of two wells and a busy trade route.

Genesis 37:18 recounts the plot of the brothers to kill Joseph. Reuben, who messed up by lying with his father's concubine, is now redeeming himself by saving Joseph from being killed. Reuben wanted to save Joseph and return him home, but his plan was foiled when the brothers spotted an Ishmaelite caravan coming. But they were foiled as well because while they were discussing selling Joseph, Midianite traders came by, drew a hollering Joseph out of the pit, and sold him to the Ishmaelites themselves. Joseph was taken as a slave to be sold in Egypt. Potiphar, an officer of Pharaoh and Captain of the guard, purchased him. The brothers kept Joseph's coat, dipped in animal blood and took it to their father. Jacob emotionally lamented that Joseph must have been torn apart by a wild beast and was dead.

Joseph's brothers were not guilty of selling Joseph themselves, or actually telling their father a lie that he was killed, but they were instrumental in both. It was all taken care of for them by circumstances. This appears to be a stroke of luck for them, but actually it sealed their dark secret and humiliation inside of them for many years until Joseph would set them free. We are always imprisoned by deceptions and set free by Truth.

CHAPTER TEN

Interruption and Change

As frequently happens in the Bible text, there is a "time-out" where another story inserted into the narrative that seems to have nothing to do with the saga in progress. In Genesis 38 the text leaves the story of Joseph to tell the story of Judah and Tamar. The book of Ruth is another example of this kind of interruption, as we will see later on. We are often surprised when, just as our lives seem to be progressing along a certain line, something happens to put us into a completely different context for a period of time.

This interruption is the famous story of Onan and the practice now known as Onanism. Onanism is when the man spills his semen on the ground to prevent pregnancy. Judah married Shua, a Canaanite. The name Judah means praise of Jehovah. Shua means longing for something higher. Since Shua was a Canaanite, Judah was marrying outside of his tribe, which metaphysically means mixed thoughts in consciousness. Judah and Shua had three sons: Er, Onan, and Shelah. Judah chose Tamar for his son Er's wife. His son Er was said to be evil and God slew him, leaving Tamar a widow.

We are told nothing about Tamar, but her name in Hebrew means victory, conquest and upright. We can see in this story that the victory consciousness carries her to success. Our own consciousness of victory and uprightness cannot be connected to evil. The name Er means watchful, attentive. But it matters a great deal what one watches or gives attention to. If one persists in focusing upon that which is evil and in error, one cannot obtain an abiding life of good.

In this story consciousness is slipping off the track and going toward the physical instead of the spiritual. Judah and Shua had the early indications of spiritual progress, but not the focus to carry it forward. Er, their offspring indicates further failing. Er died, so Judah went to Er's brother, Onan, and instructed him to go to Tamar and have a child with her to carry on his brother's name. But Onan spilled his semen on the ground instead, violating the law of Levirate Marriage. Levirate law said that a brother-in-law is required to raise up a male descendant for his deceased brother.

Again the consciousness goes further astray. Onan died and Tamar was banished to her father's house until the youngest son Shelah grew up, with the promise she would be given to him. But Judah did not keep this promise so Tamar took matters into her own hands. When she heard that Judah was going to Timnah to shear his sheep, she posed as a harlot at the entrance to Enaim. Judah came along, thought she was a harlot, and propositioned her. He offered her a kid from his flock in payment and she required of him as a surety his signet, cord and staff. She became pregnant and returned to her father's house. When Judah sent the kid by a friend to exchange it for his signet, cord, and staff, the friend could not find the harlot. When he asked, the men of the village said no harlot was there. So Judah said, *"let her keep those things as her own lest we be laughed at because we could not find her."* (Genesis 38:20) Three months later when Judah learned his daughter-in-law was pregnant he wanted to burn her at the stake. But she brought out his staff, signet and cord, and said, *"By the man to whom these belong, I am with child."* Judah had to admit his folly in not keeping his promise to her according to law.

Metaphysically, once consciousness begins slipping down into the negative or physical realm and away from spirit, no amount of covering it up will help. Error is compounded with every subsequent choice, as happened to Judah. The truth came out and Judah was obliged to admit his errors. As our errors pile up, we have to admit we have slipped away from spirit before we can go on. Tamar represents the high watch as humanity struggles back to righteousness. When we have Tamar consciousness, whose name means lofty, upright and ascending, no circumstances can bring us down. These circumstances in the story did not defeat her.

Tamar bore twins, Perez and Zerah. Zerah's hand came out first, representing the physical nature, and then withdrew back into the womb. Perez then was born past him but was still the second child representing the mental/spiritual nature. He was the ancestor of David and in the lineage of Jesus. *(Ruth 4:18-22)* Even our errors open a path to the divine because we learn from them. The experiences of Lot's eldest daughter and Tamar represent some of those errors in thought and were turned around. They all lead us eventually to the birth of the Christ nature within us.

Abruptly Genesis 39 takes us back to the story of Joseph. Joseph's predicament represents humanity's immaturity that sells it into lower material consciousness. But it has the potential to rise from this low estate just as Joseph did as he matured. He became a high-ranking manservant in the house of his master, Potiphar, the Egyptian. Potiphar and Pharaoh both mean the sun, the center of subconscious mind. Being in Egypt shows that the light of the sun is veiled by our life on the lower of sense plane. *(Metaphysical Bible Dictionary)*

The Apostle Paul said we are to mature in Christ, grow up into the head of Christ. So long as we grow and mature in wisdom and understanding of God's unending sustaining power in our lives, we will prosper in all ways. The text says, *"The Lord was with him and the Lord caused all that he did to prosper." (Genesis 39:3)* This is repeated several times. The name Joseph means *"he whom Jehovah will add to; he shall increase from perfection unto perfection."* God prospered Joseph as long as he kept maturing. Potiphar promoted Joseph making him overseer of his house and over all that he had. Potiphar knew God prospered Joseph. He had no concerns about leaving Joseph in charge of everything.

Joseph still had some difficulties to overcome. Genesis 39:6 reads, *"Now Joseph was handsome and good-looking. And after a time his master's wife cast her eyes upon Joseph and said, 'Lie with me.' But he refused."* Day after day she spoke to him in this manner and he continued to refuse. She even grabbed his garment away and he fled the house without it. She told everyone he had insulted her and she had to defend herself. She kept his garment to show her husband and repeat the accusation. Joseph was taken to the king's prison but not executed. The scripture says the Lord was with him in adversity as well in good times. He eventually found favor with the keeper of the prison and was placed in charge of all the prisoners.

There is always adversity in physical life on planet Earth. Often folks think God has abandoned them when they experience reversals and immediately abandon their faith. It is the abandoning of faith that makes things worse than they might otherwise be. Keeping the focus upon right outcomes moves them through difficulty. *"Faith is a deep inner knowing that that which is sought is already ours for the taking." Revealing Word*

A writer from Judah wrote Genesis 39. Writers from the various areas of north and south bring their versions of the stories into the Bible text. This explains a change in tone, syntax, and abrupt theme shifts. As the story continues in Genesis 40, it changes to the Ephraim or southern writer, and tells of Joseph's interpretations of the prisoners' dreams. It also contains the famous interpretation of the Pharaoh's dreams about the famine that was coming to the land. This writer continues through Genesis 41:29. From then on there is a mixture of the two strains of writing until Genesis 43 through to 45:1a. The Priestly writer inserted the temple records in Genesis 46:6 through 46:27. The temple records that are added to a text always list prosperity in the form of descendants, numbers of cattle and sheep, wives, and household slaves.

Joseph could have given up after being sold into slavery, after Potiphar's wife lied about him, and being thrown into prison. But Joseph was learning to *"make a silk purse out of a sow's ear."* When we set our feet upon the path and *"Grow up into the head of Christ"* as the Apostle Paul said, we are lifted up, prospered, and guided regardless of our circumstances.

Joseph was soon in charge of the prison inmates, the same as he had been in charge of Potiphar's household. It didn't matter where he was, in a palace or a prison. Higher consciousness had taken hold in him and blessings came forth. Higher consciousness always sets us in the highest place where we can share blessings on a grand scale in our lives.

The Joseph story is the beginning of the third cycle in human development. In Genesis 49 is a poem about Joseph and these are the first few lines:

"Joseph is a fruitful bough,
A fruitful bough by a spring;
His branches run over the wall."

That last line is indicative of the need for us to reach out beyond our comfort zone so the fruit of our efforts, prosperity, will not die of confinement and lack of opportunity to grow further.

In Genesis 40 Joseph became the famous interpreter of dreams. This signifies a higher level of consciousness developing. His statement about dreams to the men in prison was, *"Do not all interpretations belong to God? Tell them to me I pray you."* The interpretations were favorable and Joseph asked the butler, for whom he prophesied a return to his office, to remember him to Pharaoh and help him get out of the prison, *"For indeed I was stolen from the land of the Hebrews; and here also I have done nothing that they should put me into the dungeon...Yet the chief butler did not remember Joseph, but forgot him."*

In Genesis 41 it was *"two whole years"* later that Pharaoh had his dream of seven sleek cows and seven gaunt cows. When the Pharaoh needed this dream interpreted, finally the butler remembered Joseph. They cleaned Joseph up and gave him new clothes to go before Pharaoh. Joseph told Pharaoh the meaning of his dreams, and the fact that he dreamed it twice meant it was urgent and the seven-year famine would soon to commence.

Joseph laid out a complete proposal to Pharaoh of how they could survive the coming famine. Joseph gave God the credit for the interpretation and proposal, rather than himself. Pharaoh was impressed with Joseph and set him over everything save the throne. And gave him a wife, Asenath, daughter of Potiphera (sun), priest of On (city of the sun).

The name Asenath means *"the love side of natural man."*

Metaphysically Joseph, the prospered of God, unites with the light of love and the first mental tools are born of this union, affirmation and denial. Their sons were Ephraim and Manasseh, representing affirmation and denial. The name Ephraim means productive, Manasseh means forgetting the woes of the past.

Numbers always have some significance in the Scriptures. Joseph was 30 years old when he entered Pharaoh's service in Genesis 41:46. Jesus was 30 years old when he began his ministry. This is a sign of maturity and readiness to function at a higher level. In early Asian cultures, children were not to speak among the elders until the age of 30.

In Genesis 42, *"When Jacob learned there was grain in Egypt he said to his sons, 'Why do you look at one another? I have heard there is grain in Egypt; go down and buy grain for us that we may live and not die.'"*

It appeared that Jacob, in mourning for Joseph, was stuck with a bunch of not-so-brilliant sons. He did not send Benjamin, second son of Rachel, because he didn't want to lose him as he had lost Joseph. At this point, the predictions of the brash young Joseph were about to come true. His brothers would bow down to him and he would be lord over them.

Joseph recognized them, but they did not recognize him. They had come to believe their own lie to their father, that Joseph was dead. Joseph accused them of being spies and threw them into prison for three days. Joseph again tested them. They did not know he understood Hebrew so he could listen in on their conversations. In Genesis 42:22, *"And Reuben answered them, 'did I not tell you not to sin against the lad? But you would not listen. So now there comes a reckoning for his blood.'"*

"The testing involved not only verification of the brothers' words but also the discipline of suffering that would purge the evil of their hearts. The brothers were fearful and sensed that divine retribution was behind the mysterious events." Oxford RSV footnotes

The consciousness of evil, fear, and guilt cannot be allowed to stand equal with the consciousness of *"one whom God prospers."* They must be contained where they cannot escape and do harm until they are tested and the ego arrogance dissolved.

Mary Baker Eddy, founder of Christian Science, taught, *"Stand porter at your door of thought."* In other words don't let just anything into your mind. Test its truth first. Even familiar thoughts from your past, represented by his brothers, must be purged of negativity before you let them come to live in your mind.

CHAPTER ELEVEN

A Ruler Who Knew Not Joseph

In Genesis 47:5, Joseph at last met his father. Pharaoh allowed him to settle all of his brothers and their households in a part of Egypt. This area, called Goshen, is on the east side of the Nile not far from the Red Sea. The name metaphysically means unity, symbolizing unification of the *I AM* (Jacob) with all his faculties of the mind, the life energies, and the substance of the whole man. *"They dwelt in the land of Goshen"* or in a state of unity.

Joseph had more gifts for Egypt. The economic system in Egypt would not sustain prosperity after the famine. The famine was so deep and the people were going to starve before it was over. He arranged for the people to sell first their goods to Pharaoh, then their cattle, then their land, and finally themselves as slaves to Pharaoh, in return for food and grain. This contract said they would plant the grain, return 1/5 of the proceeds to Pharaoh, and keep 4/5 for themselves to replant and begin to prosper. He created an economical business system, one that would allow the people to not only survive but also thrive.

This is the manifestation of the meaning of his name, *"one whom God adds to."* Joseph didn't just prosper for himself, but for all the people of Egypt and all the people of his extended family. Those who just take and do not give must rely upon the vagaries of ego mind to continue manifesting wealth. Sooner or later it breaks down and creates a famine. Those who give rely upon the spiritual principle of giving to prosper, and are sustained by spiritual law that will not change.

In Genesis 47:29 Jacob, now more often called Israel, was closing out this era in human development. He had his whole family around him, living in prosperity and harmony. He had one more job to do and that was to set up the twelve tribes of Israel. First he adopted Joseph's sons "legally" and made them equal to Reuben and Simeon, his other firstborn sons. Joseph brought his sons to Israel to be blessed, Manasseh the first-born and Ephraim the second born.

Like Isaac his father, Jacob was now blind when he conferred the blessing. Joseph placed Jacob's right hand on Manasseh and his left hand on Ephraim. But Jacob crossed his hands and placed his right hand on Ephraim. Joseph objected, but Jacob said Ephraim the second born was to be greater than Manasseh the firstborn. Here again the first-born represents the lower or physical consciousness and the second born the mental. The second must take precedence over the first-born.

Now Israel (Jacob) confers blessing on the twelve sons who represent the twelve tribes of Israel, and their names establish the character of each tribe, representing the character of developing humanity.

1. Reuben – means strong but unstable, shall not have first born pre-eminence because he lay with his father's concubine. His territory was east of the Dead Sea and he was overcome by the Moabites.
2. Simeon – means swords of violence and his tribe was scattered among the other tribes.
3. Levi – means swords of violence and they will also be scattered among the tribes. The tribe of Levi was violent but later became the priestly tribe under the influence of increasing awareness of Divine Love. They received no territory, but were supported by the other eleven tribes.
4. Judah – means the lion's whelp, the scepter shall not depart from him. Judah becomes Judea, the northern kingdom.
5. Zebulun – means surrounded, habitation, abiding neighbor. His territory was inland even though Jacob's blessing to him was that he would dwell by the sea and be a haven for ships.
6. Issachar – means brings compensation, likes resting places and will become a slave of forced labor.

7. Dan – means righteous judgment but not yet lifted up, a viper by the path who bites at the heels, critical
8. Asher – means blessed, a rich land that yielded rich food and royal dainties
9. Naphtali – wrestling with Jehovah, a hind let loose, freedom, agility, and vitality.

Joseph – the fruitful bough is divided between his two sons:

10. Manasseh – who causes forgetfulness
11. Ephraim. – who prospers, doubly fruitful
12. Benjamin – means son of the right hand, of good fortune, prosperity, happiness, productiveness, like a ravenous wolf that devours prey and in the evening divides the spoils.

These are the twelve tribes of Israel with their blessing, purpose, and the Hebrew meaning of their names. These are twelve pillars of developing consciousness beginning to organize into a cohesive culture. They are precursors of the spiritual development as will be represented by the twelve disciples in the Gospels.

In Genesis 50:24 Joseph said, *"I am about to die but God will visit you and bring you out of this land and into the land which he swore to Abraham, to Isaac, and to Jacob."* When Jacob died the old fears of the brothers again surfaced and they sent a message to Joseph saying that Jacob had commanded Joseph to forgive his brothers for all their evil against him. Jacob made no such command. After they took their father to be buried in Canaan, Joseph went back to Egypt. He reassured his brothers that he would take care of them and all their young ones. He said the much quoted, *"You meant evil against me, but God meant it for good, so that many should be kept alive."*

Joseph died at 110 years old, was embalmed and placed in a coffin in Egypt. Over four centuries had elapsed since Joseph's death and the promise of multitudes was being fulfilled. The twelve-tribe confederacy was not yet formed. The descendants of Jacob and Joseph multiplied greatly and grew exceedingly strong so that the land was filled with them. There was still no maturing organization among the tribes and though they grew in numbers, they remained vulnerable.

In Exodus 1:8 is the ominous statement, *"Now there arose a new king over Egypt who did not know Joseph."* Scholars set this time period around the 19ᵗʰ Dynasty when Seti I was Pharaoh, 1308 – 1290 B.C. The Hebrews were living well, prospering, and expanding in numbers until it all came to an abrupt end. The Pharaoh decided to control them by making slaves of them. They were forced to build cities and pyramids for Pharaoh.

Still the Hebrews expanded in numbers, so Pharaoh decreed that all the male infants should be killed at birth. He commanded two Hebrew midwives, Shiph'rah and Puah, to do this. But they did not. They told Pharaoh that the Hebrew women were very strong and delivered before they could get there. So Pharaoh decreed that all male children should be thrown into the Nile.

Metaphysically all new ideas are quashed by this ego or material mind represented by Pharaoh, who *"does not know Joseph,"* or did not know the Hebrew God. The oppression caused growth and development in consciousness, because the people had to become more resourceful to survive. The growth in numbers continued regardless of oppressive circumstances. Humanity develops toward the spiritual regardless of the ego's desperate measures to stop it.

Exodus 2 begins the story of Moses. *"Now a man from the house of Levi went and took to wife a daughter of Levi".* We are being told right from the beginning that they were of the priestly tribe. Their son, Moses, was destined to draw humanity out of the darkness of the five senses or physical consciousness, represented by Egypt. When we are as an infant in consciousness, we are drawn out of the Nile, the river of life, and destined to move toward the higher understanding of Truth.

"Moses represents man's development in consciousness of the law of his being from the negative side…We must care for the infant thought of Truth and surround it with the ark of love and trust, right in the midst of seeming enemies. When we arrive at a degree of understanding of Truth, 'when Moses was grown,' we are zealous for our principles to the point of destroying anything that interferes with their freedom." (Metaphysical Bible Dictionary)

Contrary to Cecile B. DeMille's version, Moses did know as he was growing up that he was a Hebrew and identified with his own people. Moses could not watch his people being abused and he killed an Egyptian who was beating them. The principle was challenged when the Hebrew men turned on him, *"Do you mean to kill us as you killed the Egyptian?"*

The ego mind challenges us at every turn. At this tender time of new development when we mean to do good, we are shown other ways in which we have violated our own principles. Moses had killed with the intention to do good. We often act on impulse without prayer and wisdom. Consequently, we see only one part of the whole and our good intention backfires.

Moses fled into the desert, into the land of Midian. The name Midian means government, rule, and subjugation. It represents the experience of discipline we must undergo in seeking spirituality. He sat down by a well, symbolizing the deeper Truth we are looking for and must find in order to progress.

Moses tended Jethro's flocks and married a daughter of Jethro, Zipporah. He kept his eye on the mountain, wondering about the god they believed in who lived on the mountain. Moses climbed the mountain and stopped when an angel appeared out of a flame in the midst of a bush. Moses was mystified that the bush was not consumed in the fire.

God himself called to Moses telling him not to come near, but to take off his sandals. The ground whereon he stood was Holy Ground. Moses was still functioning from the physical mind and obeyed, not knowing who was speaking. God instructed Moses to lead Israel out of Egyptian bondage. *"I will send you to Pharaoh."* (Exodus 3:10)

Living in a polytheistic society yet, Moses wanted to know which god this was who was speaking to him and began to question and argue. He asked, *"Who am I that I should go to Pharaoh, and bring the sons of Israel out of Egypt?"* The last thing Moses wanted to do was again face the Pharaoh who wanted to kill him.

"If I go to the children of Israel and say 'God sent me,' and they ask me 'What is his name?' what shall I say to them? What is your name?"

God answered, *"I AM WHO I AM!"* In Hebrew it is designated with the letters YHWH indicating that God is *He Who Causes to Be*. God demonstrated by telling Moses to cast his rod onto ground. It became a serpent. When Moses turned to flee, God told him to pick it up by the tail. Then it again became a rod in his hand. He gave a second sign by turning Moses' hand white with leprosy and then immediately restoring it.

In Exodus 4 Moses still objected again saying, *"But they will not believe me or listen to my voice, they will say 'The Lord did not appear to you.' Oh, my Lord, I am not eloquent…I am slow of speech and of tongue. Oh, my Lord, send I pray some other person."*

Seeing that Moses definitely needed help God said, *"I will send Aaron to speak for you, he shall be your mouth…I will put words in your mouth and you will be to him as God. You will take this rod in your hand and do the signs! All those who seek your life are dead."* When we speak spiritually inspired words, we become as God. We represent God when speaking from God Mind. All the fears that seek to take away our life and happiness are dead because they cannot exist in God Mind. This is how we set ourselves free.

God warned Moses that it would be a battle. *"I will harden Pharaoh's heart."* Pharaoh was stubborn and God would harden this stubbornness so it would shatter. *"The Lord said* (to Pharaoh), *'Israel is my first-born son. Let him go that he may serve me. If you refuse to let him go, behold I will slay your first-born son.'"*

A refusal to live by principle brings consequences. In the Hebrew Testament all gifts and punishments were thought to come from God. We now know it is not a vengeful god but the law of cause and effect that brings about consequences positive or negative.

In our "teenage" level of development, we are naturally looking for something outside ourselves to blame. We see things happening in our physical world and it seems obvious to us that outer things are to blame for our circumstances. As we mature in consciousness and move into spiritual thinking, we know we are in command of the kingdom of our own being, and we must learn to think, speak and live according to spiritual law.

The first glimmerings of psychology were heavily influenced by the beliefs and traditions of the church. The church had always based its theology on the existence of sin and evil.

Sigmund Freud in the late 1880's and early1900's developed the field of psychology. Psychologists saw a pattern to human development and began to counsel people through problems according to the patterns they saw. There was a modicum of success in this.

Mid-century Carl Rogers developed the approach he coined Unconditional Positive Regard, leaving behind the belief that judgment and criticism were helpful; that people could be shamed into changing behavior. The self-help psychology field of today grew largely out of Carl Rogers' work. Self-help psychology has taught personal responsibility which aligns well with teachings of spirituality.

For this author the value of the Book of Genesis is this:

*Genesis was carefully constructed and was divinely inspired through the writers.

* It shows that the development of humanity was not haphazard, but had a pattern.

*Our Creator did not just drop us into physical existence without provision for our survival and well-being.

*The creative intention is that we should develop into mature thinking beings, and then create our spiritual body for the eternal journey; not too unlike the first fragile aircraft that opened the way to space travel.

CHAPTER TWELVE

Moses

Exodus 2 begins the famous story of Moses. Pharaoh decreed that every son born to the Hebrews should be cast into the Nile, but let every daughter live. Fearing her son would be taken and cast into the Nile, Moses' mother made a basket, covered it with pitch to make it water proof, and placed the baby in the basket. She set it among the reeds at the edge of the Nile and sent Miriam, his sister, to tend him while the basket floated to the docks of the palace of Pharaoh. Pharaoh's daughter saw the basket and told her ladies to fetch it for her. She was delighted to find it contained a boy child. She had no children and so she took him as her own.

Young Miriam was watching from the reeds and saw an opportunity. She asked the daughter of Pharaoh if she needed someone to nurse the child. She told her she knew of a wet nurse and Pharaoh's daughter sent Miriam to fetch her. No one would know this was Moses' own mother. Thus Moses' mother nursed him until he was weaned and brought him to Pharaoh's daughter.

As to the question of whether Moses was circumcised, probably if he was he would not be taken into Pharaoh's house as a son. He would have joined the male Hebrew babies in the watery grave of the Nile.

Moses' birth mother and father were Levites. *"Now a man from the house of Levi married a daughter of Levi."* In a recent book by Michael Baigent entitled "The Jesus Papers" he wrote that there was a large

Jewish temple on Elephantine Island in the Nile. All the priests there were of Levi, the priestly tribe.

God convinced Moses to go back to Egypt to set his people free. God had Moses practice these signs he was to perform before Pharaoh. The human mind always wants some kind of external proof such as performing physical signs, to assure that God is real and that spiritual principles will work.

1. God gave Moses a rod. When he cast it onto the ground it became a serpent. (and Moses fled from it) God commanded him to take the serpent by the tail, and it became a rod again.
2. God told Moses to put his hand into his robe. When Moses took it out it was leprous, white as snow. When he put his hand back into his robe and took it out, it was restored.
3. Then he was to take some water from the Nile, pour it onto dry ground, and it would become blood.
4. Then God said, *"Your brother Aaron the Levite will come out to meet you and you shall put my words in his mouth, and I will be with your mouth and his mouth, and you shall be to him as God."* *(Exodus 4:16)*

This is the first indication that we have within us the potential to be as God. We speak spiritual words of Truth, Godlike words, and we are representatives of God as us. The words of Jesus to this effect are from John 14:20, *"I am in my Father, and you in me, and I in you."*

Moses went back to his father-in-law, Jethro, and did not tell him the whole truth. He said he desired to go back to Egypt to see if his kinsmen were still alive. He did not tell him about his conversations with God. This was a time of belief in many different gods, and undoubtedly Jethro had his own household gods, just as Laban did when Rachel took them.

In human development we have many gods, many outer things we believe have power over our lives. Those gods may be money, possessions, friendships, careers and success. And it seems these things do affect our experiences, but they are not the real power that is God.

The covenant of the Jews with the One God had not yet come about. This was part of Moses' argument with God. He knew the polytheistic nature of his people. How would they know which god he was referring to?

In Exodus 4:21 God charged Moses, *"When you go back to Egypt, see that you do before Pharaoh all the miracles which I have put in your power."* This was a big jump for humanity at this stage of development. This was the first mention of miracles and that mankind should perform God's miracles. The power is given to us very early. It is always within us and we need God's guidance to know how to use it.

A strange episode shows up in Exodus 4:24. Zipporah was the daughter of the Midianite shepherd, Jethro. She probably had her own gods, so this mountain God of Moses' could have been frightening to her. She did the only thing she knew how to do probably from some ancient rites. Seeming to fear that her firstborn son would be killed, or that Moses would be killed, she quickly circumcised her son and took the foreskin to Moses. Moses was uncircumcised so she laid it on his sexual organs, declaring him a bridegroom of blood. She may have overheard something regarding this ritual that came from another culture and decided to do her best to cover all the bases for her husband and son.

"Aaron was to become the first Levite priest of Israel. The name Aaron means enlightener, the executive power of divine law and the bearer of intellectual light." (Metaphysical Bible Dictionary)

Moses and Aaron went first to their people and it was Aaron who spoke God's words to them and *"did the signs in the sight of the people."* (Exodus 4:30) Unless they could enlist the people to believe, it would be of no use to go to Pharaoh. When the people learned that God had visited Moses they believed.

When we learn of our place with God, it is essential to go to all our *"thought people,"* our own thoughts and attitudes, to convert them to the belief in God. The Pharaoh represents the great light of the subconscious mind, and will need more than a few words from conscious mind to release its grip. It will need our whole thought process to support the change.

Moses and Aaron began by telling Pharaoh to let the people go out into the wilderness to a holy mountain to make sacrifices to their god. It was not the truth but a subterfuge and it did not work. Pharaoh not only refused to grant this request, but retaliated by making the people's labors harder. Subconscious mind is not fooled and sees through our lies. We must learn to be as forthright and honest with ourselves as possible.

One way of not being truthful with ourselves is to minimize. "It wasn't *that* bad…" "I didn't eat *that* much today…" "I didn't spend *that* much money…" Our little fibs to ourselves always make things much harder. The effortless way is to speak the truth. *"I ate too much today…I spent more money than I intended…"* These statements of truth take away the judgment of our acts as good or bad, and make them simply a choice that brought an unwanted result. So we simply choose again.

In Exodus 5:22 Moses blamed God for Pharaoh's response. *"Why have you done this evil to your people?"* In this state of development, humanity looks at disasters as *"acts of God."* Some years ago the insurance companies finally matured and stopped putting that phrase in their policies. God reiterated that he was God of Abraham, Isaac, and Jacob. He gave them the Promised Land, and He will bring them out of Egypt. But the people wavered and would not listen to Moses.

When we begin to deliver ourselves out of the darkness of the "Egypt consciousness" or out of our burdens and troubles, things often get worse before they get better. Much has to break down and fall apart for the good to break through. The people of that time had the same internal processes as we do today. They had a different culture, but the internal development of humanity and of the individual is the same.

In Exodus 6:12 Moses still doubted this whole thing would work and said to God, *"If the people will not listen to me, how then shall Pharaoh listen to me."* Moses calls himself *"a man of uncircumcised lips."* Perhaps he means he was not worthy or physically he was "tongue tied."

Abruptly in Exodus 6:14 the priestly documents were entered into the text including lists of the heads of the houses of Levi and their families. The listing continues through to verse twenty-six. The wording is definitive about Aaron and Moses. In Exodus 6:26 are the priestly records and writings. *These are the same Aaron and Moses to whom the Lord said, 'Bring out the people of Israel from the land of Egypt by their hosts.' It was they who spoke to Pharaoh King of Egypt about bringing out the people of Israel from Egypt, this Moses and this Aaron."*

In Exodus 7 after Moses asked how Pharaoh could be made to listen to him, God said, *"See, I make you as God to Pharaoh; and Aaron your brother shall be your prophet."* This echoes Genesis *"We shall make man in our image and likeness."* There is no need for us to fail or fear failing if we understand that we are made as God.

Aaron cast down his rod before Pharaoh and it became a serpent. In Exodus 7:10, *"Pharaoh summoned his sorcerers and magicians and they did the same by their secret arts. But Aaron's rod swallowed up their rods. Still. Pharaoh's heart was hardened, and he would not listen to them."*

When we are attempting to change subconscious mind, we have to try a little harder, be steadfast and more convincing in our choice of thoughts, words, and actions. Moses had to continue to overcome his own doubts and fears. Getting free to occupy the Promised Land would not be a "cake walk."

The next instruction was that Moses and Aaron should meet Pharaoh on the bank of the Nile, strike the water with the rod, and turn the Nile and every other water source to blood. But again the magicians of Egypt did the same. Moses and Aaron went back to Pharaoh and threatened a plague of frogs that would swarm over everything. Again the Pharaoh's magicians duplicated the trick. Again the resistance of subconscious mind matches us act for act.

At this point Pharaoh, feeling a little more certain of himself, began to initiate a covert action of his own. He agreed to let the people go and sacrifice at the sacred mountain if Moses and Aaron would take away the frogs. As soon as the frogs were dead Pharaoh reneged.

When we see a glimmer of the change we desire, perhaps see a glimmer of prosperity, there is a tendency to slack off and subconscious mind reverts to its former state. We may be praying for a thousand dollars, and when five hundred shows up, we decide that is all we deserve and stop. We must persist and never stop the forward motion of our efforts to change.

The next plague was the gnats and this time the magicians failed to duplicate it. Then there were swarms of flies. God protected the land of Goshen where the Hebrews lived and no flies came there. Subconscious mind begins to be able to maintain our progress.

In Exodus 8:25 Pharaoh called Moses and Aaron and said, *"Go sacrifice to your God within the land."* But Moses refused. This time he saw the plot behind Pharaoh's offer. In Exodus 8:29 Pharaoh tried to bargain but Moses said, *"...let not Pharaoh deal falsely again by not letting my people go to sacrifice to the Lord."*

We are not out of the woods yet, but we are standing up to subconscious mind and demanding it let go of dodges and intrigues. Subconscious mind exists to protect us by storing memories and habits, holding us to its limited course. When we create a new path in our thinking, subconscious mind reacts to stop it. Anything new represents danger.

God sent a plague upon the cattle, camels, horses, herds and flocks, but again not the cattle of Israel.

The next plague was more personal to Pharaoh, boils and sores on every man and beast throughout Egypt. Then God sent hail. Everything left outside was destroyed. He warned Pharaoh to shelter his cattle. Now God was talking directly to Pharaoh. Again there was no hail in the land of Goshen. Pharaoh agreed to let the people go if the hail would stop. When it stopped, of course Pharaoh reneged again.

Next God brought the locusts that ate every growing thing. Now Pharaoh's servants were entreating him to let the people go. *"Do you not understand that Egypt is ruined?"* Then Pharaoh offered to let just the men go to make the sacrifice. Moses refused and the locusts came.

God sent darkness upon the land and Pharaoh said, *"take your people but leave your flocks and herds behind."* Again Moses refused. Now the Egyptian people were coming over to Moses' side against Pharaoh. Change is coming in subconscious mind, but not enough. There is uproar and confusion in subconscious mind and we experience it as unrest and turmoil.

Moses was starting to lose his temper, *"he went out in white hot anger."* This is our first glimpse of the refiner's fire that we see again in the book of Revelation. The final great plague was the death of the first born of every Egyptian family. The Israelites were instructed to be ready to move, to eat up all their food and burn what was not eaten. Put blood on the lintel of their doorways so the plague would pass over them. We need to be ready to move with the changes in our thinking, to put away the limitations of the past and move forward.

The Jews still celebrate this Passover as commanded in Exodus 12:14. *"This day shall be for you a memorial day and you shall keep it as a feast to the Lord…"* The instructions are given in great detail through verse twenty-eight.

Just where did the Israelites cross over from Egypt to the Sinai Peninsula? If you look at the maps in the back of most Bibles you will find multiple routes shown. None of the routes actually cross the Red Sea proper, but show paths that are north of the sea.

The exodus of the Israelites is described in Exodus 13:17 to 14:31. We aren't given a map of the route, but there are numerous details in the scriptures.

1) They started in the land of Goshen in the eastern part of the Nile river delta.
2) They did not go by the route of the Philistines (Exodus 13:17). This is the north/south highway along the Mediterranean coast into the land of Egypt.
3) They crossed the wilderness of the Red Sea. (Exodus 13:18) They camped near Pi Hahiroth ("mouth of Chiroth" - believed to be the entrance to a valley running from Etham to the Red Sea), which is located between Migdol and the sea. The town of Baal Zephon was on the opposite shore. (Exodus 14:2) We still don't know the location of these towns, but the mapmakers guess at their placement.
5) Pharaoh thought the Israelite's route was crazy because they were trapped by the wilderness with no escape. (Exodus 14:3) If you look at most maps, the routes they show follow major caravan routes.
6) Exodus 14:9 states the camp near Pi Hahiroth was on the edge of the Red Sea, yet the mapmakers seem to think Israel believed a lake or a swamp was the sea.

Many people do not believe the miracles recorded in the Bible really happened, so they attempt to find alternative explanations. They can't explain how three to six million people crossed the Red Sea, so they assume Moses meant the Reed Sea - a swamp just north of the Red Sea. A drought must have dried up the swamp, allowing the Israelites to reach the Sinai Peninsula. Of course these conjectures do not match the details in the Exodus account.

How did Pharaoh's six hundred chariot drivers, and uncounted horsemen and foot soldiers drown in a dried up swamp? How did God make a wall of water on each side of the path the Israelites took through the sea? This is a great example of why metaphysical interpretation is more useful to us than the literal physical perspective. The important understanding is that the Moses of our consciousness draws us out of the material traps of the physical world and onto a safe shore, drowning all our fears.

CHAPTER THIRTEEN

A Nation Being Born

In Exodus 13:18 Israel was not yet a nation. The people went out of Egypt ill equipped for battle. They carried the bones of Joseph with them. God did not lead them *"by way of the land of the Philistines, though that was near."* Development has no short cuts. God knew there was bravado but no real strength, so he led them into the wilderness of Sinai. And God went before them by day as a pillar of cloud, and by night as a pillar of fire. God made sure the guidance was clear. The pillar was always before them. This is reminiscent of the teenage years when there is bravado, but no maturity as yet. The teenager, the undeveloped mind, needs the constant reminder right before its eyes as it travels through the challenges of development into the fully adult mind.

Exodus 12:15 reads, *"Seven days you shall eat unleavened bread...."* Leaven was considered a corruption, a puffing up, so for special ceremonies and religious observations only unleavened bread was eaten. Thus in Exodus 12:14 the Passover was instituted. In Matthew 16:6 Jesus used the word metaphysically referring to falseness and puffed up egos. *"Then Jesus said to them, 'Take heed and beware of the leaven of the Pharisees and Sadducees.'"*

We aren't told exactly what the disciples asked about leavened bread, but in Matthew 16:11 Jesus clarified further. *"How is it that you fail to perceive that I did not speak about bread? Beware of the leaven of the Pharisees and Sadducees. Then they understood that he did not tell them to beware the leaven of bread, but of the teaching of the Pharisees and of the Sadducees."*

In order to escape the plagues to come upon Egypt, the Hebrews abstained from *"leaven"* and painted their door lintels with lamb's blood, indicating innocence and purity. When we are escaping the plagues of fear in the physical mind, the ego mind, we do it by being aware of its error thoughts and bloated self-aggrandizement. We keep no leaven in our house (mind), none of its fearful error thinking, and return to our innocent or original error free state of mind.

The most difficult lesson for humanity is in Exodus 14:14 which reads, *"The Lord will fight for you and you have only to be still."* But do we stand still? No, we wander in the wilderness of ego mind complaining and murmuring. We try to fight our own battles whether they are real or imagined. Mostly they are imagined. Regardless of what God did for them their faith didn't last. They sang songs of praise, but their belief soon evaporated and they began complaining again.

The forty years in the wilderness is symbolic of the time it took to mature Israel. Probably they didn't wander forty years. Sinai isn't that big. The number forty symbolizes the time it takes to get the job done. The flood of Noah's time was forty days; Moses was on the mountain forty days; forty days were required for Egyptian embalming; the Philistines ruled the Israelites forty years; King David ruled forty years. The number forty is used hundreds of times throughout the Bible. If we interpret each one this way, we will see the job that needed to be done and understand more of what we need to develop within ourselves.

In Sinai, the job to be done was to wait for the generations that came out of Egypt to die off. It takes time for our mindset of slavery and material thinking to die off before we can enter and take possession of the Promised Land. The Promised Land represents subconscious mind. In order to take possession of our subconscious mind we must conquer the negative habits, feelings, and thoughts that have lived within us all our lives. The purpose of the subconscious mind is to be a mirror for the Super Conscious or Christ Mind reflecting it into our worldly experience. If negatives of all kinds cloud that mirror, they will become our life experience rather than the clear pattern of the Christ or spiritual consciousness.

As Pharaoh's army was drowned in the sea Miriam celebrated with the people on the opposite shore. Miriam represents the soul or feminine side of the love quality that is struggling to be free of errors and selfishness of the ego mind. The names Miriam and Mary come from the same root and have a wide range of seemingly conflicting meanings. Mary is used only in the New Testament. This thread of names runs through the scriptures, because throughout human development, we are always trying to be free of error thinking. The world constantly impinges upon our perceptions and draws our attention away from Truth. The more we mature in consciousness, the more we reflect the soul that magnifies the Lord. In Luke 1:46 is the song of Mary, mother of Jesus. "My soul magnifies the Lord and my spirit rejoices in God my Savior…"

In Exodus 15:22 the journey into the wilderness began. They traveled three days before finding water. They came to the spring called Marah, which means bitter, and indeed the water was bitter. Immediately the people murmured against Moses saying, *"What shall we drink?"* God showed Moses a particular tree and as he threw it into the water, the water became sweet. God promised if the people would heed his statutes and keep the faith, nothing ill would befall them. *"… for I am the Lord your healer."*

The wandering of the Jews through Sinai was a constant cycle of facing lack, murmuring (grumbling), blaming Moses and Aaron, and God rescuing them. When humanity first began to face the growing pains of becoming a free nation, it cycled back time and again needing to learn the lessons over and over. We often have these repeat experiences because the lesson is learned only one part at a time. Growth in consciousness is step by step until our limited capacity is enlarged enough to see the whole lesson.

Next came hunger and they murmured against Moses that they would rather go back to Egypt and be slain by Pharaoh than starve in the wilderness. When we are embarking upon a new consciousness, we may be looking to have our needs filled in the same limited way as in the past. Even today people lament and long for the good old days. If they weren't good, at least they were familiar. The new way is to look to God, to the invisible substance from whence everything comes. This is a huge step and requires much prayer, meditation and spiritual practice to manifest our fulfillment in all things.

Manna fell from the sky each day for their sustenance, but they could not store it up. Of course the people tried to store it, and it was full of worms by morning. It would last only one day and that made the people angry. We must renew our consciousness every day. The thoughts of yesterday are for yesterday only and will not serve today. In the material world we have a habit of keeping extra on the shelves and filling storehouses. In the spiritual world the sustenance, the new nourishing ideas, are discovered newly each day.

In Exodus 17:8 there was a war with the Amalekites. This is the first mention of Joshua. He led the army and Moses directed the battle from a hilltop. When Moses held up his hands, the Israelites prevailed. When he put his hands down, the Amalekites prevailed. So when Moses got tired, Aaron and Hur placed a stone under him to sit on. Each held up one of Moses hands to signify victory and Israel won the war.

We need help keeping our focus upon Spirit. When we waver, the negative begins to win. We work to remain steady, building up our spiritual body and spiritual strength. God promises to banish Amalek forever, but our memory of pain hangs on. God cannot banish what we will not release. The Amalekites continued to be troublesome on into the book of First Chronicles.

In Exodus 18:10 Moses' father-in-law, Jethro saw what God had done for Moses and the Israelites, and he was converted. Not only was he converted but he was wise. He saw that Moses would not be able to endure being the only judge for all the people. People lined up at Moses' tent day and night. Jethro suggested that Moses select good men who were faithful to God, and set them up as judges, and let them decide the small matters. The name Jethro means excellence and has to do with nerves and tendons, the levers that create balance.

Humanity had developed to the level of creating in subconscious mind the balance that automatically dispels small negative habits without constantly bringing them to the conscious mind for judgment. This is equivalent to good thought patterns and habits that do the work for us. Otherwise we cannot function if we have to think how to walk every time we take a step with our feet. The new evolutionary step in the development of humanity is to consciously create good habit patterns that will become the new groove in subconscious mind and support growth.

In Exodus 19 and 20 God was going to come down from the mountain and speak to the people. But he was in clouds and spoke to Moses in terms of thunder. The people were afraid and stood afar off. They asked Moses to be their mediator. They did not want to talk to God directly for fear of death. This is the work of the ego mind that fears losing its power over us. It tells us God is a mirage, a fog, and deadly dangerous. It tells us to hide behind a shield of doubt and obfuscation.

In Exodus 19:15 the people were told to purify themselves and *"do not go near a woman"* so the Ten Commandments could be given to them. The quote means don't let your mind be distracted by the physical and material world. The same could be said of a woman not to be distracted by a man but to remain focused upon God. The way of expressing it was typical of the patriarchal thinking of the male dominated culture at that time.

More laws were laid out concerning slaves, injuries, property, and miscellaneous incidents. There was a distinction made between intentional murder and unintentional killing or accident. A man could claim asylum at an altar to protect him from the angry relatives until the case could be adjudicated.

The Decalogue, or Ten Commandments, is repeated in Deuteronomy in slightly different form. There were twelve instead of ten. According to the footnotes in the Oxford Annotated Bible, *"Originally each commandment was a short utterance lacking the explanatory comments."*

In answer to a question about the Ten Commandments, Bishop John Shelby Spong answered, *"I said there are three versions of the Ten Commandments. The oldest one is Exodus 34, the second is Exodus 20 and the last is Deuteronomy 5. It is in Exodus 34 that you will find the injunction about 'boiling a kid in its mother's milk.' This version is almost totally cultic... The fact is that these rules, like all covenant rules, emerged out of the life of the nation of Israel and probably always had several versions."*

In Deuteronomy 27:15 the same twelve commandments are written, as spoken by Moses and the Levite priests, but beginning with *"Cursed be you if you do not..."* As humanity explores, understanding is changed moment to moment, and not always for the better. This understanding slipped from being commandments needed to build a society, to the destructive threat of a curse for those who do not obey. When we send the angel of Truth out before us, destructive thinking and habits will be utterly overthrown and the reasoning of the ego mind will be broken into pieces. Once again we are told to stand in Truth, and the negatives will be destroyed before us.

In Exodus 23:23 God said, *"When my angel goes before you, and brings you to (your enemies) I will blot them out, you shall not bow down to their gods, nor serve them, nor do according to their works, but you shall utterly overthrow them and break their pillars in pieces."*

Exodus 25, 26, and 27 continue with meticulous details of the building of the Ark of the Covenant and all the tabernacle fixtures, curtains and frameworks, the making of priestly garments, the ephod, robes, and turbans.

In Exodus 29 Aaron and his sons were ordained and consecrated as priests. In Exodus 30:11 God levied a tax on everyone when a census was taken. This was "atonement money" from those twenty years old and older so the people would remember God. The tax supported the sanctuary and the military.

Much is made of anointing, anointing oils, and ceremonies. Among the Hebrews, the act of anointing with the Holy anointing oil was significant in consecration to a holy or sacred use: hence the anointing of the high priest (Exodus 29:29; Leviticus 4:3) and of the sacred vessels (Exodus 30:26). Later, Kings and Prophets were given the right to partake in this sacrament as well. It was the custom of the Jews in like manner to anoint themselves with oil, as a means of refreshing or invigorating their bodies (2 Samuel 14:2; Psalms 104:15, etc.). Humanity must refresh its movement forward, renew the vigor to advance in consciousness, lest it wane and stagnate.

In Exodus 32 Moses went back up the mountain to have a lengthy talk with God. The people became anxious because Moses was up there a long time. They decided he might be dead and they pressured Aaron to make gods for them to worship. The people donated all their gold and they made the famous golden calf. Often in waiting for our good to arrive or our prayers to be answered, we begin to doubt and settle for something physical instead of spiritual. Or we pray for the $1000 we need and settle for the first $500 that shows up. We turn our minds away and set off in another direction, a consciousness of limitation.

In Exodus 32:10 God said to Moses *"My wrath burns hot against the people."* But Moses reminded God that these are the people he brought out of Egypt with no small effort. Why kill them? *"Turn from thy fierce wrath and repent of this evil against thy people."*

At this time in human development, their god is still thought of as anthropomorphic, having human qualities and emotions. And this god can be reminded of promises made and accused of having evil intentions. Moses reminded God of his promises to Abraham, Isaac, and Jacob to multiply their descendants like the stars in the heavens. How would that come about if God killed all the people? So again God repented of his evil thoughts against the people.

In years of teenage brain development humanity tended to create a god after its own image, its own likeness and limited thinking. The peoples' explanation was that they threw their gold into the fire and out popped the calf! This is a typical dodge of the teenage level of development. It just happened! But the dodge doesn't work. And so it is written in Exodus 32:12 that God still had *"evil thoughts."* In Exodus 32:35 he sent a plague upon the people because they made the golden calf and worshipped it.

In Exodus 33 God sent Moses to continue toward the Promised Land and God promised to send an angel to clear the way of all enemies. But this god cannot control his temper and impatience toward the people, again a human trait. *"I will not go up among you, lest I consume you on the way, for you are a stiff-necked people."*

In Exodus 33:15 Moses admonished God again, *"If your presence will not go with me, do not carry us up from here. For how shall it be known that I have found favor in your sight, I and your people? Is it not in your going with us that we are distinct, I and your people, from all other people that are upon the face of the earth?"*

This is a clear example of the idea of intercessory prayer. Moses was the intercessor between a *"stiff-necked people"* and their God. My mother was my intercessor between my father and me. He had no patience with us kids, and exhibited toward us that quick fierce wrath Moses attributed to God. As children we cannot fully appreciate one who shields us from the destructive wrath of someone more powerful. It might be a mother, a friend, or an angel. Is there a difference?

"And the Lord said to Moses, this very thing that you have spoken I will do; for you have found favor in my sight, and I know you by name." The word "name" also translates to nature or way. When we are in alignment with God Mind, God knows us by our divine nature as we express it. When we recognize the nature of God, we are also recognized because we have become one with the One.

In Exodus 33:20 Moses asked to see God's face. God said, *"You cannot see my face and live…I will cover you with my hand until I have passed by; and then I will take away my hand, and you shall see my back; but my face shall not be seen."*

At this level of development, humanity has not yet the spiritual capacity to see God face to face. The Apostle Paul said we would first *"see through a glass darkly and then face to face."* Human development is still in its infancy and must progress much further until it reaches the capacity for spirituality. Moses was concerned with law and obedience, still drawing the people out of the slave consciousness into which they were born.

In Exodus 32:19 when Moses saw the golden calf he smashed the first tablets containing the Ten Commandments. When human consciousness backslides into idol worship, there is no way to progress into building a nation. Everything must stop until the groundwork is laid once again in consciousness for life in the Promised Land.

God gave Moses and the people many instructions as to how they should act and how to do things in proper order. In Exodus 34:10 the covenant was renewed and a second set of tablets was given to Moses with the same commandments as the first.

A mixture of writers is evident as the story seems to weave back and forth. At first God is the Creator of all, high and wise, and then God turns temperamental, angry, and threatens to retaliate against the people. Researchers believe the description of God as a petulant child may be evidence of a female writer from the southern kingdom writing from a family point of view. Many of the stories are told from a family perspective that would not be characteristic of male writers.

The brain at the teenage state of development creates its god as high and wise when things are going its way and stupid when things do not go its way. The ultimate adult images of God are: God as loving father, Jesus' Abba; and the Apostle Paul's Christ in you. God evolves in man's thinking from anthropomorphic to ultimate cosmic First Cause, Creative Principle. We can discern humanity's developmental maturity by the maturity of the god it creates.

When Moses came down from the mountain with the second set of tablets, his face was so radiant that the people were afraid of him. So Moses put a veil over his face when speaking to the people, and removed it when speaking to God. Moses reached radiance, a likeness to God by being in God's presence. The Fillmores and many other early spiritual teachers also had this luminosity about them. It is said people would come to Unity Village just to look at Charles and Myrtle Fillmore because of the light that emanated from them. When I met Fenwick Holmes I saw this same luminosity. He was the brother of Ernest Holmes, founder of Science of Mind. Fenwick was about five feet five inches tall with thick white hair. When he was speaking from the platform, he appeared to grow taller and taller, his hair more luminous, and his voice more thunderous. We have this luminosity when we are constantly interfaced with God Mind, when we are so focused upon our spirituality that the dense physical nature ceases to be of primary importance.

At the end of Exodus, all the vestments and ornaments for the tabernacle were made, the priests were ordained, and Moses had completed the building of the tabernacle into which they placed the Ark of the Covenant. The cloud that led the Israelites through the wilderness now settled over the tabernacle.

The tabernacle was a portable tent. When the cloud lifted they took up the tabernacle and went forward. When the cloud settled back down onto the tent everyone stopped and waited. Slowly through this obedience to guidance Israel was forming into a nation. The tribes were not yet formed, but the seeds were there. As yet the psychological twelve powers, represented by these tribes, do not function as they will eventually, but clearly they continue to develop within humanity as it matures.

CHAPTER FOURTEEN

Laws, Rituals and Murmurings

L eviticus contains all the rituals and ancient traditions to guide the people through the wilderness. Leviticus actually begins with the twenty-fifth chapter of Exodus and continues on into the book of Numbers. The division of books, chapters, and verses does not follow any specific pattern, or signify the beginning or the ending of a complete thought. Divisions were arbitrarily inserted, sometimes dividing a sentence leaving the first part in one chapter and the second part appearing in the next.

Leviticus starts out with burnt offerings. There are offerings for everything and details on how to prepare and present them. There are sacrifices for every growth event in the consciousness of man. In order to have love, we must give up fear. In order to have abundance we give up thoughts of poverty and lack. In order to be happy, we give up thoughts of resentment and jealousy.

In Leviticus 6:1 the sacrifice of guilt caught my attention. There was a way provided to relieve people of their guilt. They were to make restoration in full plus adding one fifth and giving the whole sum to the one they wronged. Humanity cannot develop and prosper by stealing, deceiving or otherwise causing hurt to another.

Today humanity is still developing ways of recognizing errors and eradicating them. In today's world, the twelve step programs contain a step to make reparation for wrongdoing. This and the other eleven steps must be carefully considered and worked through before one can complete the process of healing from an addiction.

This harkens back to ancient writings that mirror the fear of men about women. Every cave man knew that while hunting, if he were wounded and bled, he would die. But women bled every month and did not die. Women bled after birth and did not die. This mysterious power of women was so feared that many laws were created to subdue women and protect the men from some imagined threat. This fear is mirrored in the torture of Middle Eastern women and other cultures by religious extremists down through the ages. In Leviticus 12:1 if a woman bore a male child, the period of purification was one week. After the birth of a female child she was considered to be unclean for at least two weeks, sometimes more, and then she was required to take a sacrifice to the priests before being declared clean.

Many of the laws were created for physical survival and diagnosis of ailments. In Leviticus 13 are instructions for careful examination of skin conditions to determine if leprosy was present and bodily discharges that would render the person impure and unclean.

Metaphysically we must keep the mind as clean and healthy as possible to insure survival and progress. There are many dis-eases in thinking because humanity has deep fears that produce imbalance in the body systems. Race consciousness is the great reservoir of human thought that contains absolutely everything humanity has thought, good, bad and all between. Humanity constantly names and describes each symptom meticulously and that keeps it rooted in the race consciousness. All those thoughts are still available should someone delve into it with a strong negative mindset. Perhaps this explains, as Carl Jung discovered, why many people have scary images, strange dreams, and thoughts that are completely foreign to them.

The continued fear of sexual power is expressed in Leviticus 18, containing the twelve sexual prohibitions. The other sexual activities are described as *"uncovering nakedness."*

They include incest, homosexuality, bestiality, coveting your neighbor's wife, or any kinswoman. The chapter begins with the words, *"You shall not do as they do in the land of Egypt and you shall not do as they do in the land of Canaan."*

As humanity develops in consciousness toward building a nation and living in an orderly way, sexual activity is not to be the focus but to be lifted to a higher place in society. It was for the begetting of children in order for the tribe to continue to exist and increase in numbers and prosperity. Homosexuality is mentioned as an abomination because it does not produce children. Children died in great numbers in their first year of life, and a childless couple would be an impoverished couple in every way. Communities were fragile and could quickly be wiped out, during wars, famines, and plagues.

In that time there was no such thing as romantic love, marriage for love, or freedom to choose one's own mate. In today's world we can choose to court and marry for love, and now there is no need to continue overpopulating the world. Even though homosexuality was an abomination in the biblical times, their reasons no longer exist in the modern world. When Jesus said, *"Love your neighbor,"* he didn't say only men or only women. We have risen to an agape form of love that includes everyone, and may lead to courtship between any two consenting adults.

New ideas for survival and expansion must be born all the time. To focus the mind on unproductive carnal thinking is to kill the creativity necessary to live in higher ways. Human consciousness must constantly shift toward higher more expansive awareness.

Leviticus 19:2 is called the *"Holiness Code"* beginning with *"you shall be holy; for I the lord your God am holy."* These are the rituals for moral holiness. Today we use meditation, prayer and some ritual services to help us stay aligned with our progress toward spiritual understanding and expression.

In Leviticus 19:18 is the commandment alluded to by Jesus, *"You shall love your neighbor as yourself."* It is embedded in the Ten Commandments and restated here. This is the third time the Ten Commandments have been repeated in the early scriptures. To recap, the first time was when Moses came down from the mountain with the set of stone tablets. The second was when he came down with a second set after he smashed the first ones.

In Leviticus 24:19, *"When a man causes a disfigurement in his neighbor, as he has done it shall be done to him, fracture for fracture, eye for eye, tooth for tooth; as he has disfigured a man, he shall be disfigured."* This has been practiced literally among some peoples.

In metaphysical understanding, we know that what we do to others we have already done to ourselves because it is first in our own consciousness. We can do only what exists in our own thinking. We can only be willing to hurt someone else when we are living and acting out of that damaged place within ourselves.

In Leviticus 25:2, *"When you come into the land which I give you, the land shall keep a Sabbath to the Lord. Six years you shall sow your field, and six years you shall prune your vineyard, and gather its fruits, but in the seventh year there shall be a Sabbath of solemn rest for the land..."* It shall lie fallow every seventh year. In our country we have not always followed that commandment. Humanity has worn out the land by constant cultivation.

We give our minds to holiness for barely an hour on Sunday. There is a metaphysical equivalent in keeping the Sabbath for our minds and devoting the seventh day to holiness. Many people work right though the Sabbath, work six and seven days a week, subjecting themselves to disease, burn out, depression, and many other maladies. They become depleted just as the overworked land becomes depleted.

For the Jews it is Shabbat, a twenty-four-hour time period when no work is to be done. All food is prepared before the Sabbath begins. Even travel was forbidden in early times. The Jews greet and say farewell with the words Shabbat Shalom from sundown Friday to sundown Saturday. It is a reminder that means *"peaceful Sabbath."*

When in scripture it is written the Lord will smite us, it is talking about our own abuse of our minds, bodies, and resources to the point that we sicken all three. It is not God punishing us, but the result of ignoring physical and spiritual law. It is not the Lord but violation of the law that smites us because we have not lived by it. If we jump off a building and are injured when we hit the ground, it is not God injuring us. It is our own lack of observance of the law of gravity.

Leviticus 27 is an appendix concerning religious vows and evaluation of what was being vowed. People, property, and animals could be vowed or consecrated to the temple. An arbitrary monetary value was placed on each one and that would be the price of redemption. One could consecrate something to the temple and receive the set value in cash. If one wished to redeem something consecrated to the temple, such as a son or daughter, he would pay back the cash he received plus one fifth of the value to the priests. *"All the tithe of the land... is the Lords; it is holy to the Lord. If a man wishes to redeem any of this tithe, he shall buy it adding a fifth to it."* (Leviticus 27:30)

The words redemption and redeem first show up in Exodus. This whole system of redemption is spelled out in detail in Exodus and Numbers. At this early stage of development, humanity is redeemable only at the physical or monetary level. But in Psalms, redemption has to do with redeeming the soul. This is a later advance in development.

The book of Numbers initially refers to the numbering of the people, the census, in each tribe except the tribe of Levi. All in the tribe of Levi were the priests and did not own land. This was the great ordering of tribes and people forming them into the foundations of a nation. There were strict laws for the Nazirites and cruel laws for women suspected of adultery, all written in the most graphic terms. The fears of ego mind are always cruel and punishing, even unto death.

In Numbers 6:24 is the blessing of Aaron to the people that is still used today as a benediction:

"The Lord bless you and keep you,
"The Lord make his face to shine upon you, and be gracious to you.
"The Lord lift up his countenance upon you and give you peace."

In Numbers 11:10, the people complained about their hardships and it is written *"the Lord blazed hotly and Moses was displeased."* Moses blazed hotly, too, and again upbraided God for being cruel to the people. *"Why have you dealt ill with your servant? And why have I not found favor in your sight, that you lay this burden of all the people upon me? Did I conceive all this people? Did I bring them forth, that you should say to me, 'carry them in your bosom...' If you will deal thus with me, kill me at once..."*

We get really frustrated with our concept and image of God. At this stage of development humanity wants a god that will rescue them, see to their needs, and treat them like a loving parent. When this doesn't happen, humanity assumes it is being punished. But God is Principle, First Cause, the Divine that moves through us as we see to our own needs. What seems to be punishment is simply not using the Principle correctly to bring what we need into our lives. Whatever we focus our minds upon the Principle will bring into our experience.

In Numbers 12:1 is the story of Miriam's punishment. Miriam is one of the few whose life story is told from childhood in Egypt to her death in Kadesh noted in Numbers 20:1. We meet Miriam again at the crossing of the Red Sea as she celebrated with the women the success of their escape from Egypt. She seems to have become a spiritual leader side-by-side with Aaron.

She became disgusted with the constant complaints and murmuring of the people and feared God would punish them all. Moses let his Midianite wife continue with her own religion, which Miriam thought angered God against them. The faith of the people was still fragile. They criticized Moses and blamed him for their troubles. Miriam had worked herself into such a negative state of mind as to criticize God for speaking only through Moses. Another thing that upset her was that Moses was so laid back. The text says he was *"very meek, more so than any other man on the earth." (Numbers 12:3)*

Aaron and Miriam went to Moses' tent and challenged him. They asked if God could speak only through Moses. *"Has he not spoken through us also?"* Aaron was with Miriam in speaking against Moses, but evidently Miriam somehow went a step too far and suffered the consequences. We are not told what exactly she did that caused the leprosy. It may have been that she became angry and bitter at the people who were so difficult, and as a result brought leprosy upon herself. Bitterness will eat at a person physically as well as emotionally and cause illness or dis-ease. Miriam was set outside the camp for seven days, during which time she was healed and able to rejoin the people. It is good to give ourselves a time-out when frustrations become too much, and heal ourselves before the difficulty takes deeper root in the consciousness.

In "Stories from Martha's House" is a fiction story I wrote about Miriam. She had let hardship take over and harden her. The people began to hate her. She had blamed God for her bitterness and was immediately struck with leprosy. While she was exiled outside the encampment in the Sinai, she began to see the truth. She had let the joyous Miriam at the crossing of the Red Sea slip away. She had spoiled her own happiness by choosing bitterness. When she saw clearly what she had done, repented her error state of mind, and she was restored to health and to her people. They greeted the restored Miriam with joy because she was again the Miriam they knew at the crossing of the Red Sea.

It is so easy to get caught up in this world and let our struggles overtake us. TV shows and Internet blogs are full of utter lack of civil interaction and respect for others. When we allow ourselves to get caught up in the negativities of the world, we bring upon ourselves illnesses and difficulties. When we see the truth, we turn our thinking around, take responsibility for our life experiences and regain our joy, and the difficulties begin to fade away. Repent means to turn our thinking around.

In Numbers 13 the story abruptly turns to spying out the land of Canaan. Canaan represents our subconscious mind. This is the beginning of revealing the contents of subconscious mind. There are a lot of fears in our subconscious minds. Moses sent out twelve scouts, the heads of the twelve tribes, and all their names are listed. The leaders of this expedition were Caleb and Joshua, son of Nun. The name Joshua means the savior, the same as the name Jesus. In the Hebrew Testament they represent precursors of the Christ consciousness.

In Numbers 13:17 Moses told them what they needed to look for and what evidence they needed to bring back to him. The instructions are quoted here because there is a great opportunity for us to use them as a guide to the content of the subconscious mind.

"Go up into the Negeb yonder, and go up into the hill country, and see what the land is, and whether the people who dwell in it are strong or weak, whether they are few or many, and whether the land they dwell in is good or bad, and whether the cities that they dwell in are camps or strongholds, whether the land is rich or poor, and whether there is wood in it or not. Be of good courage and bring some of the fruit of the land."

We must search the contents of our subconscious minds. Are the fears large and threatening or small and inconsequential? Are they grouped and protected by walls of emotion? Are they grounded in truth (good land) or in misperception (bad land)? Is the land rich and can good be built there? And what are the fruits or the results of these contents for your life?

The clearing of subconscious mind is a task that must be undertaken throughout our lives. Mary Baker Eddy said, *"Stand porter at your door of thought."* We must learn to keep out harmful thinking while at the same time releasing what we have already let in from the past.

In Numbers 13:25 *"at the end of forty days they returned."* Forty again is symbolic of the time it takes to get the job done. All but two of the spies *"gave an evil report."* They said the land was full of walled cities and descendants of Anak. There were Amalekites, Hittites, and Amorites. Anak was father of a tribe of giants called the Nephilim. *(See Genesis 6:4)* Ancient mythology describes them as giants with superhuman thought power resulting from divine and human intermarriage. But Joshua and Caleb were not afraid. Caleb in Hebrew means bold, fearless, and impetuous. Caleb wanted to attack but the time was not right.

Numbers 13:30 *"We are well able to overcome it."*. Joshua and Caleb reported, *"the land we passed through is an exceedingly good land…it flows with milk and honey…do not fear the people for they are bread for us… do not fear them."*

The other men said, *"We are not able to go up against the people for they are stronger than we…the land devours its inhabitants…we seemed to ourselves as grasshoppers, and so we seem to them."* They saw themselves as diminished by those they perceived as greater. Our fears argue with our courage, our doubts with our faith and we see ourselves as less than or diminished before others.

Again the people wanted to choose another leader and go back to Egypt. In Numbers 14:10 they wanted to stone Caleb and Joshua, so the *"glory of the Lord appeared to all the people"* and God complained to Moses that the people still despised him. God wanted to smite them all with pestilence and disinherit them. But Moses reminded God once again of his promises and all he has done for them. God complained, *"these people put me to the proof ten times and have not harkened to my voice…"* (Look at all I've done for my kids and they still hate me.)

This again is considered the writing of a southern kingdom writer, depicting God as a petulant child or angry parent who laments all he has done for the people and still they don't love him. Humanity is still in the teenage level of development. Biologically the teenage brain is not the same configuration as the adult brain, so adult thinking is not yet available.

God said again as he said once to Noah, make meat sacrifices to create *"an odor pleasing to the Lord."* The image here is still of an anthropomorphic god. This God demands numerous physical sacrifices to appease him. Again you can tell the maturity of a person or a people by the god they create. Is their god a parent, a punisher, a giver of gifts, or a lover/redeemer?

You can see how important it is to create in your mind God as Principle or the Divine Creator. And not as a parent who punishes, as Santa Claus that will bring you things you ask for, or an oracle to whom you take your complaints. You seek to align your consciousness with the All Good of Creative Principle, God Mind. The degree to which you accomplish this determines the level of power you will have as you answer your own prayers.

CHAPTER FIFTEEN

Joshua Commissioned to Lead

Because the people were so disobedient, God threatened to kill them all in the wilderness. Once again Moses reminded God of his promises. In Numbers 14:17, *"And now I pray thee, let the power of the Lord be great as you have promised, saying, 'The Lord is slow to anger, and abounding in steadfast love, forgiving iniquity and transgression...' Pardon the iniquity of this people, I pray you..."*

In Numbers 14:1, *"All the congregation raised a loud cry; and the people wept that night. And all the people murmured against Moses and Aaron; the whole congregation said to them, 'Would that we had died in the land of Egypt! Or would that we had died in this wilderness! Why does the Lord bring us to this land, to fall by the sword?'"*

They wanted to choose a captain and return to Egypt. Joshua convinced them that the land was good and they should wait for the Lord to give it to them. Soon the people regretted their murmuring against Moses and God. Now they wanted to see God face to face to atone for their sins. They still would not listen to Moses and thought they could deal with God on their own terms. In Numbers 14:39 *"Do not go up lest you be struck down before your enemies. God is not among you!"* But they charged up the mountain anyway. The Amalekites and Canaanites then come down from the hills and defeated Israel and chased them to Mount Hormah.

The name Hormah means a sanctuary of destruction. We are driven to a place where error thoughts are taken in and utterly destroyed. Humanity keeps hitting its head against the brick wall of error thinking, trying to redeem itself by throwing itself at the feet of God and then not waiting for guidance. We cannot escape error thinking without consciously changing it and acting according to the change.

"God is not among you." God is not among our error thoughts. God cannot take away our erroneous thoughts and fears. We must do that ourselves and open the way for Truth to help us. This part of the story displays the continuing adolescent willful thinking. When disaster happens, the adolescent mind simply shouts, *"I'm sorry!!!"* Humanity butts its head against circumstances over and over until its consciousness develops beyond this stage.

The god of the Hebrew Testament appeared as a demanding and cruel god. A man gathered sticks outside the camp on the Sabbath day and God ordered him stoned to death so the story goes. Humanity creates a cruel god according to its own lack of development, self-hatred and worst fears. We create God in the image and likeness of our own minds. As humanity grows, it images an ever-uplifting idea of God the Creator and not God the punisher.

In Numbers 16:31 Moses finds that Korah, Dathan, and Abiram were disobedient. *"The ground under them split asunder; and the earth opened its mouth and swallowed them up with their households... and they went down alive into Sheol; and the earth closed over them and they perished in the midst of the assembly."*

The idea that hell was underground somewhere comes from this and other mythologies. In Greek mythology a person who died had to pay their fare to Charon the ferryman to cross the River Styx and enter the *"underworld."* Persephone was kidnapped by Hades and carried down to the underworld. Words used for hell are also Hades, Sheol and the inferno. Hell is not a place but a state of mind. We create heaven or hell right here in our lives according to our own predominant thought.

God was still angry and began to destroy his people with a plague. Moses ran to put on incense, *"And he stood between the dead and the living, and the plague was stopped."* Our Moses consciousness that draws us out of the darkness of the purely physical nature still stands against the darkness to shepherd us forward in our development and defend us from our own misperceptions of God.

In Numbers 17 the duties of the priests are outlined. All Levites were responsible for the sanctuary. Only Aaron and his sons were responsible for the priests. The priests were allowed to eat the temple offerings that God gave them as a *"perpetual due."* This was how the Levites were sustained for all time without having to work the land.

Numbers 19 contains Purity Rituals necessary for the health and survival of the community. *"He who touches the dead body of any person shall be unclean seven days; he shall cleanse himself with water on the third day and on the seventh day, so to be clean."* These were health rituals. Dead bodies were to be buried quickly. They could contaminate with diseases those who touched them. Humanity must maintain its purity in thought as much as possible and not entertain deadly thoughts of the past if progress is to continue.

Numbers 20 begins with Miriam's death. *"The people stayed at Kadesh; and Miriam died and was buried there."* Kadesh is on the southern border of Canaan. Miriam's life story is told sporadically from when she was a child guiding Moses' basket in the Nile River until her death. If she ever married, it is not mentioned. Evidently she was not a widow. It was unusual however that a prominent woman who had no husband should play a prominent role in events of that time.

The name *"Miriam in Hebrew means contradiction, outcry, protest, rebellion, bitterness, grief, and also amiable, aromatic, sweet-smelling, fragrant, exaltation. There is no name that offers a wider range of seemingly conflicting ideas…smell is associated with spirit, breath, understanding, inspiration. Miriam, Mary, and Myrrh come from the same root."* *(Metaphysical Bible Dictionary)* This is the soul's struggle to break out of mental constraints into spiritual freedom and understanding. The struggle is life-long symbolized by the telling of her life-long story. This is a facet of our being we would do well to pay attention to and allow our struggles to teach us. Miriam symbolizes our ever-developing consciousness.

In Numbers 20:2 the people were again murmuring and threatening to go back to Egypt because they had no water. So Moses struck a rock twice and water came forth. Later on this would be the reason given that Moses would not be allowed to enter the Promised Land. Striking the rock twice indicated that he was impatient and didn't trust God to respond. I suppose this is like kicking a flat tire out of anger and frustration. When you are in anger trying to force something to happen, you are outside of the Kingdom of Heaven. He could not enter the Promised Land in that lower state of mind.

Moses sent a message to the king of Edom asking for safe passage and the king refused. Edomites were the descendants of Esau who lost his birthright to his brother Jacob. They became the enemies of Israel. In our first foray into subconscious mind, we will be repulsed by the negative attitudes and habits that have no birthright in God, but have dwelled there unchallenged until now. But this was not the time for Israel to attack head on as Caleb desired to do. When we first see what is in subconscious mind, we are not to attack it unprepared. Numbers 20:21 says *"Israel turned away from him* (Edom*). They journeyed from Kadesh to Mount Hor."*

Aaron died on Mount Hor. In Hebrew Hor means *"to be in a high state of mind, to think, mountain of mountains."* In this high state Aaron passed his executive powers to his son, Eleazar to carry on. *"Eleazar means God has surrounded. Spiritual strength through the individual's recognition of God as his supporting, sustaining power."* (Metaphysical Bible Dictionary) The higher state of mind is not static. The Aaron level of development, the mouth for Moses, sinks back into the subconscious and a new level of consciousness, Eleazar, steps forth.

In order to avoid going through Edom, they set out by way of the Red Sea and again the people were impatient and spoke against God and Moses. God sent fiery serpents against the people. Moses again prayed to God not to destroy the people. The people promised God they would defeat Arad if God would take a hand in it. The Israelites did defeat the Canaanite king of Arad.

Growing into a higher state of mind is not necessarily smooth sailing. We encounter many negative thoughts and habits that are quite powerful. Israel kept moving until they arrived north of Moab on the east side of the Dead Sea. The list of places they camped is in Numbers 21:10. Again Moses asked for passage through the land of the Amorites and was denied. Israel defeated the Amorites and dwelt in their cities. They fought their way through tribe after tribe up the east side of the Dead Sea to the territory that is now modern Jordan.

There are some obscure poetry fragments in this chapter from *"the Book of the Wars of the Lord."* This book is lost. Numbers 21: 14

through18 are all that remain of it. It may seem at times that we have a flash of an ancient memory that does not become quite clear in our minds. It may be a fragment from a past lifetime or a time that is long lost to present consciousness.

In Numbers 22:1, the Israelites killed everyone who came against them and *"camped in the plains of Moab beyond the Jordan at Jericho."* Jericho is on the west side of the Jordan, in the land of Canaan. The inhabitants of those tribes sent a messenger, to Balaam, who practiced the art of divination, to place a curse on the people coming out of Egypt. Babylon was a well-known city of diviners. But God came to Balaam in a dream and said *"You shall not go with them; you shall not curse the people, for they are blessed." (Numbers 22:12)*

We discover again that Moses is not the only one that God talks to. Now anyone who sought contact with the divine was responded to. However Moses was the only one who held arguments and conversations intimately with God.

In Numbers 22:18 the ruler, Balak, sent even higher officials to Balaam, but Balaam said, *"Though Balak were to give me his house full of silver and gold, I could not go beyond the command of the Lord my God, to do less or more. Pray now tarry here this night that I may know what more the Lord will say to me. And God came to Balaam and said, '…go with them, but only as I bid you, that shall you do.'"*

Balaam is an interesting character. His name means foreigner, lord of the people. He is a prophet and soothsayer of the Midianites. Although *"he strives for ascendancy, he discerns the superiority of Spirit and cannot fight openly against the Truth. He represents sense man that tries to destroy Truth thoughts in subtle, devious ways." (Metaphysical Bible Dictionary)* Sense man is the person who lives in the world of the five senses, the physical, and has not yet risen in consciousness to the spiritual.

In Numbers 22:21 is the famous story of Balaam's talking ass. *"In the East the ass is especially remarkable for its patience, gentleness, intelligence, meek submission and great power of endurance…a symbol of peace…"* *(Smith Bible Dictionary)* Jesus rode an ass into Jerusalem for the Passover Celebration.

In Numbers 23:11 Balaam refused to curse the Israelites and Balak said to Balaam, *"What have you done to me? I paid you to curse my enemies, and you have done nothing but bless them."* Balaam launched into slippery words of prophesy to put Balak off and probably keep the fee. Ego mind has many reasonable sounding ways of arguing us out of the Truth.

In Numbers 25, the Israelites were living in the land of Moab and were intermarrying with the Moabites. It symbolized a corruption of Israel's faith. Moabites worshipped Baal, the Canaanite god of storm and fertility. God was said to be jealous and God sent a plague that killed 24,000. The word jealous also translates to zealous. After the plague God ordered another census. Of those who wandered in the wilderness, only Joshua and Caleb were left.

Once again we take stock of our thinking after slaying all the foreign and negative thoughts. Only the leading pure thoughts remain, Joshua and Caleb. *"Caleb means one who unceasingly wars against error, is fearless and zealous. Joshua means Jah is savior, deliverer."* In the Hebrew his name is identical with the Greek Jesus. So this is the part that survives to lead humanity to the new thoughts of Truth. In Numbers 26 the names of the leaders are listed from the Priestly records.

Numbers 27 marks a new thought coming forth. Until this time women were not permitted to inherit. If their family males all died, the property went to others in the tribe. But the daughters of Zelophehad went to Moses and said, *"Our father died in the wilderness; he was not among the company of those who gathered themselves together against the Lord in the company of Korah, but died for his own sin; and he had no sons. Why should the name of our father be taken away from his family, because he had no son? Give to us a possession among our father's brethren."*

Moses went to God and God said to give them their share of the inheritance and henceforth give a portion to any woman whose father dies and has no sons. So for the first time women were given the right to inherit. They could not marry outside their tribe because their land could not be transferred outside the tribe. This restriction was for the survival of the tribe. Survival often requires a sacrifice. The feminine aspect of humanity is given its rightful place in Divine inheritance.

At the end of Numbers 27:18, Joshua was commissioned by God through Eleazar, son of Aaron, to lead the people. Joshua went to war against Midian and its corrupting influences and defeated them. The land was distributed to the tribes of Reuben, Gad, and Manasseh upon their promise to stay true to God and the leadership of Joshua.

In Numbers 33, the stages of Israel's journey are again retold in detail. The Levites, the tribe of priests, are given cities but not territories.

The concluding statement in Numbers 36 covers all the laws given in Moab. *"These are the commandments and ordinances which the Lord commanded by Moses to the people of Israel in the plains of Moab by the Jordan at Jericho."*

CHAPTER SIXTEEN

Deuteronomy

In 2 Kings 22:8 (repeated in 2 Chronicles 34:14) the house of the Lord was being cleaned and a book was discovered in a storage place. It was taken to King Josiah who sent it to Huldah the Prophetess for authentication. She authenticated the book as the word of God and it became known as the book of Deuteronomy.

The first three chapters of Deuteronomy consist of a recounting of the history of the Israelites up until they occupied Moab, as we have already read. Moses was getting the people ready to enter Canaan. Again he admonished them not to take on the beliefs and the worship rituals they would find among the Canaanites.

In Deuteronomy 4 *"And now, O Israel, give heed to the statutes and the ordinances which I taught you, and do them; that you may live, and go in and take possession of the land which the Lord the God of your fathers, gives you."* Moses went over everything, including the Ten Commandments, but this time there are eleven.

In Deuteronomy 6:4 is the *"Great Commandment,"* the beautiful shema.

"Hear, O Israel; the Lord our God is one Lord; and you shall love the Lord your God with all your heart and with all your soul, and with all your might. And these words which I command you this day shall be upon your heart; and you shall teach them diligently to your children, and shall talk of them when you sit in your house, and when you walk by the way, and when you lie down, and when you rise. And you shall bind them as a sign

upon your hand, and they shall be as frontlets between your eyes. And you shall write them on the doorposts of your house and on your gates."

The sign upon your hand indicates you are the hand of God. The frontlets between your eyes indicate you see with the eyes of God. The doorposts and gates are your state of mind that shall be focused upon this teaching. Mary Baker Eddy said, *"Stand porter at your door of thought."* Don't let error in.

The passage goes on to say take heed that you do not forget this when you continue on your life journey, when you are occupying cities you did not build and eat of orchards you did not plant. Many years hence keep this commandment before your eyes as a guide similar to the pillar of fire that led the people through Sinai. Or it is like railroad tracks that keep you from going astray so you will surely reach your destination of spiritual unfoldment.

Starting in Deuteronomy 7, Moses told the people exactly how to live in the land of Canaan, what it meant to be God's people in a new land. This is the symbol of humanity moving out of the child mind and toward the pre-adolescent mind. We train our minds by speaking words of spiritual Truth at all times. By doing this we engrain in our consciousness the basic commandments of living. The shema has long been the guiding teaching of people even today. This and several other wonderful invocations in the scriptures are very useful to center one's self for meditation or in any situation that needs focus, a quiet mind, and blessing. People also use Psalm 23 and the Psalm 91, as we will see later in the chapter on Psalms.

In Deuteronomy 12 is the centralization of worship. The Canaanite shrines were to be torn down and the central place of worship chosen by the Lord. It is a sign of early development in psychological consciousness that will eventually progress to spiritual awareness. This was turned around when Jesus told the woman at the well that God was to be worshipped in spirit in the valleys and the mountains and everywhere.

In Deuteronomy 15 is the famous Year of Release. *"At the end of every seven years you shall grant a release…every creditor will release what he has lent…Any servants will be set free in the seventh year…Remember that you were a slave in Egypt and your Lord redeemed you."*

This is a teaching of compassion, that you release yourself from hard-hearted thoughts, enslaving ideas and limiting beliefs. We release ourselves from binding judgments we have placed upon ourselves such as believing we must be poor, sick, and declining in strength in our later years. We have other judgments as well such as thinking ourselves guilty, stupid, ugly or shameful. As soon as these beliefs appear they all must be released never to return to our thinking. This is a continuing process that seems enormous at first but becomes easier as time goes on. Subconscious mind eventually becomes the *porter at our door of thought,* trained to automatically discard error thinking.

Deuteronomy 16 is about the appointed feasts: The feast of weeks, the feast of booths, etc. It reminds us that there are many famines in our lives, but there must also be feasts and celebrating. Psychological humanity is a feast and famine critter. Until we rise into our spirituality as expressed in the Gospels, life experiences go up and down.

In Deuteronomy 19 Cities of Refuge are established. Anyone who has accidentally injured or killed another person may flee to the city of refuge to escape revenge of the brothers. If someone intentionally murders, they may not find refuge in these cities but be turned away. Hard as it can be, we learn to create a place of refuge in consciousness where we can sort out our thoughts with a cool head to avoid pronouncing ruinous sentences of guilt and self-hatred upon ourselves. This is a beginning of the practice of self-forgiveness.

Deuteronomy is a renewal of the Covenant, or the "Second Law." It decreed that worship be centralized in one place, the temple in Jerusalem, so the Jews would not be worshipping in the Canaanite shrines, bowing down to Canaanite gods, and diluting the Mosaic teaching.

Mixed thoughts cause us to be imprisoned by the ones that are not Truth. Often we allow this situation to exist in our consciousness for a very long time before we learn to spiritually interpret who we are and the meaning of our lives.

In Deuteronomy 27 is a negative rendering of the Ten Commandments, only there are twelve this time. The Commandments start with *"Cursed be he…"* and the same wording of the ten follows. Again all the laws are repeated. We repeat the Truth teachings or spiritual laws to our minds over and over until they become second nature. We must be careful not to turn an affirmation into a negative, and instruction or command to a curse. For example we make a healthful resolution to lose weight and then curse ourselves when it doesn't happen. Jesus began the beatitudes with "Blessed are you…."

In Deuteronomy 31 God told Moses he would not be allowed to cross over the Jordan with the people. Again Moses told them *"Be strong and of good courage. The Lord your God himself will go over before you and will destroy the nations before you…"* God prophesied that the people would turn to pagan beliefs again and again. God then commissioned Joshua to lead the people and Moses died, or as said in early biblical times, went to sleep with the fathers.

In Deuteronomy 32 is the Song of Moses and in chapter 33 is the Blessing of Moses on the tribes of Israel. God buried Moses in a secret place in Moab. *"Moses was 120 years old when he died; his eye was not dim nor his natural force abated."* This is the denial of the judgment humanity has placed upon itself, that we should decline in our senior years. When the body is laid to rest, we step out in full power to continue into our next expression of eternal life.

The Book of Joshua

This book symbolizes humanity entering a whole new world, the world of the teenage mind. We don't just skip from infancy to full adulthood. It is a learning process. The kids are going off to college and being on their own for the first time. There will be frat parties, credit cards over the limit, car accidents, football injuries, girls getting pregnant and many students flunking classes.

In this process humanity moves from being guided by a visible person, symbolized by Moses, to being guided by the invisible God. Mom and Dad are far away, and the not yet mature internal moral compass takes over. Humanity still looks to the outer world for power. The invisible God at this time of development is a nationalistic God, a God of battles, whose power is chiefly manifested in prosecution of Holy War. University classes are battles to be won, academics to be understood and grades to be wooed.

God laid out the rules for waging Holy War in Deuteronomy 20, and they might be surprising. *"When you go forth to war against your enemies and an army larger than your own, you shall not be afraid of them for the Lord your God is with you... When you draw near to a city to fight against it, offer terms of peace to it..."*

In the cities of ego mind, offer terms of peace and make ego mind your servant instead of your enemy. You need right thoughts and helpful habits to empower your life experiences. The power is in subconscious mind and must be wooed and trained to serve your highest good.

Canaan represents subconscious mind. Your fears will be large and you may feel small like the first twelve men Moses sent to spy out Canaan. They came back fearful saying, *"We are to them as grasshoppers!"* Subconscious mind seems huge like big schools and universities that can be overwhelming to the new student.

The first battle was against the city of Jericho, thought to be the oldest city known. Joshua sent spies to Jericho and they found a welcome in the house of Rahab. Rahab was characterized as a harlot, but that could simply mean she was unmarried or widowed and on her own. She ran her own business, probably textiles since she had flax stored on the roof, and she operated an inn. She lived in the wall built around Jericho. Walls were double, an outer wall and an inner wall, with a wide space between them. Many merchants set up their shops in this space between the city walls.

Rahab knew the whole history of the Israelites. She represents the freedom within us that recognizes spiritual Truth. She hid Joshua's spies and lied to the king's men about harboring them. She tricked the soldiers into going out of the city gates to pursue the spies to the Jordan and while they were gone, the gates were closed giving Joshua's spies time to assess the city's strength. We always need to chase away and close the doors against negative thoughts, and take stock of the content our minds.

Rahab made a bargain with the spies to spare her and her family from death in exchange for her help. She surely knew that her life was forfeit as soon as she lied to the king's men. She let the spies down by rope from her window and told them to escape into the hills for three days so they wouldn't encounter the king's men returning. They told her to tie a scarlet cord to her window and gather her family there so Joshua's men could identify them and keep them safe. Always we need a plan and help to progress through difficult times to our goal of spiritual development. We will read more about the importance of plans when we get to the book of Nehemiah.

The Ark of the Covenant was carried by the priests into the middle of the Jordan River and the water stopped while the Israelites crossed on dry land, reminiscent of the crossing of the Red Sea. The Jordan can be a quiet little river except in the spring when the snows on Mount Herman melt and turn the river into a torrent. Twelve leaders of twelve tribes were instructed to pick up a stone from where the priests stood in the river, and carry it with them as a memorial to when the waters were stopped.

Later in the Book of Judges, the reality seemed to be that Joshua's victories were not so comprehensive or decisive as the book of Joshua reports. There is a heavy theological theme to this book to show what God does for the people. *Oxford RSV Introduction to Joshua, p. 263*

The Hebrew Torah was written as saga to show what God had done for his people. So it is not meant to be historically accurate. Bible stories were written to make a point, not write history. The Book of Acts is the first book in the Bible written deliberately as a history of the Acts of the Apostles.

In Joshua 5:2, the Israelites camped at Gilgal and placed the stones there. Since the men were of generations born in the wilderness, they were not circumcised. The place of this mass circumcision was called Gibeath-haaraloth, or the hill of the foreskins. Our new generation of thoughts must be updated, upgraded and opened to the Truth of being.

In Joshua 5:14, the commander of the Lord's army came to Joshua as he was looking at the walls of Jericho. The commander said to him, *"Put off your shoes from your feet, for the place where you stand is holy."* Some part of this story seems to be lost, according to the *RSV footnotes*, because no other command or explanation was forth coming. This perhaps was a reminder of God telling Moses to take off his sandals because the ground whereon he stood was holy, connecting Joshua to Moses in the covenant.

In Joshua 6, Joshua received the instructions directly from God, and not this angelic commander, about attacking Jericho and destroying the walls. The sacred number seven is used repeatedly in this chapter. This is an indication of the theological intent of the writing. We don't follow the directions of some imaginary realm now but go directly to God.

CHAPTER SEVENTEEN

The Promised Land

Joshua 6:1 *"Now Jericho was shut up from within and from without…"* No Truth came in or went out. The name Jericho means *"sweet breath, animation, spirit, soul, mind, the moon renewing. These words stand for the intellectual rather than spirit. Just as the moon has only reflected light, so Jericho represented the moon and not the sun."* (*Metaphysical Bible Dictionary*)

When the intellect becomes egotistical, it believes it is the actual light of God, and not just reflected light. This belief must be completely eliminated or remain forever a stumbling block to development. The idea that the ego is substantive forms a consciousness referred to as the devil, Satan, or carnal mind. Thus this idea must be destroyed completely and never rebuilt.

The number seven is a powerful symbol indicating completeness, the Alpha and Omega of a cycle. In completeness there is no process or conversation. This powerful symbol is used to obliterate the deeply rooted carnal idea that ego mind is the light of God. On the seventh day, seven circuits were made around the city. There were seven trumpets, seven priests blowing the trumpets continually all of the seven days. After the seventh day and the seventh time they marched around Jericho, Joshua commanded the people to shout and the walls fell flat. They destroyed everything in the city including men, women, children, and animals. Only Rahab and her family were unharmed. Joshua's men got them out just before they burned the city. Only the "Rahab thought" that recognizes Truth and acts upon it is saved.

Metaphysically, the destroyed were all error thoughts, negative emotions, young error thoughts that would grow up to spawn more error thinking. And animals represented negative habits. All silver, gold, and iron were taken to the Lord's treasury. The people and military were not permitted to loot the city.

In Joshua 6:26, *"Joshua laid an oath upon them at that time saying, 'Cursed before the Lord be the man that rises up and rebuilds this city, Jericho. At the cost of his first-born shall he lay its foundations and at the cost of his youngest son shall he set up the gates.'"*

This prophecy came true in 1 Kings 16:34. Hi'el of Bethel was rebuilding Jericho. His eldest son was murdered and buried in the foundation of the city, the second murdered and buried under the gate. *"It was customary to bury the bodies of children under the foundations of buildings for good luck." (Oxford RSV footnotes p. 442)* The idea of good luck is the creation of the ego mind, neither of which is substantive.

"The gate of the city was the place where the council of the elders met and where business was transacted. The gate was not merely an opening in the city wall, but an enclosed structure sometimes containing several rooms and more than one story high." From Oxford RSV footnotes p. 286

In Joshua 7 after the defeat of Jericho the capture of the city of Ai looked like a cakewalk. It was small and spies advised Joshua to send only two or three thousand men and not his whole population. But the Amorites of Ai rose up and defeated Israel easily. Joshua was dumbfounded. He demanded of God why he let them fail. Some of the Israelites did not obey God and took some of the gold articles, "devoted things" for themselves and hid them among their own belongings. *"Devoted things"* are those things that are dedicated to be offered to God. *"The unitary view of society caused the entire group to be blamed for the sin of one of its members." Oxford RSV footnotes, p. 269)*

Metaphysically we know that a few saved error thoughts, trying to go against the divine, can defeat our whole purpose and stop our progress. Before Joshua went to attack Ai again, he rooted out the family (the thought people) responsible for taking the items and they were stoned and burned to death. The cruelty with which people were treated who disobeyed God is not a description of God, but a symbol of the intensity with which we must go after those thoughts that harm our whole being.

In Joshua 8, he tried again to take Ai. This time Joshua was more careful. He brought 30,000 *"mighty men of valor,"* and they lay in ambush outside the city on three sides. Then the people with Joshua approached the walls and the people of Ai came out after them, they ran and drew them into the ambush of the hiding soldiers. Joshua took the city and was instructed to do the same to it as they did to Jericho. Kill and burn everything.

Ai and Bethel were very close together, so those who came out to do battle with Joshua were from Bethel as well. Joshua's men killed all the people from Ai and Bethel and burned the cities behind them so there was no retreat or escape. They took the king of Ai alive and brought him to Joshua. They hanged him from a tree and buried him at the gate to his city. This time the Israelites were allowed to take booty for themselves. The prosperity principle is the first tenth goes to God and the rest is for our living. Those who do not give the tenth or the tithe will not be able to keep it. Rev. Edwene Gaines taught prosperity principles and said the Universe always reclaims its tenth through various means if it is not given.

Joshua built an altar on Mount Ebal and again read all that Moses commanded to the people. Altars are markers, important turning points. We are to completely obliterate all negative thoughts, feelings, and habits from subconscious mind. At every turning point, the people were reminded again of all the commandments and laws. We remind ourselves periodically of the Truth of our being lest we get lost in the battles and booty strewn on our path.

All the peoples of Canaan heard of the victories of the Israelites and banded together to fight. But the Gibeonites acted alone to trick Joshua into an alliance with them. They dressed in rags, worn out sandals, torn wineskins and carried moldy food to convince Joshua that they were on a long journey, *"from a very far country."* Joshua, believing them, made the covenant, an oath for their safety and they would be servants of Israel. When Joshua found out the truth, that they were actually close neighbors, it was too late. The oath could not be broken. So they were allowed to labor among the Israelites.

Ego mind is tricky. Ego mind will present seemingly positive thoughts to gain a legitimate place in your mind. Once they have taken root among your thoughts they grow like vines wrapping around everything, laboring among your positive thoughts, and they are difficult to root out. It will tell you things such as - gambling is prosperity and you deserve to win so buy more lottery tickets. Gambling is not prosperity. It is hoping to get something for nothing, to be lucky rather than faithful. Again luck is not substantive, it has no power or positive effect. It is nothing.

In Matthew 13:25 is the story of an enemy who dropped the seeds of tares among the wheat. The servants wanted to immediately rip up the poisonous weeds, but the owner told them to wait until the harvest and then separate the tares from the wheat. Ripping up the tares immediately would uproot the wheat as well. If we are focusing on rooting out every *"thought weed"* while we are just getting started on our journey, we will disturb the tender roots of the true thoughts and destroy the whole crop. Our focus should not be on destroying the weeds when it is the thoughts of Truth that need our attention and nurturing.

Every stranger and enemy knew the details of the entire history of the Israelites starting with their release from Egypt. There were no newsletters or mass communications except story telling. Rahab, the Gibeonites and others were able to recite the whole history of Israel. Memory in subconscious mind continues to recite our history. When we neutralize any negative thoughts and feelings that were part of it, our history becomes a helpful learning tool.

In Joshua 10:13 there is reference to a lost writing, the Book of Jashar, or Book of the Upright. It follows the Bible almost word for word with a lot more detail inserted. There are many websites referring to it, most determining the one that emerged and was published in 1625 is a forgery.

In Joshua 10:16 he defeated the kings from southern Palestine. The five kings hid in a cave. Joshua killed them, threw them back into the cave and sealed it with rocks. *"And Joshua took all these kings and their land one at a time..." (Joshua 10:42)* Joshua also wiped out the Anakim from Israel although some still resided in Gaza, Gath and Ashdod. Philistines occupied those three coastal cities.

In Joshua 11 he went on to defeat the northern kings. The most prominent was Jabin, king of Hazor. Jabin is the king mentioned in Judges 4 and 5, and Sisera was his general. Deborah and Barak defeated Jabin and Sisera. Later on David the shepherd boy would defeat Goliath, a giant of the Philistines.

We can vanquish tribes of negative thinking, but there are always some thoughts left around the edges of our minds. Joshua accidentally allowed Gibeonites to live among his people and the Anakim still existed along the Mediterranean coast of Canaan.

In Joshua 12 is the long list of all the kings Joshua defeated. In Joshua 13 are lists of all the lands yet to be conquered. Joshua 13:13 indicates they did not drive out the Geshurites or the Ma-acathites. So, Joshua did not defeat and *"utterly destroy"* all in the Promised Land as God commanded him to do. Joshua reiterated Moses' allotments of the territories east of the Jordan, and he distributed to the remaining the nine tribes all cities, towns, villages, and areas, which are listed in detail. It is likely the priestly writer added these temple records to the text.

In Joshua 17 the tribes of Joseph's sons, Manasseh and Ephraim, complained to Joshua that their portion was too small for the size of their tribes. Joshua also gave them the hill country where the Canaanites had chariots of iron and were strong. He told the tribes to clear the hill country and take the territory, but the sons of Joseph delayed for fear of the iron chariots. The young undeveloped adolescent consciousness still wants to be given more and more without taking the necessary steps to earn it.

Starting in Joshua 17:3, again it is mentioned that the daughters of Zeophchad were given land. The daughters of Manasseh received an inheritance along with his sons. The daughters represent the feminine aspect of human development now demanding to be recognized as meriting equal value with the masculine.

In Joshua 18:3 it seems that seven of the tribes were not eager to possess the territory given them. *"How long will you be slack to go in and take possession of the land which the God of your fathers has given you? Provide three men from each tribe to go up and down the land and write a description..."*

Humanity is slow and even resistant to take possession of its God-given opportunities to grow. Men from each tribe took tablets and wrote detailed descriptions of the land like surveyors. Each territory is meticulously described throughout several chapters. Then the tribes cast lots for each territory. The cities of refuge were appointed and the cities for the Levites, since the Levites would have no territory of their own. This again is an inkling of the value of making a plan before charging forward to assault the negatives in subconscious mind.

The organization in mind is now beginning to take shape. There is still reluctance to change and often fear to move deeper into the more unfamiliar areas of consciousness. Our cities of refuge are our affirmations and denials, the tools that keep us safe and progressing. We affirm the good and deny the negative any power over our lives, keeping the way open for good to manifest and consciousness to progress.

In Deuteronomy, the land of Canaan was strictly west of the Jordan. The tribes of Manasseh, Ruben and Gad were given land by Moses on the east side of the Jordan in Moab. So there became a contention between those in the east and those in the west. In Joshua 22:10 *"the tribe of Manasseh built an altar of great size by the Jordan."* This caused a squabble from the western tribes as to whether they were allowed to build an altar.

In Joshua 22:16, *"Thus says the whole congregation of the Lord, 'What is this treachery which you have committed against the God of Israel in turning away this day from following the Lord by building yourselves an altar in rebellion against the Lord?'"* and on and on it went.

The three eastern tribes responded, *"The Mighty One, God, the Lord! He knows; and let Israel itself know!... We did it from fear that in time your children might say to our children, 'What have you to do with the Lord, the God of Israel? For the Lord has made the Jordan a boundary between us and you. You Reubenites and Gadites, you have no portion in the Lord...'"*

The ego mind goes to great lengths to disempower the spiritual nature that is taking root in consciousness. But that holy one within us comes to the rescue with Truth. Phineas the priest determined that there was no treachery against the Lord, there would be no sacrifices burnt. It would be a memorial...and the report pleased the people of Israel and spoke no more of making war against them.

The name *"Phineas means oracle, mouth or prophecy, metaphysical, spiritual revelation and power. One must be spiritually lifted or become the mouth of brass."* (*Metaphysical Bible Dictionary*) The altar is a marker, a crucial junction. The mouth of spirit speaks and people are satisfied. Only spirit can heal the rifts and fears created by the ego mind. Inner war in the developing mind is abated. Only spirit can turn the battlefield into a place of peace.

In Joshua 23:11, Joshua was old and gave a charge to Israel. *"Take good heed to yourselves to love the Lord your God. For if you turn back and join the remnant of these nations left here among you, and make marriages with them… know assuredly that the Lord your God will not continue to drive out these nations before you; but they shall become a snare and a trap for you, a scourge on your sides and thorns in your eyes, until you perish from off this good land which the Lord has given you."*

Negative thinking is still within and all around us. It will be easy to let that creep in and muddy the consciousness. God will not intervene, but will sustain us through our dark night of the soul. Ultimately we alone will have to choose the pure thoughts of spiritual Truth. This will take practice, dedication, and pure love of Truth.

In Joshua 24, Joshua again reiterated the whole story from Egypt to the present. He admonished them again to put away foreign gods. And he died at 110 years old.

CHAPTER EIGHTEEN

The Book of Judges

This introduction to the Book of Judges is from the Oxford RSV Bible. *"Plainly many parts of Canaan were never subjugated, while the rest of the book is largely an account of battles which had to be fought through several generations before the land was securely in Israel's hands. The enthralling tales the book contains are traditions preserved by various tribes about the exploits of their particular heroes – the 'judges' of whom the title speaks.* The book is mostly concerned with *"a moral lesson. Loyalty to God is the requisite for national success. Disloyalty is a guarantee of disaster."*

The eleven judges are Othniel, Ehud, Shamgar, Deborah, Gideon, Abimelech, Jepthah, Elon, Ibzan, Abdon, and Samson.

There are some discrepancies noted by researchers, one being that in Judges 1:8 Judah fought against Jerusalem and conquered it. It is recorded that Jerusalem was not conquered until David became king in 2 Samuel 5:6. Again this indicates that these books are not chronological history but saga, stories told to teach a moral point.

The subconscious mind, represented by Canaan, is far vaster that one can imagine. A battle with a few negative thoughts and emotions is only the beginning. Just about the time we think we have done a pretty good job of reclaiming subconscious mind, more error thoughts come up from deeper down to be healed that were not obvious before.

In Judges 1:13 is an interesting short story about Achsah, wife of Othniel. *"The name Achsah means anklet, a charmer, a serpent-charmer.*

Her father, Caleb, symbolizes spiritual faith and enthusiasm. Serpent-charmer is one who has power over serpents usually by a kind of personal dominion, assurance, and magnetism...Serpents refer to sense life, wisdom that is gained through the senses...Achsah was given land to the south, or lower area, and the springs above and below represent the spiritual consciousness and the material life." *Metaphysical Bible Dictionary*

The feminine nature is taking a stronger stance in requesting its inheritance. Women are to accept more than just an arid token out of life, but the full measure of life itself. This is the third time in the Hebrew Testament the feminine nature rises to be recognized and valued. It is developing along with the masculine. Achsah would not accept the arid land of the Negeb without also having springs of water, wellsprings of life from above and below.

In Judges 1:16 the Israelites did not conquer Canaan and clear out all the inhabitants as God commanded Joshua. Joshua 1:19 reads, *"Judah could not drive out the inhabitants of the plain because of their iron chariots."*

Verse 27, *"Manasseh did not drive out the inhabitants of Beth-Shean and its villages."*

Verse 29, *"Ephraim did not drive out the Canaanites who dwelt in Gezer."*

Verse 30, *"Zebulun did not drive out the inhabitants of Kitron or Nahalol."*

Verse 31, *"Asher did not drive out the inhabitants of Acco, Sidon, Ahlab, Achzib,*

Helbah, Aphik, or Rehob."

Verse 33, *"Naphtali did not drive out the inhabitants of Bethshemesh or Beth-Anath."*

Verse 34, *"The Amorites pressed the Danites back into the hill country."*

Instead the Israelites dwelt among the inhabitants taking them as servants. Consequently the servants brought their own gods into the houses of Israelites.

We fail to clear out all the negative thoughts and feelings from subconscious mind immediately because it is a huge endeavor. In Joshua 10:42 *"And Joshua took all these kings and their land one at a time..."* While we are clearing one area of thinking, another is growing. They multiply birthing more error thoughts all the time. This is where we need God's help or the all-knowing, all-seeing, all-powerful wisdom of the Holy Spirit.

In Judges 2 again we are told of the burial of Joshua and of the wrath of God because the Israelites again turned away and served Baal. In Judges 2:14, *"God gave them over to plunderers…so that they could no longer withstand their enemies."*

Baal is the generic term for all the gods of Arabia. When we turn from spirit to focus on material living we are weakened and our good thoughts plundered. From Judges 15, *"and they were in sore straits."* When we are ruled by the physical world, which has no compassion or wisdom for us and we are indeed *"in sore straits."*

Worship means *"pay divine honors to."* (Dictionary) *"The worship of Baal leads the negative mind deeper and deeper into bondage. This bondage is belief in luck, chance, sorcery, wizardry, etc. In modern times Astrology, palmistry, guidance of spirits, mesmerism, and hypnotism, are some of the many forms of denial of God."* Metaphysical Dictionary

In Judges 3:9, after eight years God called up the first judge or leader, Othniel, from the tribe of Judah, to save them from the power of those who plundered them. Othniel means strength of God. And yet they did not listen to their judge. When they ignored the judge, still God raised them up from their errors, but God did not drive out the other nations. God is always there to give us the power to solve our problems, but does not solve them for us.

In Judges 3:1 *"Now these are the nations which the Lord left, to test Israel by them, …and to teach war.."* They are listed and after Othniel defeated the enemies, he died 40 years later and Israel had peace for those 40 years. His cycle or rule ended in peace and was complete.

Ehud, from the tribe of Benjamin, fought the Moabites and slew Eglon, king of Moab. on the roof chamber and locked the doors to the chamber when he left. In Judges 3:24 After Ehud escaped and when the roof doors were locked the servants surmised Eglon only went into the closet of the cool chamber to relieve himself. *"When the servants finally entered the chamber there lay their Lord dead on the floor."* Ehud escaped and sounded the trumpet in the hill country of Ephraim. All the men came to him and they went to the fords of the Jordan where they slew the Moabites.

After Ehud died came the judge Shamgar. There is only one sentence about Shamgar. In Judges 3:31 *"And after him was Shamgar the son of Anath, who killed six hundred of the Philistines with an ox-goad; and he too saved Israel."*

In Judges 4, the people of Israel again did evil in the sight of the Lord, and God sold them into the hand of Jabin, King of Canaan, who was living in Hazor. The commander of his army was Sisera. Most notable about Sisera was that he had chariots of iron. *"The Israelites were not yet familiar with the art of working iron."* Oxford RSV Footnotes

From *Easton's Bible Dictionary* about Jabin, *"Another king of Hazor, called 'the king of Canaan,' who overpowered the Israelites of the north one hundred and sixty years after Joshua's death, and for twenty years held them in painful subjection. The whole population was paralyzed with fear, and gave way to hopeless despondency, until Deborah and Barak aroused the national spirit, and gathering together ten thousand men, gained a great and decisive victory over Jabin in the plain of Esdraelon (Judges 4:10). This was the first great victory Israel had gained since the days of Joshua."*

From the *Jewish Encyclopedia*, *"Harosheth was where Sisera's army was quartered. The city is supposed to have stood near Hazor, in the northern part of Canaan, afterward known as Upper Galilee, or Galilee of the Gentiles. It was so called on account of the cosmopolitan character of its inhabitants. Harosheth was the home of Sisera, general of the armies of Jabin, King of Canaan, whose seat was Hazor. The ruins of Hazor are still highly visible northwest of the Sea of Galilee, and are an archeological tourist attraction."*

We are constantly battling the mind of the flesh, the ego mind, the material mind. This will be with us and we will overcome it time and again, until we are able to claim the whole subconscious mind. Subconscious mind contains habits, groups of thoughts or attitudes, memories mental and emotional, perceptions we are taught, snippets of stories about our history, stuff others have told us about ourselves and the world, impressions from childhood, fears and anxieties. When these things present themselves, we choose to let them live or destroy them. If we do not destroy the negatives or the enemies, they will continue to grow thought families and expand in the subconscious mind.

In Judges 4, Deborah the prophetess was the next judge. Her name means "a bee" or fine spiritual discernment and great activity. She was married to Lapidoth whose name means a torch or light bringer. Nothing is said about him other than he was Deborah's husband. The judges are those spiritually discerning thoughts that jump up in your consciousness to defend you and vanquish your enemies when you are in danger of attack from negative thoughts and feelings.

Deborah summoned Barak and told him God commanded him to gather his men at Mount Tabor, taking 10,000 from the tribes of Napthali and Zebulun. She would draw Sisera to the Kishon River. Barak made the famous declaration that he would not go into battle without her. She promised to be with him, but the glory would not be his because God said Sisera would be delivered into the hand of a woman.

The Kishon River flows into the Mediterranean Sea at the port of Haifa. The Kishon is a small mountain stream unless it is roaring in the spring and making a swamp out of the Plain of Esdraelon. Sisera drove his nine hundred iron chariots into the soft swampy area of the river and they became mired and useless. Barak and Deborah defeated his army there, but Sisera escaped. The text says he alighted from his chariot, which was also mired and useless.

The woman God referred to was not Deborah, but Jael. Sisera ran to the tent of Heber the Kenite where he thought he would be safe, not knowing that Heber had broken away from the Kenites and their alliance with King Jabin. Jael invited him into her tent and he lay down and went to sleep in exhaustion. Then she drove a tent peg through his head *"til it went down into the ground." (Judges 4:21)*

Jael could not be seen to be a murderess with no reason to kill. Also if her husband found a man in her tent, he would kill her. She invited Sisera into her tent so she would have a lawful reason to kill him and her husband would praise her instead. Barak pursued Sisera to Jael's tent and became her witness that Sisera was indeed in her tent and was dead by her hand.

In Judges 5 the story of Deborah and Barak is repeated in poetry or song style. It is called *"the Song of Deborah and is the oldest remaining fragment of Hebrew literature"* according to the Oxford RSV footnote p. 298.

At the end of the poem is this interesting image of Sisera's mother, waiting in a window for her son to return. This *"woman in the window"* is a motif that appears in many stories depicting a woman of great power. As queen mother she ruled when her son was away. These images of the feminine aspect coming into its own power are Deborah, the woman who defended Israel; Jael, the woman who defended herself; and the ruling mother, the woman who waited.

The Book of Ruth

In the midst of the books of Judges and Kings, of wars and struggles to build a nation and to keep foreigners out, is the Book of Ruth. Ruth was from Moab and the Moabites were particular enemies of Israel. The introduction in the Revised Standard Version of the Bible states that it may have been inserted here to engender sympathetic feelings for foreigners. Despite all the efforts to keep foreigners out, this story opens the door to them.

Naomi, her husband Abimelech and their sons left Judah because there was a famine. It is symbolic of abandoning the God of Israel to seek after abundance. This echoes the story of Abram who abandoned the Promised Land because there was a famine and traveled on into Egypt.

Unlike Abram who prospered, Naomi lost everything and decided to return to Bethlehem of Judah. She was a pauper and bitter. She told the people to no longer call her Naomi, a name of happiness, but Mara, the name of bitterness. She said the Lord had dealt bitterly with her.

For Ruth it certainly must have been the winter of her life when her husband, brother-in-law and father-in-law all died within a short time. Her life as she had known it was suddenly over. Orpah, her sister, chose to stay in their homeland and return to her family hopefully to remarry. Many people give up in the face of a challenge and choose to return to the comfort of old ways.

Naomi, Ruth's mother-in-law, planned to return to her homeland to live out her days in bitterness hoping her kinsmen would take her in. But Ruth was looking at what held the greatest promise. She loved Naomi and insisted upon going with her and serving her as she always had done when their husbands were alive. She allowed love to lead her and followed the thread of that love. She followed Naomi into a new experience even though she would be a stranger in an unwelcoming culture. Naomi tried to dissuade her, but Ruth loved Naomi and was certain this was her heart's desire. Love will always return us home to God.

In a hostile land and knowing nothing of the customs in Bethlehem of Judah, she clung closely to Naomi and followed her every instruction. Naomi taught her to prosper by gleaning in the fields. It was a lowly job but the only activity available to widowed women. She taught her how to conduct herself in the presence of the other gleaners and ultimately the proper way for her to show her love to Boaz.

Boaz fell in love with Ruth and married her. Naomi was joyful that once again she had a real family with Ruth, Boaz and baby Jesse. They became the ancestors of King David and eventually of Jesus who first expressed the Christ nature. Wherever you are in life whether in despair or hope, remember to follow the thread of love as you make your way.

Ruth and Boaz were ancestors of Jesus of Nazareth, an early part of the thread that led to the eventual development of the spiritual nature introduced in the Gospels.

Ruth's heritage being Moabite went back to Lot's eldest daughter who bore Lot's child and named him Moab. Moab became the father of the tribe of Moab and the Moabites. Out of this interesting lineage, came Ruth who married Boaz. Their child was Jesse, referred to as *"the root of Jesse."* Jesse was the ancestor of King David. This story thread developed within humankind through succeeding generations, to culminate in the birth of Jesus who lived and taught the Christ nature.

We can always learn from the processes shown to us if we know where to look for them. Ruth's process is one of the early cycles of learning true prosperity.

1. She was faithful to Naomi helping turn her life from one of despair to joy.
2. She persisted in her inner work of obedience and love
3. She worked joyously gathering small prosperity experiences
4. She was present to the love principle wherever she was
5. She followed guidance and wisdom
6. She claimed abundant good as her rightful inheritance

Her commitment in the words *"Entreat me not to leave thee"* has been set to song and sung even today. *"Your people will be my people, and your God my god."*

CHAPTER NINETEEN

First Samuel

Hannah, wife of Elkanah, was barren and after much supplication to God was with child in her old age. The child was named Samuel and they made a vow to dedicate him to God. This same theme applied to Sarah, Rebekah, Rachel, the mother of Samson, and Elizabeth of the New Testament. *"It is thought this theme signaled the birth of a person of importance in later life." Oxford RSV footnotes, p.330*

"Samuel means name of God, heard of God; instructed of God; God has heard. He was the last prophet and judge of Israel before kings ruled over Israel. Samuel represents both wisdom and judgment that come from the still small voice at the heart center." (Metaphysical Bible Dictionary)

Samuel was so quickened that he heard the word of Spirit as a child. When Samuel first heard the voice of God calling *"Samuel, Samuel!"* he thought it was Eli, the High Priest of Israel, calling him and said, *"Here am I, for you called me."* In 1 Samuel 3:4 Eli finally caught on that it was the Lord calling Samuel and he told Samuel to reply these words the next time God called him, *"Speak Lord for thy servant hears."*

Humanity becomes so busy complaining to God, telling God what it needs and how God should accomplish it, that the request becomes the demand, *"Hear Lord, for your servant speaks."* We must learn to become still and listen, allowing wisdom to come to heart and mind. When we do this all else comes into divine order in our experience.

God called Samuel three times. Peter denied Jesus three times, and three times Jesus asked Peter to answer the question *"Do you love me?"* Jesus knew that Peter was the one to carry on his ministry and released him from the effects of his denials by canceling them out with affirmations. We can cancel our error thoughts in the same way. We can replace any negativity with an affirmation of spiritual Truth repeated three times. When we need prosperity, we affirm prosperity rather than envision lack. When we are afraid we affirm poise and courage, always replacing the negative thought with the positive.

In 1 Samuel 2:26 we are told *"Samuel continued to grow in stature and in favor with the Lord and with men"* This is a precursor to Luke's comment about Jesus who was growing up *"increased in wisdom and stature, and in favor with God and man" (Luke 2:52).* This indicates their lives were sanctified, even though Samuel and Jesus were still young boys.

Samuel may have been twelve at the time the Lord spoke to him. *(Josephus, Antiquities 5, 10, 4).* Jesus was said to be this same age when he taught in the temple. *(Luke 2:46)* The age of twelve is the end of the childhood cycle and the beginning of the next level of maturity. For Samuel and Jesus, this was a time when they were no longer driven by childish emotion and personality, but led by spirit.

Eli was very old and his sight was diminishing. For all his spiritual wisdom, he could not control his own sons who were doing evil things *"to all of Israel."* Eli could do nothing more than admonish his sons who paid him no attention. God caused both of the sons to die on the same day, as punishment on the house of Eli, *"for it was the will of the Lord to slay them."*

"The house" represents the consciousness, the mind, where we harbor destructive thoughts along with the constructive ones. The contrast of the sons of Eli and Samuel is between unconsecrated evil thoughts and the consecrated spiritual thoughts. The evil thoughts must die before they contaminate the whole mind.

Humanity was still in the psychological phase of development, moving toward adolescence. The seeds of spirituality were there but had no strength to influence the whole consciousness, like the acorn that is not yet ready to grow into the mighty oak. There was still a battle between good and evil that went on in the developing conscious mind.

Physical things easily consume us, letting the spiritual sight grow dim. It is said in the story that the Lord killed. That is the ancient way of indicating that evil is not eternal and dies. The spiritual is eternal and grows in favor with God because it matches the high vibration of God Mind.

God told Samuel in a dream what would befall the house of Eli. Samuel was afraid to tell Eli, but Eli told him to withhold nothing. *"It is the Lord; let him do what seems good to him."* Eli had complete faith that all would be well. Living without fear and not hiding from the truth is the first step in developing toward the spiritual nature. The ego mind loves to keep us in fear, convincing us that the shadow on the path is actually a bear.

In 1 Samuel 4, Samuel was confirmed by God in the first verse, *"The Lord revealed himself to Samuel at Shiloh...And the word of Samuel came to all Israel."* At this point the story of Samuel was set aside and the focus became the Ark of the Covenant and the battle with the Philistines.

Israel still believed that God lived in the Ark and they had to carry God with them. The Ark held the two tablets given to Moses. Some passages say it also carried Aaron's rod and a jar of manna, but in 1 Kings 8:9 it is stated that the Ark carried only the two tablets. Humanity was still not ready to let go of an external God that could be carried in a box. The Ark was carried by priests going before the people through Sinai, up the east side of the Dead Sea and across the Jordan River to Jericho. This was the symbol of the power of Israel and that God was with them. When we carry God only in the intellect, in a box, it can be easily stolen by thoughts foreign to Spirit.

The name Philistine means transitory, wandering, deviating, infidels, strangers to Spirituality. The five great cities of the Philistines ruled by "lords" represent the five senses under the dominion of ego mind, thoughts foreign to Spirit.

"When the five-sense man gives himself up to sense desires and makes no attempt to live in spiritual consciousness, he is ruled by Philistine thoughts... under such rule the soul will finally be crowded out of its rightful domain." Metaphysical Bible Dictionary

The Israelites were defeated by the Philistines in the first battle so they decided to bring the Ark from Shiloh to the battlefront. When the

Ark arrived in the Israeli camp there was a great shout. The Philistines heard it and thought a whole bunch of gods had arrived, the ones that brought all the plagues on Egypt. But they didn't want to be slaves of the Hebrews, so they prepared to fight anyway. Israel was defeated and the Ark was captured.

Eli was ninety-eight and blind at the time. At the news of the Ark and the death of his sons, he fell over backward, broke his neck and died. He had judged Israel for forty years, the number forty indicating his work was complete.

It was not a happy capture for the Philistines. Every time they set the Ark beside their god, Dagon, a part of the statue of Dagon broke off. When the people were afflicted with tumors they moved the ark to Gath, and the people there were also afflicted. The same happened when it was sent to Ekron and there was panic. After seven months the Philistines called their priests to ask what they should do. They put the Ark on a cart with two golden images inside, one of their tumors and one of mice that overran them, as a guilt offering. They headed the oxen toward Israel, slapped them on their rumps and let them go. They sent a message to Kiriath-jearim that the Philistines were returning the Ark and to come and get it!

This probably inspired the short story entitled the Ransom of Red Chief. A young boy was kidnapped for ransom. The kid made so much trouble for the kidnappers that they begged his parents to come and get him.

In 1 Samuel 7 Israel put away the gods of Baal and the Ashtaroth and then served the Lord only. They gathered at Mizpah and fasted and prayed. The Philistines decided to attack at Mizpah, but *"the Lord thundered with a mighty voice and threw them into confusion…and the men of Israel pursued them and smote them as far as Beth-car."*

Metaphysically this is *"the place where we consciously abide and rejoice abundantly in the overcoming power of Spirit and in realization of the omnipresent substance and life. This is a genuine milestone for our spiritual progress. We have conquered all the ground that our consciousness grasps of that which is real in ourselves and in the universe as well." Metaphysical Bible Dictionary*

Now the writers returned again to the story of Samuel. The Philistines did not enter the territory in all the days of Samuel and all the cities were restored to Israel. Samuel traveled all over the territory until he became old and made his sons judges over Israel. The sons took bribes and perverted justice, and the people hated them. The people demanded that Samuel give them a king! So God gave up trying to be their king and told Samuel to listen to the people. The adolescent consciousness was gaining in momentum, but not in wisdom.

In 1 Samuel 8:10, Samuel told the people all the evil things a king (ego mind) would do to them. The king would take their harvest, their daughters, their sons, cattle and lands. He would require a tenth of everything and make slaves of them. *"And when you cry out because of your king, whom you have chosen for yourselves; the Lord will not answer you in that day."*

In 1 Samuel 8:19, *"But the people refused to listen and they said, 'No! We will have a king over us, that we may also be like all the nations, that our king may govern us and go out before us, and fight our battles.'"* So the people gave up their freedom and turned their responsibilities over to someone else. That someone would not have their best interests at heart, but only his own. Many want to have someone else be responsible for them, to fight their battles and to make their decisions for them. This struggle between freedom and rule still goes on in conscious mind today.

In 1 Samuel 9 there was *"a man of Benjamin who had a son whose name was Saul, a handsome young man. There was not a man among the people of Israel more handsome than he; from his shoulders upward he was taller than any of the people."*

Humanity again looks to the external, the physically attractive, to the appearance and not to God. The teenagers at this stage of development pick the tallest best-looking athlete to be the king of the prom.

In 1 Samuel 12:9 *"And when they forgot the Lord their God, he sold them into the hand of Sisera, captain of the host of Hazor, and into the hand of the Philistines, and into the hand of the king of Moab…And they cried unto the Lord, and said, 'we have sinned, because we have forsaken the Lord, and have served Baalim and Ashtaroth: but now deliver us out of the hand of our enemies, and we will serve you.' And the Lord sent Jerubbaal, and Bedan, and Jephthah, and Samuel, and delivered you out of the hand of your enemies on every side, and you dwelled safe. And when you saw that Nahash the king of the children of Ammon came against you, you said to me, 'Nay; but a king shall reign over us when the Lord your God was your king.'*

"Now therefore behold the king whom you have chosen, and whom you have desired! And behold the Lord hath set a king over you. If you will fear the Lord, and serve him, and obey his voice, and not rebel against the commandment of the Lord, then shall both you and also the king that reigns over you continue following the Lord your God. But if you will not obey the voice of the Lord, but rebel against the commandment of the Lord, then shall the hand of the Lord be against you and your king."

They had declared that they wanted a king, an authority over them who would shape their lives, who would tell them what God wanted from them and be in charge. They could relax, grow food and have no worries. The prophet Samuel told them to work on their relationship to God, but no, they believed they needed a king! Ego mind at this stage of development is strong and demanding, and does not heed impending consequences.

We have many kings in our thinking that we allow to rule us. They can be in the form of money, religion, career, a relationship, a guru, fitness, and anything else we believe will keep us safe and solve our problems. These come between God and us because we let them be our authority. We are successful for a while and things seem to be going our way. But then things change as these kings become our corrupt masters, truly limit our freedom, curtail our success, destroy our happiness, and we are left with nothing.

In 1 Samuel 13 the Philistines were gathering to attack and the people of Israel were hiding in caves, tombs, holes and behind rocks. For some reason Samuel did not arrive on the scene at the appointed time and they started leaving and running away. Saul tried to force the favor of God by making a burnt offering that was supposed to be done only by priests in a consecrated setting. Samuel was furious with him saying, *"What have you done?"* And Saul was full of excuses as he was every time he disobeyed God. This is the ego mind that just blunders on in its own way, grabbing for power, giving reasons and excuses as to why failures weren't its fault.

In 1 Samuel 15, Saul still continuing on his ego-driven way, *"went to Carmel and set up a monument to himself."* The ego requires a physical image because it has no reality in God Mind. It needs a physical marker.

God said to Samuel that he regretted making Saul the king over Israel. Samuel never saw Saul again.

In 1 Samuel 16 God sent Samuel to the house of Jesse to find the new king that God would indicate. Jesse had seven sons that he passed before Samuel, but Samuel did not see God's chosen among them. Then Jesse's youngest was brought in from tending the sheep. *"And the Lord said 'arise, anoint him, for this is he'...and the Spirit of the Lord came mightily upon David from that day forward...Now the Spirit of the Lord departed from Saul, and evil spirit from the Lord tormented him."*

When humanity starts on the path toward God and then departs, there is a void that is filled with darkness. Without God there is no light. But it is not God that sends the darkness or the "evil spirit" but the ego mind that loves to blame everything on God. David was hired to play the lyre for Saul to lighten his moods. Saul alternated between intense love and hate for David, eventually trying to kill him. This kind of love/hate state of mind has its roots in violence and is not really love, but attachment and possession.

In 1 Samuel is the story of Goliath the giant. Saul placed all of his armor on young David but it was too big and heavy. Instead David picked up five stones and his shepherd's sling to go meet Goliath. There is much speculation about what these stones represented. But the stones represent ideas. Goliath's strength was in his ability to engender fear because of his size and his blustering. David was armed with faith and Goliath had only fear as a weapon. Fear is actually very fragile and can be destroyed with one well-aimed idea right into the center of its forehead or thought process. Faith is indestructible.

Saul's hatred for David grew as the people celebrated and loved David. Saul's attempts to kill him failed, so Saul sent David into battle against the Philistines hoping they would kill him instead. David was victorious and Saul now feared him. Saul's son Jonathan and David were like brothers and loved each other, so when Saul instructed Jonathan to kill David, Jonathan hid David to keep him safe from Saul. Jonathan spoke to Saul and Saul promised not to kill David, but it didn't last. David had to escape through a window and fled to Samuel. The chapters continue to tell the stories of how Saul pursued David everywhere he went.

In 1 Samuel 24 when Saul fell asleep in a cave, David was hiding there and could have killed Saul, but he would not. When Saul realized this, he said to David, *"You are more righteous than I; for you have repaid me good, whereas I repaid you evil…I know that you shall surely be king, and that the kingdom of Israel shall be established in your hand."*

In all this difficulty with Saul who chased him all over the land, David found it necessary to gather a considerable number of men and they became as outlaws. He committed many acts of treason, sedition and violence. At one point he fought beside the Philistines against his own people and shared Israel's military plans with them.

In 1 Samuel 25 is the story of Abigail and Nabal. David and his men also protected the people who helped him and kept them from harm. Nabal was a drunken lout and when David's men came to ask politely for food, Nabal thoroughly insulted them and turned them away. Abigail heard of Nabal's behavior from her servants and that David's men treated Nabal's people kindly regardless. She knew David and his men could eventually come and destroy her entire household and fields for this insult but there was a good side to David as well.

Abigail hurriedly packed generous amounts of food and supplies on pack animals and started out for David's camp. She knew she would be in terrible danger. He could kill her but she persisted. When she met David she begged his forgiveness. She spoke to him what she knew of his activities, even mentioning a hollow sling, his shepherd's sling, used against his enemies. She reminded him that he was appointed a prince over Israel and of his favor with God. Rather than being in fear, she was courageous and appealed to his higher nature. Nabal died at hearing her recount the story. David remembered Abigail and she became the first of David's wives. The name *"Abigail means joy and abundance, and would rightly be joined with love, represented by David."* Nabal on the other hand means *"empty, evil, stupid, a corpse." Metaphysical Bible Dictionary*

David was still in his renegade mode, going to the Philistines and then claiming he was just spying on them. Again David caught Saul sleeping and had his men take the water jar and spear that lay beside Saul's head. Again Saul was aware that David could have killed him but did not. Meanwhile Samuel had died, and Saul was up to his old ways, sending his men to find a medium, the witch of Endor, so he could inquire of her. He asked her to conjure up the spirit of Samuel. Samuel was awakened from death and was angry that Saul had the medium disturb his sleep. This is an interesting commentary on death, that the dead could be awakened, have emotions, and prophesy. Samuel's spirit berated Saul for all his disobedience to the Lord, and predicted that Saul and Jonathan would die on the battlefield with the Philistines that next day.

CHAPTER TWENTY

Second Samuel

In 2 Samuel 3:6 Isbosheth accused Abner of lying with one of Saul's concubines. Abner became very angry and told Isbosheth *"I keep showing loyalty to the House of Saul your father, to his brothers, and his friends, and have not given you into the hand of David; and yet you charge me today with a fault concerning a woman?"*

Isbosheth was afraid of Abner and did not answer him. Abner sent messengers to David asking him to make a covenant with him and he would hand over Israel to David. David agreed if Abner would give him Michal saying, *"Give me my wife, Michal, whom I betrothed at the price of a hundred foreskins of the Philistines."*

This was a political move on David's part to keep his connection to the throne of Saul. Abner traveled to Hebron to tell David that all Israel and the tribe of Benjamin were willing to have David as their King. David and Abner made an agreement between them and *"David sent Abner away in peace."*

Without David's knowledge, Joab sent messengers to bring Abner back and then killed him at the Hebron city gate. David cursed Joab and his household forever, and set up public mourning for Abner so the people of Israel would know David had nothing to do his murder. However, making David king over Israel was put aside for the time. Often our plans are interrupted by a catastrophic event and we are required to deal with it, to put a few more right thoughts in place before we can move forward.

In 2 Samuel 5 David finally became *"king over all Israel and Judah. He was 30 years old and he reigned 40 years. At Hebron he reigned over Judah for 7 years and 6 months; and at Jerusalem he reigned over all Israel and Judah 33 years."*

"The rulership is withdrawn from the head, or will (Saul), and is gradually transferred to the heart, or love (King David)... When you find that your willful (Saul) rule is not proving harmonious, call upon the Spirit of the Lord for His anointing. You will receive the baptism of Spirit if you are sincere in your asking, and this spiritual anointing will prove to be the first step in setting up a new reign in which love will be king." MBD

2 Samuel 5:19 reads, *"And David became greater and greater for the Lord, the God of hosts was with him."*

In Judges 1:8 it reads that Judah and Simeon captured Jerusalem. But it was David who actually captured Jerusalem and established a stronghold called the City of David. Earlier in human development we may think we have captured the city of peace, or the mind of peace, but it slips away without humanity knowing what it really was. It takes the movement into the heart, represented by David, to recognize the mind of peace and make it the capitol of consciousness.

In 2 Samuel 5:17 the Philistines learned of David's anointment over Israel. They realized he was now a powerful enemy and came after him. So David went to his stronghold and asked God if he should attack them. The answer was yes. David defeated them and said, *"The Lord has broken through my enemies before me, like a bursting flood."*

Scholars are not sure what the stronghold was, but to the metaphysician it is the presence of God within. We turn within to realign our consciousness with God Mind and ask for guidance. Notice the dramatic words, *"like a bursting flood."* There was exuberance in the expression of joy in the work of the Lord as he experienced it. We might consider how we respond when we manifest our good. Do we exult in our success in practicing spiritual law and seeing the great outcome? Or do we just go right on barely noticing it.

The Philistines fled and as they fled they left their idols behind. David's men carried the idols, their symbols of power, away. The Philistines came after David again, and again David inquired of the Lord. The Lord told David exactly what to do this time; giving him a battle plan. And David was successful.

The more we accustom ourselves to asking for guidance, and establish that communication more strongly, the more specific the response is. The more we ask for guidance, the more we do it automatically until we start to live in that place of simply knowing guidance is there.

In 2 Samuel 6 King David wanted the Ark to be brought to Jerusalem, but perhaps his heart was not quite pure at that point. He wanted Jerusalem to be a religious center as well as a political and military center, consolidating his power. As they were bringing the Ark to Jerusalem, the oxen stumbled and Uzzah put out his hand to keep the Ark from falling, and it is said *"God smote him and he died."*

Uzzah's death made David very angry with God and he refused to let the Ark come into Jerusalem. He instead stored it outside the city at the house of Obedeom. The Ark blessed the household of Obedeom with much abundance. When David heard that, he changed his mind and had the Ark brought into Jerusalem. Being angry with God is not a prospering attitude. When we are angry the prosperity goes to where there is a consciousness of happiness.

In 2 Samuel 7 while David was resting from all his enemies and battles, God decided he wanted a real house instead of a tent and complained to the prophet, Nathan. God seemed to ignore the temple built for him at Shiloh. In metaphysics, house refers to state of mind and these could refer to the size of different states of expanded consciousness.

In verses 4 through 16 God reminded David of all the things he had done for David. David was contrite and promised to build God a house. Then David reiterated to God all David had done for Him as well, and prayed that God would bless David's house forever.

Humanity still has a very primitive idea of God. They think of God as they would a king or householder. And their God in return exhibits all the traits of humanity. All the great leaders exhibited a bargaining power with God. You do this for me and I will do this for you. Now bless me forever and ever. This is an early idea of a god that rewards, punishes, has fits of temper, complains, needs to be reminded of who he is, likes the smell of meat cooking, wants a house in which to dwell, anoints kings and kills people who disobey him.

King David saw Bathsheba bathing on her roof top and desired her. The writer is quick to say her bath was her ritual cleansing. *"She was purifying herself from uncleanness."* They did not want us to think she lured the king on purpose.

When she told David she was pregnant with his child, David tried to cover it up by ordering Uriah home to sleep with Bathsheba to make it look like this was Uriah's child. When that did not work he had his general, Joab, place Uriah her husband in the front of a battle where he was sure to be killed. The ego mind does not want to be caught with its hand in the cookie jar, so it devises a plan to cover up the act.

Bathsheba was not particularly disturbed by the death of her husband. She completed the mourning formalities, then married David and bore him a son. Nathan told David that God was displeased and the child would die. So David fasted and prayed as the child grew weaker. When the child died, David got up from the ground, bathed and changed his clothes, and continued on with his life.

The child represents a thought and this child was conceived in deceit and deception. A thought conceived in deception will not thrive. This child was not named, not given any identity in human development. This thought had no life and was forgotten.

David and Bathsheba were criticized for their quick recovery from the death of Uriah and the death of their child. But love does not linger in the past. It moves forward into new expression. There is much sexual tension now in the stories, and those tensions are played out against a background of David's battles. The military serves as a framework in which to place these public episodes. Sexuality at the physical level will always be played out in a framework of battle until it is spiritually understood.

In 2 Samuel 13 is the story of the sons of David, Absalom, Tamar, Amnon and Solomon. Solomon was far down the line of succession to the throne, but these stories pave the way for Solomon to gain the throne. David's first born was Amnon, then Chileab (Daniel) who may have died young because he was never mentioned again. This left Absalom the next in line to the throne after Amnon.

In 2 Samuel 13 Amnon desired the beautiful Tamar, Absalom's full sister. Tamar would have nothing to do with him. So Amnon turned to his cousin, Jonadab, who was a "clever man." Jonadab advised him to pretend to be ill and ask his father to send Tamar to care for him. When Tamar came Amnon grabbed her and raped her. She resisted him but was not strong enough. Then she begged him not to put her to shame, but to marry her for both of their sakes. *"Then Amnon hated her with very great hatred."* And he threw her out and had his servant bolt the door behind her. Absalom found her, told her to keep her peace about it and took her to his house to live. Absalom bided his time, *"two full years,"* while he plotted the death of Amnon. There was always a celebration at the time of shearing and men got drunk. Absalom begged King David to send Amnon to the shearing with him. Then Absalom commanded his servants to kill Amnon *"while his heart is merry with wine."*

Shimei, from the house of Saul, showed up to curse David and his entire household. He ran along the opposite hills throwing stones and dirt and shouting curses. David's servant wanted to go remove the guy's head, but David said to leave him alone. David and his people continued to the Jordan where they all refreshed themselves. David never assaulted the house of Saul, no matter what happened, and he was not going to let this character change his mind. Saul was the anointed of God, the first king, for as long as his reign lasted. David honored Saul because he was the anointed of God and would not attack the house of Saul then or now.

Some negative thought from our past may come up cursing us, throwing stones and dirt (hard dark negative thoughts). We do not veer from our spiritual path by giving these thoughts power by attacking them. To do so would stop our spiritual progress.

Absalom was King David's third son and he was described as physically beautiful. The name Absalom means peace, but the meaning of his name was not born out in his actions. In 2 Samuel 15, Absalom gathered an army and planned to move against his father, King David. Hearing of Absalom's conspiracy, David fled Jerusalem but he kept a cool head. He empowered his friend, Hushai from the house of Saul, to stay in Jerusalem and to spy on Absalom. Hushai not only reported to David, but gave Absalom the wrong advice that causes Absalom's eventual defeat. *"Absalom's hastily assembled forces were no match for David's standing army." Oxford RSV Footnotes p.399*

Often our long held favorite thoughts and habits no longer serve our highest good. When they have gotten us into deep trouble, it is prudent to remain cool headed, assess the situation by observing from a distance, and using our standing army of trained thoughts to go against the trouble. Just as Absalom was a favorite of son David's, so these thoughts may be our dearest held favorites and we will mourn their loss.

There was still a strong division between Israel, the northern kingdom, and Judah, the southern kingdom. David was still King over Judah, but not yet Israel. Israel represents the religious law or intellectual side and Judah the celebratory or emotional side. They are still contending for supremacy and have not yet learned to work together as one nation. Love, represented by David, has not yet been able to draw them together.

God told David there would be a famine in the land because Saul put Gibeonites to death. So David went to the Gibeonites and asked what they wanted to bring peace. They asked for seven sons of Saul so they could hang them. *"Gibeonites, thoughts of the sensate or carnal phase of the subjective consciousness, that aspire to higher and more spiritual ideals and try to reach these ideals by making an alliance with man's real true thoughts (Israel)." (Metaphysical Bible Dictionary)*

David was always about making things right if he could. If we look at this as a thought process, the first capacity of love that is now developing in humanity brings with it the action of righting wrongs. The ego mind will want to convince you that it is O.K. to hurt someone while you right a wrong. In this case King David delivered Saul's grandsons to them. One of the Twelve Steps of Alcoholics Anonymous (AA) says to make amends except when to do so would injure someone. *"Made direct amends to such people wherever possible, except when to do so would injure them or others." (AA)*

God instructed King David through Araunah to build an altar on the threshing floor of Araunah's property. This was to be a holy place and later became the location of Solomon's temple. Araunah wanted to give the place to King David, but David insisted upon purchasing it. This is reminiscent of when Abraham purchased the site for Sarah's burial in Hebron. The Hittites offered to give the place to him as a gift and argued with Abraham several times, but Abraham insisted upon paying a fair price for it. Abraham needed to have sole possession of the Cave of Machpelah before burying Sarah there. We need to honestly own the spiritual ground upon which we stand and not borrow it from another's consciousness or have it always be subject to ego mind. Your understanding must come from Higher Mind, from God Mind only, without interference from cultural or religious prejudice.

CHAPTER TWENTY ONE

The Adolescent Brain

In 1 Kings 13:11 is a story about the "Man of God" and an old prophet from Bethel, who refused to eat and drink with King Jeroboam. To do that would have meant the Man of God condoned all that Jeroboam had done. The old prophet rode out after the Man of God and invited him to his house to dine and drink water. Again the Man of God refused saying God had told him not to return by the way he came.

"The old prophet lied to the Man of God saying an angel came to him and told him to bring the Man of God to his home. So the Man of God came to his home with him. Then the Lord spoke to the old prophet saying the Man of God had not kept what God commanded him. As the Man of God rode away, he was attacked by a lion and killed.

The old prophet put the body in his own grave and told his sons to put him there also when he died."

Metaphysically, when we are on the spiritual path, we cannot turn back, even at the insistence of an angel or a prophet. Notice the liar was not harmed in this story. It is our responsibility to stay on the path and not blame anyone else for our failing to do so.

The invitation to turn back is always false regardless of who gives it. Anyone who calls you to forsake what you know to be true is a false prophet, regardless of his or her credentials or position. Jesus said, *"No one who puts his hand to the plough and looks back is fit for the Kingdom of God." (Luke 9:62)*

In 1 Kings 13:33 Jeroboam reigned over Judah, continuing in his errant ways. He appointed priests from among the common people *"any who would."* This was the sin of his house, and his kingdom was destined to be *"cut off and destroyed."* Metaphysically the *"sin of his house"* is referring to a pervading error state of mind. We appoint thoughts that are not spiritual to a high place of mental priesthood in our minds that can never lead us to spiritual understanding.

Jeroboam's son Abijah became ill. Jeroboam sent his wife in disguise to the prophet Ahijah to inquire about this son. But Ahijah, even though he was nearly blind, recognized her footstep. He told her that Abijah would die as soon as she returned home. After twenty-two years on the throne Jeroboam died and his son, Nadab, ruled in his place.

The next verse immediately speaks of Rehoboam, son of Solomon, reigning over Judah, in Jerusalem. Judah and Israel, all twelve tribes, continued to do evil in the sight of the Lord. These represent the adolescent years of human development, the teenage brain that has not yet developed into the adult brain. It continues on the same track toward destruction not realizing the consequences.

In the fifth year of King Rehoboam, Shishak king of Egypt invaded and took away the treasures of the house of the Lord and the king's house, all the gold and shields Solomon made. The entire material world upon which we place high value is soon taken away or destroyed. Adolescents quickly lose their cell phones, smash up their cars and max out their credit cards.

In 1 Kings 15:6 there was continual war between Jeroboam and Rehoboam. Rehoboam died and his son Abijam reigned in his stead. Abijam was no better than his father. War continued and Abijam died leaving his son Asa to reign in his stead.

Asa did what was right in the eyes of the Lord in regard to religious things. He put away the male cult prostitutes, removed the idols his father had made, removed his idolatrous mother from being queen. He brought votive gifts of gold and silver back into the house of the Lord. Despite all the warring ideas within us, there is the will to heal that pulls together and reconstructs the good and keeps humanity developing.

"Asa means physician, healer, binding up, making whole, the will working constructively. In body consciousness the work of Asa is the

rebuilding process that goes on in the subconscious mind, directed by the will to be well." (Metaphysical Bible Dictionary)

Baasha became king of Israel and built Ramah to block Asa. Asa took all the silver and gold, gave it to his servants and sent them to Benhadad in Damascus to make a pact with him to defeat Baasha. Benhadad accepted the agreement and began taking the cities in Israel. A shocked Baasha stopped building Ramah and fled to Tirzah. Then Asa's troops carried away all the stones being used to build Ramah and built Geba of Benjamin and Mizpah. When Asa died, his son Jehoshaphat reigned in his stead.

Nadab is briefly mentioned in 1 Kings 15:25. He reigned over Israel two years, did evil in the sight of the Lord, and *"made Israel to sin."* Baasha assassinated him. Baasha died and his son reigned in his stead.

In 1 Kings 16:8, *"in the twenty-sixth year of Asa king of Judah, Elah the son of Baasha began to reign over Israel..."* His commander Zimri killed him and reigned in his stead. Zimri immediately destroyed everyone in the house of Ba'asha. Zimri reigned seven days when he attacked the Philistines. All Israel made Omri king over Israel. Omri went to Tirzah and when Zimri saw all was lost he committed suicide, burning his own house down over his head. All of this represents the ego mind error thoughts struggling to have all the power, hormones running roughshod through the still adolescent brain and body, and its slowly maturing mindset.

Again there was a division, with half the people following Tibni and half following Omri. But Omri soon overcame Tibni, and Omri was made king over Israel. Asa was still king over Judah. Omri was worse than Jeroboam. He founded the City of Samaria, and then married his son Ahab to Jezebel, daughter of the king Ethbaal of the Sidonians. *"This was a good political policy, but it turned out to be a religious disaster."* (Oxford RSV p. 442)

In 1 Kings 16:33, *"Ahab did more than all the kings to provoke the anger of the Lord."* Ahab turned to worshipping Baal and erected an altar in the house that he built in Samaria. Then Ahab erected an Asherah, a wooden pole, symbol of the Canaanite fertility goddess, Asherah. His wife Jezebel was strong and demanding whereas Ahab was weak and fearful. Jezebel worshipped Ashera.

"Jezebel means intact, untouched, unproductive, the ruling emotions on the physical plane of consciousness. She met a violent death; passion and appetites burn themselves out." (Metaphysical Bible Dictionary)

Ahab helped Hiel build Jericho, and Hiel killed his first-born Abiram and placed his body in the foundation of the city, and killed his second son Segub and placed his body under the gates of the city. *"The bodies of children were often buried under the foundations to bring good luck to the building project." (Oxford RSV p. 442)*

In 1 Kings 17, it was believed that Baal controlled the rain. Elijah the prophet set out to prove to Ahab that he, Elijah, controlled the rain, not Baal. A famine came upon the land and Elijah said it would not rain until he gave the word. The Elijah consciousness was interfaced with God Mind to the point where he controlled the kingdom of his own being completely. No negative force could enter his experience. He was a precursor of the Christ experience as humanity continued to develop an initial spiritual capacity, but not yet abandoning the ego struggles with evil Jezebel.

The adolescent years of development are filled with turmoil and wars. The brain is still developing and has not reached the physical adult configuration yet. Humanity at this stage swings wildly from good to evil and back. King after king, error thought after thought, reigns in the mind, starting wars, killing each other and taking power. The mind is divided as symbolized by Israel and Judah that are still two different kingdoms, not yet united into one Israel. More development in humanity is needed.

CHAPTER TWENTY TWO

First Kings

In 1 Kings 19:1, it is written, *"And Ahab told Jezebel all that Elijah had done, and how he had slain all the prophets with the sword. Then Jezebel sent a messenger to Elijah, saying, 'So may the gods do to me, and more also, if I do not make your life as the life of one of them by this time tomorrow.'*

"Then he (Elijah) was afraid, he arose, and went (ran) for his life, and came to Beersheba, which belonged to Judah, and left his servant there. But he himself went a day's journey into the wilderness, and came and sat down under a broom tree; and he asked that he might die, saying, 'It is enough; now, O Lord, take away my life; for I am not better than my fathers.'"

Fear does not keep us from dying. Fear keeps us from living. Fear takes away our drive to continue on. Elijah used all his energy to debunk the lies of Baal, slay the priests, and convince the Jews to be faithful to God. But the Jews still sacrificed to Baal, so Elijah considered himself a failure. When we cannot combat all the evil we think we should in our world, a human reaction is to think, *"What's the use?"*

"And he lay down and slept under a broom tree; and behold, an angel touched him, and said to him, 'Arise and eat.' And he looked, and behold there was a cake baked on hot stones and a jar of water. And he ate and drank, and lay down again. And the angel of the Lord came again the second time, and touched him, and said, 'Arise and eat,' else the journey will be too great for you.' And he arose, and ate and drank, and went in strength of that food forty days and forty nights to Horeb the mount of God."

Our angelic thoughts minister to us. Help is always there within us that we might be able to accomplish what needs to be done, the time it takes symbolized by the forty days and forty nights.

"And there he came to a cave, and lodged there; and behold, the word of the Lord came to him, and he said to him 'What are you doing here, Elijah?'" We might continue to lodge in a dark cave, a gloomy state of mind. But God comes and asks what we are doing in a depressed state of mind instead of our natural buoyant spiritual state.

And he said, *'I have been very jealous (zealous) for the Lord, the God of hosts; for the people of Israel have forsaken thy covenant, thrown down thy altars, and slain thy prophets with the sword; and I, even I only, am left; and they seek my life, to take it away.'"* He is still moaning and feeling sorry for himself. The word for jealous can better be translated as zealous. He tried so hard. Now everything was destroyed and he was feeling lonely and bereft. *"And I, even I only, am left."*

"Elijah means Jehovah God, the spiritual I Am of man's consciousness. Elijah championed the cause for God with such zeal that he became violent and destructive. This is the Jezebel aspect of our character. He slowly learned the lesson that one must receive the Kingdom of God as a little child. He started out with the roar of the whirlwind and ended with the whisper of a still small voice." (Metaphysical Bible Dictionary)

In 1 Kings 19:11 God showed Elijah the great whirlwind, an earthquake, and a fire *"but the Lord was not in them."* God is in the silence and quiet. God came to Adam in the quiet of the evening, not in the heat and turmoil of the day. We must be calm in the face of the whirlwinds and earthquakes of our lives and stay focused on God.

We all have a dark side of our character represented by Jezebel. Everyone in the Bible, for better or for worse, represents part of our psychological makeup. There is violence in everyone, but many channel it as energy and enthusiasm for the benefit of all, not as Elijah and Jezebel did, trying to destroy each other. Had Jezebel endeared herself to the people, and worked to help and benefit them, been loving and kind, she might not have come to a violent end.

Both of them were claiming they were working for the good. Neither could accomplish good through violence. God is not in the whirlwind, the fire, and the earthquake of violence. Triumph means to receive the kingdom of God, and evil is thereby defeated. Regardless of how lost we get, how we burn ourselves out, how long we sulk in the cave of despair, we are not abandoned. We are nurtured until we are back to health. The angel urges Elijah, *"Eat for you still have a long way to go!"* Probably that was not what Elijah wanted to hear right then, but he did eat. And he did regain his strength.

In 1 Kings 19:15 God sent Elijah to anoint Hazael king of Syria, and Jehu king of Israel, and Elisha who would be a prophet in his place. Hazael and Jehu continued the battle. Hazael means *"all seeing, to restore order in the confused consciousness."* Jehu means *"the self existent God."* Ahab means a mind-set that is thoroughly corrupt and evil. Jehu completely destroyed the house of Ahab. According to the meaning of their names, Hazael and Jehu were anointed to clean up the evil and restore order, so humanity could continue to develop toward spirituality.

In 1 Kings 19:19, God sent Elijah a friend, Elisha. God always sends us a friend, a higher thought, when we need one. Elijah found Elisha plowing a field with twelve yoke of oxen and he walked beside the twelfth. "Elisha means to whom God gives victory, God is a savior, God of deliverance. The spiritual I AM."

We know from the description that Elisha was extremely important in human development. He plowed the field of life with double the twelve tribes, or elementary twelve powers, and he was at the head. Elijah cast his mantle upon him, and he left the oxen and ran after Elijah. Elijah told him to go, take care of his family, and return to him *"for what I have done to you. I have done something very important to you." (Oxford RSV p.447)* He slew the oxen, fed his people, and then he followed Elijah and ministered to him.

Elisha was stepping up to a higher way, leaving the lower way behind. Once we have the mantle of spirit, we cannot go back but must continue forward into higher understanding. When the founder of a healing center was learning energy healing, her teacher was an elderly man who was dying. She went to visit him in the hospital. He pulled up her shirt and put his hand on her midsection. She said she felt a jolt of energy and from that time on she had noticeably stepped up power. This was similar to the mantle of Elijah being thrown over Elisha. When Elijah asked him what he wanted of him, Elisha asked for only a double portion of Elijah's spirit. In asking for spiritual power, we are always lifted up.

In 1 Kings 20 Elisha and Elijah disappeared from the narrative for a time. It takes up the story of Ahab and his war against Benhadad, king of Syria.

"In the spring, Benhadad mustered the Syrians and went up to Aphek, to fight against Israel. And the people of Israel were mustered, and were provisioned, and went against them; the people of Israel encamped before them like two little flocks of goats, but the Syrians filled the country." (1 Kings 20:26)

Aphek was a strategic fortress because of its geographical location. The two coastal routes south of Aphek were forced to converge here to continue to Mount Carmel. Aphek was at a narrow pass where great armies had to go through single file leaving them vulnerable to even small enemies who could pick them off a few at a time and be victorious.

A man of God whispered to Ahab that God would give the great multitude into Ahab's hands. When Benhadad was defeated he hid in the city of Aphek, but his men encouraged him to come out and beg forgiveness from Ahab. Benhadad came in sack cloth to Ahab's chariot and promised to return to him the cities his father took from Ahab's father, and would allow him to establish bazaars in Damascus. This was quite lucrative for Ahab. He agreed to the terms and forgave him. In 1 Kings 20:35-43, he was violently criticized for what he thought was a noble act. Ahab returned to his house in Samaria resentful and sullen. Samaria represents intellectual perception, a mixed or confused state of consciousness.

In 1 Kings 21:5 is the well-known story of Naboth and the vineyard that Ahab coveted. *"But Jezebel his wife came to him, and said to him, 'Why is your spirit so vexed that you eat no food?' And he said to her, 'Because I spoke to Naboth the Jezreelite, and said to him, 'Give me your vineyard for money; or else, if it would please you, I will give you another vineyard for it; and he answered, 'I will not give you my vineyard.' And Jezebel his wife said to him, 'Do you govern Israel? Arise and eat bread, and let your heart be cheerful; I will give you the vineyard of Naboth the Jezreelite.'"*

Ahab was always in a weakened, confused state and easy prey to the lower mental forces. He forgave those he had conquered but left himself vulnerable. He allowed Jezebel, the lower emotional state, his licentious counterpart, to take over his power and position. She did not hesitate to use deception and murder to get this vineyard for Ahab. He was so divided between Jezebel his power hungry queen and Elijah the powerful prophet that he fearfully and constantly ran back and forth between the two of them.

In 1 Kings 22:5 false prophets counseled Ahab telling him that he would be victorious in a war he was planning. He denied and imprisoned the one truthful prophet who told him he would be defeated. He heard only what he wanted to hear. He went into battle ill advised by the false prophets and was defeated and killed.

The Book of Second Kings

In 2 Kings 1:3, Elijah predicted the death of Ahaziah and mocked him. *"Is it because there is no god in Israel that you are going to inquire of Baalzebub, the god of Ekron?" Baalzebub means lord of flies. It is a mocking distortion of Beelzebub that means either lord of the divine abode or Baal the prince." (Oxford RSV p. 454)*

Ahaziah kept sending men to inquire of Elijah, and Elijah sent fire from heaven and consumed them. The power of Elijah continued to be symbolized by fire. He had not quite let go of his own violent ways. Human consciousness had not yet developed beyond needing a physical show of force. Even in 2 Kings 2 that reads *"Now when the Lord was about to take Elijah up to heaven by a whirlwind, Elijah and Elisha were on their way to Gilgal."* Again the whirlwind, a symbol of lower power, is Elijah's way even to be taken up to heaven.

The book of 2 Kings 2 continues the story of Elijah and Elisha. Elijah told Elisha to wait for him while he went to Bethel to pray. But Elisha would not leave Elijah, so he went with him. He knew that Elijah was going to die momentarily. Then Elijah wanted Elisha to stay in Bethel while he went to Jericho, but again Elisha would not leave him.

"The sons of the prophets who were at Jericho drew near to Elisha and said to him, 'Do you know that today the Lord will take away your master from over you?' And he answered, 'Yes I know it; hold your peace.'" (2 Kings 2:5)

Again Elijah wanted Elisha to stay in Jericho while he went on to the Jordan River and again Elisha would not leave him. So they and fifty men went to the Jordan and the fifty stood some distance from them. Notice the three times Elijah tested Elisha. The three denials of the disciple, Peter, were cancelled with three affirmations. Jesus asked Peter three times, *"Do you love me?"* We can cancel out the effects of negative thought with three affirmations.

"The Elijah took his mantle, and rolled it up, and struck the water, and the water was parted to each side, and the two of them went over on dry ground." (2 Kings 2:8)

Then when Elijah asked him what he wanted, Elisha asked only for a double portion of Elijah's spirit. Elijah warned Elisha that this was a hard thing he asked. *"..if you see me as I am being taken from you, it shall be so for you; but if you do not see me, it shall not be so."* Elisha must be of sufficiently high consciousness to receive the double portion. And he was. He saw the chariots of fire come down and take Elijah up in a whirlwind to heaven.

This is also the third parting of waters. The first was Moses, where God did it for him. The second was Joshua, where the priests holding the Ark held back the Jordan so the people could cross. This time Elijah did it alone. This is a gradual stepping up of spiritual awareness and the power that comes with it. Commanding the waters showed up in Jesus' story of calming the stormy waters of the Sea of Galilee. Water represents the unformed substance of the Universe, the Kingdom of God, that we are to learn to command. But we must earn it by right of consciousness, not by some magical fluke.

Elisha had passed the test. He saw Elijah, the chariot, and the fire. In 2 Kings 3:12 Elijah cried out, *"My father, my father! The chariots of Israel and its horsemen!"* And then he was gone. *"He (Elisha) then took off his own clothes and tore them to pieces. And he took up the mantle of Elijah that had fallen from him, went back and stood on the bank of the Jordan. He took Elijah's mantle and struck the water saying, 'Where is the God of Elijah?' The water parted and he went over on dry land."*

In taking off his own clothes Elisha shed his personal consciousness and took up the mantle of Elijah, the pathway to pure Spirit. Humanity must shed its limited personal mind and take up the Christ Mind. At that time God was still referred to as the God of Elijah, Abraham, Isaac, Jacob, and/or David. Humanity still saw God through the eyes of earlier leaders and not as yet through their own experience. God was not referred to as "my God" until Jesus proclaimed God as Abba, his father.

CHAPTER TWENTY THREE

Elijah and Elisha

Beginning in 2 Kings 2:7, there were fifty men, sons of prophets from Jericho, who followed Elijah and Elisha to the Jordan River. However the fifty did not cross over with them, but waited on the western bank.

Elijah warned Elisha if he were not of sufficient consciousness, he could not receive the double portion of Elijah's spirit, and this would be indicated by whether or not he would be able to see him leave in the chariot and horses of fire. But Elisha was confident and he did see Elijah leave. The fifty were not of sufficient spiritual advancement to see where Elijah went. When Elisha came back over the river, the men bowed down to Elisha, but then wanted to go and see where the chariot of God had dumped Elijah. Was it on a mountain or in a valley?

All aspects of our consciousness at that period of development are not completely in alignment. Humanity still sees only the physical. Because this was a spiritual event Elisha knew they would find nothing remaining in physical form. They indeed came back to Elisha disappointed that they did not find Elijah and Elisha said, *"Did I not say to you, do not go?" (2 Kings 2:18)* There is no point in looking for the spiritual at the physical level. There was no need to chase after the physical body of Elijah when his spirit stood right before them in the person of Elisha. How far do we travel only to discover what we are looking for is right in front of us?

In 2 Kings 2:19 the men of the city still doubting wanted to test Elisha. *"Behold the situation of this city is pleasant, but the water is bad and the land unfruitful."* He ordered them to bring a new bowl with some salt in it. He tossed the salt into the waters and they became sweet *"... according to the word which Elisha spoke."*

"It is not difficult to see in Elisha an incarnation of the Christ, and he was in a certain degree God manifest. Jesus was a fuller manifestation of the same spirit." (Metaphysical Bible Dictionary)

Elisha went up to Bethel and some boys came out of the city to jeer him. *"He turned around and cursed them in the name of the Lord, and two she-bears came out of the woods and tore forty-two of the boys."* (2 Kings 2:23)

The story is meant to inculcate a respect for the power residing in holiness. Elisha cursed lower thought and it was swallowed up in the physical realm. The number forty-two is used in regard to how many boys were maimed. It doesn't say they were killed, but torn. Forty-two is an ill omen, used again in 2 Kings 10:14 when Jehu slew forty-two at Betheked. He was supposed to let them live but he did not.

Revelation 11:2 reads, *"The nations will trample over the holy city for 42 months;"* Revelation 13:5 reads, *"The beast was allowed to exercise authority for 42 months."*

Again these are ill omens that evil would be loosed upon the world until God was honored as Lord over all.

In 2 Kings 1, Mesha, the king of Moab, rebelled against the new king of Israel once Ahab died. He had been required to send huge tributes to Ahab, but now they would send nothing. So King Jehoshaphat of Israel, King Jehoram of Samaria and the king of Edom prepared for battle against Moab. They marched in circles for seven days without water for man or beast, striving at the lower levels of consciousness for completion or victory. The king of Israel, Jehoshaphat, seeing that it wasn't working became desperate and shouted, *"Alas, the Lord has called these three kings to give them into the hand of Moab! Is there no prophet of the Lord here through whom we may inquire of the Lord? One of the king's servants answered, 'Elisha, the son of Shaphat is here, who poured water on the hands of Elijah.'"* (2 Kings 3:10)

The kings represent the ego nature that rides high and rules in early development, but the ego nature is not wise. It operates out of fear and is blind. It was the servant of the king, and not the king himself, who knew where the prophets were located. In 1 Samuel 28:7 this happened also in the story of King Saul where he sent his servants to find the witch of Endor. There is a part of us, the way of wisdom that we have not yet valued as other than a lowly servant, but it always knows the location of the power.

Elijah and Elisha refused to be brought down to the level of the kings and their demands. Elijah waited at the top of a mountain and vanquished those who would demand that he come down. This precursor of Christ consciousness is not to be brought low, but always rises up. The ego's lowly demands fall down into the dust of nothingness.

*"And Elisha said to the king of Israel, 'What have I to do with you? Go to the prophets of your father and the prophets of your mother (*meaning Baal*).' But the king of Israel said to him, 'No, it is the Lord who has called these three kings to give them into the hands of Moab.' And Elisha said, '... Were it not that I have regard for Jehoshaphat, the king of Judah, I would neither look at you, nor see you."* (2 Kings 3:13)

The prophet, the holiness within us, will let the ego nature know in no uncertain terms that the ego is not in charge! Neither do the kings know the will of God, but only their own foolish fear. Jehoram, who reigned after the death of his father, Jehoshaphat, did all the good he could possibly do to rectify things in the sight of the Lord. He removed the pillar of Baal his mother had erected but was still not in good standing with the Lord because mere physical changes are not enough.

Elisha ordered a minstrel to play while he summoned the Power. We play meditation music to quiet the atmosphere while we move into the silence where the Power of God resides within us. He summoned a pool of water that would be filled so the men and cattle could drink and then prophesied that the Moabites would be delivered into the hands of these three kings. They were instructed to fell every tree, stop up every spring of water, ruin every good piece of land with stones, and offer a blood sacrifice.

"Behold the water came from the direction of Edom, until the country was filled with water." The Moabites saw the water as being red like blood and thought the three kings had already slain each other. So the Moabites shouted *"to the spoil!"* and charged ahead to the camp of the Israelites. The Israelites rose and attacked the Moabites and slaughtered

them as they ran away. The king of Moab, seeing all was lost, sacrificed his son and heir to the throne by burning him on the wall of the city.

"Human sacrifice, common in many ancient religions, was not unknown among the people of Israel and Judah. When the king of Moab made the supreme sacrifice of his son, the forces were filled with the fear of the god of Moab, Chemosh, and they gave up the victory that was within their grasp and returned to their own land." (Oxford RS p.458)

The confusion that plagues the ego mind causes fear and misinterpretation. In the present time we might call it fear of success where people unwittingly sabotage their own efforts as they near their goal. Fear drove some kings to take up the practice of human sacrifice. In 2 Kings 16:3, *"King Ahaz burned his eldest son according to the abominable practices of the nations who the Lord drove out...(or made his son to pass through the fire)"* is an alternative translation, but probably means the same thing.

In 2 Kings 4 is a collection of the miracle stories of Elisha. The writers were writing miracle stories to indicate the spiritual importance of Elisha, just as in the Gospel writers told stories of the miracles of Jesus for the same reason. Elisha's miracles began with the famous story of the widow and the jar of oil. She had one vessel of oil left and tax collectors were coming to take her and her sons into slavery. Elisha instructed her to gather as many empty vessels as possible and begin pouring the oil she had into them. As long as there were empty vessels to be filled the oil poured. When there were no more empty vessels the oil stopped. When we open ourselves to be filled, abundance pours out for us. When we believe we are limited in how much we can have, it stops.

Gathering the empty vessels means gathering thoughts and ideas. We close the door of our minds against doubts and fears, and fill the vessels with the oil of life. When she ran out of empty vessels, the oil stopped flowing. She had enough to pay her debts and she and her sons could live on the rest. The prosperity stops flowing when we are satisfied with filling only our minimal daily needs and no more.

In the psychological development stage, humanity still focuses on the limitations of the physical. So the holy thoughts poured into borrowed ideas will bring only enough to sustain us for a limited time, but this is not true abundance. In the Gospels, the water became and continues to flow as long as we are focused on our unlimited spiritual potential.

In 2 Kings 4:8 Elisha continued to Shunem to stay. A woman there fed him and had her husband build a small chamber where Elisha could stay whenever he passed through. He wanted to do something for her, so he had his servant go to her and ask what she wanted.

In 2 Kings 4:30 is a familiar theme that a woman who was past the age of bearing children longed for a son. A child was born to her and growing when he suddenly became ill and died. She rode an ass, an animal known for its swiftness, to Mount Carmel to meet the holy man. Her husband thought it would be better to wait and meet the holy man on a holy day as was the custom, but believing it would be acceptable she went immediately.

Elisha saw her coming and sent a servant to meet her. When she told him of her son, Elisha sent his servant ahead of them with his staff. He said, *"Don't stop to talk to anyone, but go and lay the staff on the child's head."* When we are on a holy mission, it is easy to dissipate the energy by chatting with others about it and letting the energy drain away. The child did not awaken until Elisha performed the same ritual that Elijah had used, and later the Apostle Paul. He laid down on the child, mouth upon mouth, eyes upon eyes, and hands upon hands, and the child became warm. Then Elisha got up and walked to and fro in the house and performed the same ritual again. The child sneezed seven times and opened his eyes. Walking to and fro is the way that energy healers amp up the energy within them when they need to do extensive work with a patient. He used all his energy to warm the child and needed an extra charge to complete the task. The number seven, the seven sneezes, indicates the task was complete.

A new story begins in 2 Kings 4:38. Elisha went to Gilgal, a high and holy place near the Jordan above Jericho. He ordered his servant to set a great pot on the fire and others went out to gather herbs. But they also gathered gourds and some poisonous plants that they were not familiar with. The pottage soon began to poison the men. Elisha dropped some meal into the pot, *"And there was no harm in the pot."* It mirrors the story of the bad water at Jericho when Elisha threw salt into the water and it was sweetened. Also in Exodus 15:25 Moses threw a tree into the brackish water at Marah and the water became sweet. Applied higher consciousness changes events from poisonous to sweet.

One day I made an illegal left turn in the city, and a police officer stepped out in front of my car. He was angry and berated me and went to the back of my car to get my license number. I asked God what I could do to make the interaction sweet and the answer came to take off my sunglasses. They were the mirror glasses that police hate. I threw them on the seat beside me and smiled up at the officer when he came back. I explained that I was from out of town and was so excited to find the store I was looking for which was on the left. The no left turn sign was on the right and I just didn't see it. I realized it was clearly my fault. His anger melted away and we had this lovely conversation and nearly hugged. Did I get a ticket? Yes, but that was not important. The ticket was merely the admission fee to the sweet interaction I asked for and that spirit manifested.

In 2 Kings 4:42 is the story of a man who brought bread to the Man of God. Elisha said to spread it before the men that they might eat. But the servant brought only 20 loaves and said, *"How am I to set this before 100 men?"* Elisha told him they would eat and have some left over. And it was true. This is a precursor to the six stories in the Gospels where Jesus fed the 5000 and the 4000, and where there were twelve baskets left over. Many teachings were brought forward from the Hebrew Testament into the Gospels because the symbolism to be applied is the same. It represents Principle that cannot change but is expressed at many levels of consciousness as humankind develops. We are to look past appearances of lack and affirm abundance.

In 2 Kings 5 is the story of the healing of Naaman, the commander of the army of Syria. He was a leper. Again it was a servant girl from the land of Israel who knew where the holy man was who could cure Naaman. The holy man referred to was Elisha. The king of Israel mistook himself to be the holy man referred to in the letter and he rent his clothes and shouted, *"Am I God, to kill and make alive, that this man sends word to me to cure a man of his leprosy? Only consider, and see how he is seeking a quarrel with me!"*

The ego mind always thinks it is the center of everything. It takes everything personally and is always ready for a quarrel. Elisha came to the king and said send the man to me. So Naaman with chariot, horses, and a retinue, arrived at the house of Elisha. Elisha sent a servant out to tell him to *"Wash in the Jordan seven times, and your flesh will be restored, and you will be clean."* Again the number seven is symbolic...seven sneezes, seven washes, the completion of healing.

But Naaman also got angry and went away. In 2 Kings 5:11 he said, *"'I thought he would come out to me and stand and call on the name of the Lord his God, and wave his hand over the place, and cure the leper. Are not the rivers in Damascus better than the water of Israel? Could I not wash in them and be clean?' So he turned and went away in a rage. 'My father, if the prophet commanded you to do some great thing, would you not have done it? How much rather, then, when he says to you, 'Wash and be clean?'"* So he went down and dipped himself seven times in the Jordan according to the word of the Man of God and his flesh was restored and he was clean.

Now the servant Gehazi saw that Elisha refused the rich gifts offered by Naaman for the healing. So secretly he ran after Naaman and asked for the gifts to give to two men who were coming to the holy man's house. Naaman gave Gehazi the gifts. Gehazi hid them in Elisha's house, not giving them to the two men, and tried to lie about it to Elisha.

In 2 Kings 5:25 Gehazi declared, *"I went nowhere!"* But Elisha said, *"Did I not go with you in spirit when the man turned from his chariot to meet you?' Then Elisha said to him, 'The Leprosy shall now be yours,' and Gehazi went from his presence a leper, as white as snow."*

Humanity still thinks it can hide from God and pursue material gain illicitly. Now humanity begins to gain some understanding that the consequences of deceiving itself regarding spiritual law are dire. We may not get leprosy, but the deceptive thinking will gnaw at us just the same and destroy our progress.

In 2 Kings 6:5 is a short story of a man who was chopping down trees for a house when the axe head flew off into the waters of the Jordan. He ran to Elisha in a panic because the axe head was borrowed. So Elisha cut off a stick and threw it into the water where the iron axe head was lost and the axe head floated to the surface.

Elisha did not discriminate between large and small in using spiritual power to help someone. Some folks think their prayer requests are too small or foolish with which to be bothered. But that power comes through for anything at all that we need. It does not pick and choose what it thinks is worthy, but serves our every need.

CHAPTER TWENTY FOUR

Rewriting The Past

In 2 Kings 22:1, Josiah was eight years old when he began to reign and reigned thirty-one years. *"Josiah did what was right in the eyes of the Lord, and walked in all the ways of David, his father, and he did not turn aside to the right hand or to the left."*

In the eighteenth year of Josiah's reign he sent Shaphan to Hilkiah the Priest to reconcile the funds and pay the repair workers. Hilkiah found a book of law in the dust and Shaphan took it to the king and read it to him. It was the book of Deuteronomy, the covenant with God. The king immediately sent it to Huldah the Prophetess to be authenticated. She sent a message back to the king that this was the true covenant with God and the people were far from obeying the law.

In 2 Kings 23 the king had the priests take all the vessels of Baal and Asherah out of the House of the Lord outside the walls of Jerusalem and burn them in the fields of the Kidron Valley, the garbage dump of the city. They took out the Asherah and burned it and stomped it into the ground. They broke down the houses of the male prostitutes. They burned down the statue of Moloch that stood over the Kidron Valley that no more infant sacrifices would be made.

In 2 Kings 23:11, *"He removed the horses that the kings of Judah had dedicated to the sun at the entrance to the house of the Lord…he burned the chariots of the sun."* He pulled down and smashed Manasseh's favorite Babylonian altar and essentially made a complete political break with Assyria. To get rid of the pagan cults he ordered that all worship must be in the temple at Jerusalem and nowhere else. There is an echo of this when Jesus met the woman at the well in Samaria. She reminded him that Samaritans were not allowed to leave their borders and could not worship in the temple in Jerusalem. Jesus told the woman at the well *"those who worship God must worship in spirit and in truth"* everywhere. *(John 4:21)* We do not have to be in any special place because God is within us and everywhere present.

In 2 Kings 23:21 Josiah re-instituted the Passover, slew the wizards and mediums, and any other abominations to God. It seems Josiah was trying to do the right thing, but it was too late. God never forgave Judah for its transgressions. Is it any wonder that the Jewish and Christian teaching even today is that God remembers our sins and even holds a grudge? This is the ego mind's grand attempt to forever enslave the human mind to guilt. The ego mind depicts God as a terrible judge that only punishes and never forgives. How many guilty thoughts have people carried for decades and humanity for centuries? They become so deeply rooted in subconscious mind, that they create an underlying platform of guilt in race mind that has become the foundation of human non-spiritual thinking. *"Race mind is the totality of beliefs, thoughts, memories, feelings and experiences of the entire race of humanity."* *(Revealing Word Dictionary, Unity)*

Everything for Israel, Judah, and Assyria was crashing at this point. Nineveh of Assyria had fallen before Medes and the Chaldeans, but Assyria was still fighting. Egypt was an ally of Assyria, so Pharaoh Neco of Egypt went to Assyria to help. Josiah got into the fray against them and lost his life at Megiddo. This was the end of his reforms and Judah then became a vassal of Egypt. Now the somewhat divided kingdom was completely divided. Israel was deported to Assyria, which itself was falling apart, and Judah was enslaved to Egypt.

Guilt, punishment, jealousy, murder, and revenge all serve to shatter the cohesiveness of the development of the psychological nature and pollute the subconscious mind. We popularly call it a midlife crisis or nervous breakdown, but the material nature we have worshipped has exposed its temporal side and it seems we are falling apart. The religion we thought would save us turns out instead to place stumbling blocks in our spiritual development. Humanity loses its belief in God and even loses its faith that good will happen.

When Jehoahaz began to reign he did all the evil that former kings did. So Neco Pharaoh jailed him and put Eliakin, son of Josiah, on the throne and made him change his name to Jehoiakim to symbolize his vassalage to Egypt. Jehoiakim became ruler in Jerusalem and did all the evil of the former kings. King Nebuchadnezzar, king of Babylon, besieged the city of Jerusalem and Jehoiakim surrendered to him.

Zedekiah was 21 years old when he ruled in Jerusalem for a short time and rebelled against Nebuchadnezzar. So the king of Babylon laid siege to Jerusalem, carried off all its riches, burned it to the ground, and tore down the walls around it. They carried away the people who were left alive and exiled them to Babylon. Many were executed when they got to Babylon as well. Gedaliah became governor of what was left. His advice to others was, *"do not be afraid of the Chaldean officials; dwell in the land and serve the king of Babylon, and it shall be well with you." (2 Kings 25:4)*

But Ishmael and ten men attacked and killed Gedaliah. Everyone else fled to Egypt except Jehoiakim, king of Judah, who was graciously freed from prison by Evilmerodach king of Babylon. *"Evilmerodach means fool of Mars, foolish destruction; A central ruling thought in the Babylon state of consciousness in man. This thought is foolish in that it looks upon worldly price, pomp, and power as worthy of one's effort to attain; it also believes in outer, limited, error conditions as real." (Metaphysical Bible Dictionary)*

In 2 Kings 25:27, *"The king spoke kindly to him, gave him a seat above the seats of the kings who were with him in Babylon. So Jehoiakim put off his prison garments. And every day of his life he dined regularly at the king's table; and for his allowance, a regular allowance was given him by the king, every day a portion, as long as he lived."*

The teaching in Amos 3:11 is to agree with your adversary quickly lest you be jailed and must pay to the last farthing. We do not need to agree with what they say and do, but we do need to be agreeable and strike as comfortable and harmonious a relationship as possible. We can even make an adversary into a friend and a great teacher.

"Jehoiakim means whom Jehovah has appointed, whom Jah has set upright, stability of Jah, Jehovah's creation." (Metaphysical Bible Dictionary)
"This story of Jehoiakim was partially confirmed by archeological researches. The writer may have used this information to end his book with a note of

modest hope, as though to say the Davidic dynasty has not been snuffed out."
(Oxford RSV p.494)

The Book of First Chronicles

"The purpose of 1 and 2 Chronicles, unlike that of 1 and 2 Kings, is theological and idealistic. There is practically no attempt to present history as we understand the word. The Chronicler wishes to advocate a certain pattern of religious life for his own day, and to indicate what a proper kingdom of his people under God would be like. He does this by describing the reigns of David and Solomon in particular, not as they actually had been, but as they ought to have been. David, especially, is highly idealized and becomes the real founder of the temple and its ritual." (Oxford RSV p. 495, the Introduction to First Chronicles.)

The first nine chapters of 1 Chronicles start with Adam and follow the genealogy to the return of the exiles from Babylon. All who returned from Babylon were listed as well. Jabez was one in a list of hundreds of names, some of which were heads of tribes and powerful, but he was not notable. This is the only time he is mentioned in the entire Bible.

In the midst of 1 Chronicles 3:9 is the now famous prayer of Jabez. The name Jabez means *"he brings pain and sorrow,"* so we know his life didn't start out well, but he knew where to turn to change things.

"Jabez was more honorable than his brothers; and his mother called his name Jabez, saying 'Because I bore him in pain.' Jabez called upon the God of Israel, saying, 'Oh that you would bless me and enlarge my border, and that thy hand might be with me, and that you would keep me from harm so that it might not hurt me!' And God granted what he asked."

Jabez may not have had a good start, but instead of letting his mother's pain or his brothers' lack of honesty define his life, he asked God to bless him with greater consciousness. Then he asked God to be with him and keep him from harming himself out of ignorance of it. And God granted his prayer. When we ask for greater consciousness, greater territory, larger experience, like Jabez we are asking for something that will be new to us. So it is wise to claim God's presence in it with us so we do not cause harm. If we are not accustomed to great riches, faster cars, sharper knives, we can do others and ourselves great harm. If we are born in pain and limitation, we must have honor and a sense that God must be in the picture or we will allow the pain to expand along with our borders.

In 1945 we exploded the first atomic bomb. We had developed a bomb that could destroy the world without the consciousness to use and control that magnitude of power. At this stage of human development we were gaining the awareness of power, without the awareness of the dangers of ego mind turned loose with it.

In 1 Chronicles 8:17-34, through the list of descendants the chronicler established the idea that David, with the help of Samuel, established all the arrangements and rituals of the temple. Since David did not build the temple they must be referring to the tent of the Lord. Once again this is an idealization of the life of David.

In 1 Chronicles 10, the chronicler wrote a quick overview of Saul and all his descendants in order to create a contrast with David, to the greater glory of David. It doesn't mention that Saul and Jonathan fell in battle, only that the Lord slew them for disobedience.

In 1 Chronicles 11 there is a brief story, only 9 verses, of how David became king over all Israel concluding with, *"And David became greater and greater, for the Lord of hosts was with him."* In verse ten begins the list of *"David's mighty men."* The book of 1 Chronicles ends at David's death and the succession of Solomon to the throne.

The book of 2 Chronicles begins with the reign of Solomon. Solomon received wisdom and built the temple and the book continues to the exile into Babylon. It ends with King Cyrus of Persia issuing a proclamation that those who wished to rebuild the house of the Lord at Jerusalem should go and do it.

The scholars enjoy comparing Kings and Chronicles because they find information in one that is not in the other. They reference the prophets and the Judges in an intellectual exercise that can be fascinating. For our purpose of interpretation we will not go through these two books, but think about how a complete rewrite of our lives, or an autobiography written about the ideal parts of our lives would serve us. This we can do in the form of rewriting our thoughts about past events and neutralizing our feelings about them so we are free to move forward unencumbered. Too often we indulge in painful memories, guilt and self-criticism and continue to live in the effects of them. We can all use the opportunity to rewrite our story freeing us and lifting us toward spiritual understanding.

There is a fascinating promise in Joel 2:25. *"I shall return to you all of the years the locust has eaten."* This would mean that all the good things in our past that have been covered over by the locusts of guilt, disapproval of self and others, feelings of failure, and a sense of wasted years are restored. If I mention to my sons the times when I was unhappy about the way I was in their early years, they always bring up the good things about that time. They are in a sense the chroniclers of my good. They reset my consciousness about the past. They restored my soul and set me free of all that covered the good.

From Isaiah 65:17, *"For behold, I create new heavens and a new earth; and the former things shall not be remembered or come into mind. Only be glad and rejoice forever in that which I create."* God creates only good and we are the children of God. Not only is all made new, but we won't even remember the former feelings and thoughts.

In A Course in Miracles on page eighty-three in the Text Book it reads, *"How can you who are so holy suffer? All your past except its beauty is gone, and nothing is left but a blessing. I have saved all your kindnesses and every loving thought you ever had. I have purified them of the errors that hid their light, and kept them for you in their own perfect radiance. They are beyond destruction and beyond guilt. They came from the Holy Spirit within you, and we know what God creates is eternal. You can indeed depart in peace because I have loved you as I loved myself."*

CHAPTER TWENTY FIVE

Ezra and Nehemiah

"*In the Apocrypha Esdras (Ezra) says that he was quickened of Spirit. He saw the building of the body temple. The Book of Ezra then, is a lesson in the building of the house that is 'not made with hands.' It really describes the building of our consciousness, a house for God.*

"*Ezra was a priest and scribe of the Jews who brought a large number of Jewish exiles back to Palestine from the Babylonian captivity. He did much to establish the Truth among the people and helped to rebuild the Temple and all of Jerusalem. He worked with Nehemiah.*

"*Ezra in Hebrew means 'help.' There is a faculty of the mind that receives and transcribes upon the tablets of memory every wave of mind that touches consciousness, whether from the flesh or from spirit.*" (Metaphysical Bible Dictionary)

King Cyrus of Persia was inspired to send out a written proclamation that the temples should be rebuilt, and the temple in Jerusalem should also be rebuilt for the god who is in Jerusalem.

"*Cyrus represents the ruling idea in consciousness that was stirred up by the Lord...The Lord inspires people who are open to Truth, wherever they may be found.*

The name Persia means horse, cloven, splendid; and Medes means the middle land, the psychic realm. The two are usually mentioned together. The psychic apart from true spiritual understanding leads to piercing, cloven, inharmonious experiences." (Metaphysical Bible Dictionary)

Regardless of how far afield we may go in consciousness, we can be stirred by spirit at any moment and find ourselves returning to spiritual thoughts. Everything is returned that we lost when we went into mental exile. Everything is supplied for us to return and rebuild our inner temple. Humanity is developing to the point of realizing its need to rebuild and maintain the sacred inner sanctuary of the soul.

Ezra 1:5 reads *"Then rose up the heads of the houses of Judah and Benjamin, the priests and Levites, every one whose spirit God had stirred to go up to rebuild the house of the Lord..."* The phrase, go up, is similar to rise up and go.

In Ezra 2 the whole census is written listing the numbers of those returning from exile and their names including the servants, male and female, singers, mules, horses, asses, etc. Many of the families had prospered in Persia and gave 61,000 darics of gold (Persian gold), 5000 minas of silver and 100 priest's garments. When the altar was set for the Jewish observances, sacrifices and feasts, the rebuilding could properly commence.

Everything was done meticulously according to the directions in 1 Chronicles 29. When we begin to rebuild our inner temple it is to be done carefully according to the best spiritual instruction we can find. We cannot skim over or ignore the deep teachings when rebuilding our inner temple. Those directions came from King David who represents our faculty of love. Humanity is learning to look at and think more deeply about its development of the capacity to love to satisfy its longing for God. The casual observer cannot understand the directions or even see the need for them.

In Ezra 3:10, the builders laid the foundation of the temple and there was a huge celebration. This alerted neighbors who came and asked to join in the rebuilding of the temple. They considered themselves observant making all the sacrifices. But they were of mixed races. They were the people who were transplanted there from other places during the exile of the Jews to Assyria. The Jewish leaders refused to let them help, so the neighbors opposed the rebuilding forcefully and the people of the land of Judah became afraid to continue.

The neighbors wrote a letter of accusation to Artaxerxes 1, King of Persia. They said in Ezra 4:6 *"Jerusalem was always a wicked city and if the temple were finished the people would not pay taxes, the city was rebellious and the royal treasury would suffer..."* The king wrote back and ordered the rebuilding to cease until he could research their accusations. The rebuilding ceased at the end of Ezra 4:24, *"until the second year of Darius' reign."*

In Ezra 6:1, King Darius dug up the original decree of Cyrus in the house of archives in Media and reinstated it, so the rebuilding could continue. In Ezra 6:11, *"Also I make a decree that if anyone alters this edict, a beam shall be pulled out of his house, and he shall be impaled upon it, and his house shall be made a dunghill. The house of the Lord went forward and was finished in four years by command of the God of Israel and by decree of Cyrus, Darius, and Artaxerxes 1, kings of Persia."*

Opposing mixed thoughts throw all sorts of doubts and fears in the way of our spiritual work, and can even stop us for a time. The intellect through memory goes back to the original inspiration and gathers those powerful truths to restart the work. It takes powerful destroyers of the negative thought patterns, three kings, to clear the way. These kings represent light at this level of human development but not the spiritual light. They are still subject to error, but manage to do good as well.

God moves through Cyrus (*the sun - light*), Darius (*upholding the good*), and Artaxerxes the Great King (who wrote the stop order and then the order to continue). They represent the will, open to both error and right thought, each acting according to that which appealed to him at the time, to bring about the completion of the temple. Humanity is still in the psychological realm reaching for the spiritual as best it can and is subject to the swings of mood and circumstance. In the Gospels the disciple Matthew resents the faculty of will that is spiritualized as it comes under the direction of the Christ nature.

The kings and others referred to Jerusalem and Judah as the *"province beyond the river."* Since the exile, Israel was no longer a kingdom, but a province of Persia and beyond the river referred to beyond the Jordan.

In Ezra 10:16 Ezra was set in charge of selecting the council that would meet and consider what was in alignment with righteousness and the question of mixed marriages came up. There was no divorce so Shechaniah proposed to Ezra a covenant whereby those mixed marriages were declared not true marriages and that all foreign wives and children would be abandoned. The multitude of Jews standing in the square before the House of the Lord agreed. A list was drawn up of all men who had married foreign wives and the men put away their wives and children. We do not know exactly what "put away" meant, whether they were sent to their homes of origin or killed. The law was enforced and guilt offerings were made to signify that the mixed marriages were illegal. The wrong had been righted.

Positive and negative thoughts mixed together, love and hate, faith and fear, are not true spiritual thinking. Negative thoughts and feelings must be "put away" or erased for the development toward spiritual life to move forward. All of the error thoughts we espoused and emotions born of that error must also be *"put away."*

The Book of Nehemiah

This is the diary of Nehemiah, the memoirs of Nehemiah the Cupbearer. Some verses belong back in the Book of Ezra and some in Ezra belong in the Book of Nehemiah. Some parts run parallel. The story begins when Nehemiah served King Artaxerxes 1, son of Xerxes.

Nehemiah believed in divine possibility. His potential to succeed was limitless as long as he worked with God. Nehemiah was a slave in Persia and was the king's most trusted servant. As cupbearer he tasted all of the king's food to be sure it wasn't poisoned. This position took courage and a mind that was well honed to stay focused in faith and wisdom.

Like Nehemiah we must not step out of faith or we will be poisoned with guilt and disappointment instead of being successful. Our condition of success and prosperity can also turn into lack if we fall into a money consciousness of greed that creates poisonous fear and doubt. A powerful success consciousness demands our steadfast focus and faithfulness.

Nehemiah heard that the walls of the temple were falling apart. He wept and mourned for days. In this way he released the shock and grief of the news before he took action. When we find that the sacred temple within us has fallen to neglect and disrepair we must first clear the mind of shock, guilt and anguish. We purge fear thoughts and clear our minds of all doubts and useless chatter. Depending upon the depth of the disaster, it may not happen in a few days or weeks. Nehemiah took the time to purify himself from December to April. He made a plan and prayed asking for guidance and specifically for success. We must concentrate on God and also ask for guidance and success in our plans.

He then approached the king (ego mind) who knew him well. Nehemiah did not put on a brave face but showed his deep concern for *"the place of my father's sepulchers."* He set his plan with exactly what he needed before King Artaxerxes 1. He needed letters of passage from King Artaxerxes to the kings of the territories through which he must pass to get to Jerusalem; a letter to the keeper of the king's forest to get lumber to rebuild. The king was so impressed that he gave Nehemiah everything he asked for. The king sent his officers of the army and horsemen to escort him and insure his safety. The ego mind is very cooperative and generous when you incorporate it into your initial plans. It sends all the helpful ideas from subconscious mind to accompany you and guards you from enemy thoughts.

Nehemiah did not reveal all of his plans but just the ones the king, needed to hear. He was not actually upset about the sepulchers of his father as he said, but the very walls of Jerusalem. If he had told the king he was going to also rebuild the walls, that would sound like a rebellion and the king might have changed his mind and perhaps had him killed. We pick thoughts and words for our prayers carefully to affirm our good.

Once he was outside the jurisdiction of the king he could contemplate his next moves. Approaching the outskirts of Jerusalem he went alone at night to inspect the walls and the extent of the damage. The damage was so great that the walls were flattened and the boulders so thick that he could not ride his horse into Jerusalem. He then knew that before he started rebuilding the temple, he had to repair the walls because the temple would never be safe until there were walls to keep enemies out. Before we can repair the sacred temple within us, we need to build a wall of prayer and affirmative thinking to keep our doubts and fears from destroying our efforts.

There were mixed race enemies all around Jerusalem at that time and they would surely attack. Anyone who was not a full-blooded Jew could not be part of the rebuilding. Sanballat, Tobiah, and Geshem were Arabs representing our most powerful enemy thoughts. Many Jews around Jerusalem had intermarried with the Arab inhabitants and their families were not full-blooded Jews. They represent mixed thoughts within us that vacillate between good and evil. The three accosted Nehemiah with their rage and ridicule but Nehemiah turned them away. Rebuilding your inner sacred temple must be done using only the pure spiritual thoughts and we literally turn our minds away from the ridicule of enemy thinking.

Nehemiah divided the jobs among the workers, some building gates and some hewing stones. He taught the workers to be ready for attack. They built with one hand and held a spear in the other. The old people and children were sent to watch the weak places in the walls. They were to sound an alarm if the enemy approached. Then the workers who already had spears in one hand would race to defend the wall.

There will be ridiculing thoughts in our minds, served up by the ego. It will call us feeble and stupid, unable to do the job. Nehemiah 4:1 reads, *"When Sanballat heard we were building the wall he was angry and greatly enraged, and he ridiculed the Jews. And he said in the presence of his brethren and the army of Samaria, 'What are these feeble Jews doing? Will they restore things? Will they sacrifice? Will they finish up in a day? Will they revive the stones out of the heaps of rubbish, and burned ones at that?'"*

The walls and temple were rebuilt while Nehemiah meticulously set up a government, wrote the laws, and created all the infrastructures needed for the city of God. He kept records of everything. All the names of the priests, officials, and workers were listed.

Carefully we must design and set up the kingdom of God within us! We must keep the thought patterns cleansed, stay the course despite doubts and fears, and carefully plan the steps we will take to create all the elements required.

The signers of Nehemiah's covenant to support God's house are these. Notice how the meanings of their names correspond to the characteristics we must have to rebuild our sacred inner temple. There are no mixed messages among them.

Priests:

Zedekiah - Uprightness. Jehovah vindicates
Seraiah - Jehovah hath prevailed
Azariah - Whom Jehovah aids
Jeremiah - Whom Jehovah establishes
Pashhur - Surrounded by prosperity
Amariah - Jehovah enlightens
Malchijah - Jehovah's king

Hattush - Increased
Shebaniah - Jehovah makes youthful
Malluch - Counselor, king
Harim - Consecrated dedicated
Meremoth - Exaltations, glories
Obadiah - Worshipper of Jehovah
Daniel - Judgment of god
Ginnethon - Great protection
Baruch - Blessed and prospered
Meshullam -Devoted friend of god
Abijah - My father is Jehovah
Mijamin - Fortunate, happy, faithful
Maazial - Strength of god
Bilgai - Rejoicing
Shemaiah - Obedience to god

Levites:

Jeshua - Deliverance, freedom
Binnui - Rebuilding, family-ship
Kadmiel - Eternal god
Shebaniah - Powerful, mature
Hodiah - Splendor, glory
Kelita - Take into one's self
Pelaiah - Mediator
Hanan - Compassionate
Mica - Assimilate Jehovah
Rehob - Broad-visioned
Hashabiah - Purpose of Jehovah
Zaccur - Mindful, remembering
Sherebiah - Light of Jehovah
Shebaniah - Youthful, powerful
Bani - Begotten
Beninu - Our posterity

When all was accomplished the Book of Nehemiah ends with this prayer. *"Remember me, O my God, for good."*

CHAPTER TWENTY SIX

Nehemiah, Esther and Job

There was a famine while Nehemiah was rebuilding the city. In order to get grain the people were forced to mortgage their fields, which would force them into slavery. In Nehemiah 5, Nehemiah would not allow this so he took charge of the economy. He decreed that interest could be charged to non-Jews, but they could not exact interest from their Jewish brothers. They took no food from foreign governors who had impoverished their people by requiring a food allowance or payment.

Nehemiah did not purchase land for himself but focused on the building of the wall. He wanted no distractions. Seeing that the wall was almost finished, Sanballat, Tobiah and the Arabs, tried to lure Nehemiah away to the plain of Ono where they planned to kill him. He refused to go, telling them the finishing of the wall was his priority. When their plan did not work, they sent a letter accusing him of plotting a rebellion because he was building walls. They thought this would frighten the workers, that they would drop their tools and not complete the wall. They were not correct.

A man sent by Sanballat and Tobiah urged Nehemiah to hide in the temple, but he refused. *"Should a man such as I flee? And what man such as I could go into the temple and live? I will not go in!' and I understood and saw that God had not sent him. He was hired that I should be afraid, act in this way and sin, so they could give me an evil name in order to taunt me." (Nehemiah 6:11)*

These are great illustrations of how the ego mind plots the demise of your strength and your progress toward building spiritual consciousness. It brings a famine upon you with ideas of lack and desires to enslave you with guilt. It tries to scare you with lies about your intentions to cause your faith to waver. It encourages you to hide for your own safety behind the outer trappings of religion. It plots to draw you off into a dangerous territory of deadly traps from which you may not escape.

Sanballat from Hebrew means hatred, secret enemy. Tobiah was a servant of Sanballat.

Tobiah means deceptive thought, not of a true spiritual character. He was from the Ammonites and could not prove his Jewish lineage. They pretended to have Nehemiah's best interest at heart, but they were enemies. Ego mind always wants you to think it has your best interest at heart, but its only goal is its own preservation.

The returning exiles were registered and counted. They were carefully sorted: Levites, priests, servants in the temple, and servants of the sons of Solomon. Some could not find their names in the genealogies and could not prove their lineage to be included in the priesthood. There were lists of those living in Jerusalem and those living in their family towns from before the exile. Nehemiah organized every area and set overseers to manage them. We sort out in our minds what we believe and what we do not believe, what is of great importance and what is of minor importance, what are priestly thoughts and what are merely servant thoughts.

Nehemiah went to visit King Artaxerxes and when he returned he found that mischief was done in his absence. Eliashib tried to sneak Tobiah into a chamber in the courts of the house of God, but Nehemiah found him and threw Tobiah and his furniture out. He also found that the Levites had not been given their portion of the tithes and had fled to their own fields to survive. So Nehemiah gathered the Levites in, set them at their stations and gave them their portion of the tithes. He cleansed the priesthood of everything foreign.

Then he saw the men of Judah running their presses and selling their produce on the Sabbath. The men of Tyre brought in fish to sell. So Nehemiah had the gates in the walls closed before the evening of the Sabbath and not to be opened until after the Sabbath. They tried to camp outside the gates to set up a market there, but Nehemiah ran them off. He even physically contended with the women of condemned mixed marriages who refused to leave.

We need to keep the whole spiritual law, not just bits and pieces of it, letting go of all error thinking. We need to devote our lives to the study and pure practice of it. Humanity at this level of development continues to struggle to observe the law and still finds many distractions that lead down false paths.

The Book of Esther

"This book was disputed by rabbis when it was entered into Scripture. It is not history. It does not mention God or things precious to the Jewish religion. It celebrates a secular feast for the deliverance of Jews from an anti-Semitic pogrom. It is a legend intended to explain the origin of Purim. There are also additions to the book in the Apocrypha intended to supply religious components to the story." (Introduction to the book of Esther, Oxford RSV)

The divine feminine within us is our heroine. It faces any danger to insure the progress toward our spiritual growth. Stories of this important and powerful aspect of our nature are created as reminders of its existence in a highly patriarchal world.

The story begins with a celebration wherein King Ahasuerus (his name means lion king), wanted to impress those attending with the beauty of his queen, Vashti. She refused to be paraded naked past a bunch of drunks, suffering their leers and comments. She would not leave an important feast she was holding for her women. The king consulted his counselors about the law when she refused to come. He banished Vashti for her disobedience, then later regretted it when he sobered up. However his decree was irreversible. Ego mind is under the influence of its own intoxication and makes decisions that are vastly destructive.

The servants set about looking for all the most beautiful virgins in the land so the king could choose another queen. Mordecai was the uncle of the beautiful Hadassah. He probably tried to hide her when the edict came out but she was found. Before she was taken to the palace Mordecai hurriedly renamed her Esther so the king would not know she was a Jew. Before the women in the harem went before the king they were given their choice of a dazzling display of jewelry to wear. Esther asked for nothing and took nothing as the king's eunuch, Hegai, advised her. As a result of her purity she was chosen to be the next queen and a huge banquet was given in her honor.

Mordecai sat at the palace gate and heard of a plot to kill the king. He told Esther and she told the king in Mordecai's name. It turned out to be true and the plotters were hanged. Then the king appointed Haman the Agagite to be set above everyone except the king. Haman hated the Jews, especially Mordecai because Mordecai would not bow down to him. Haman received unlimited power and funds from the king.

Haman sent out an order in the king's name to the princes that all Jews were to be killed. Mordecai sent a message to Esther to go before the king and entreat him for her people. Esther knew she could not go before the king unless she was summoned by the king. To do so could mean her death. Mordecai reminded her that she would not escape death either, if it became known she was a Jew. Esther 4:14 he wrote to her in, *"If you keep silence at such a time as this relief and deliverance will rise for the Jews from another quarter, but you and your father's house will perish. Who knows whether you have come to the kingdom for such a time as this?"*

He was saying her time had come, her big moment. If she passed it up, she and her family would pass into oblivion and someone else would save the people and get the credit. A more modern wisdom saying is, *"On the plains of hesitation bleach the bones of countless millions who, at the dawn of decision, sat down to wait, and waiting died."*

(*Sam Ewing*) Someone else will do the job. Someone will manifest the idea. Do you want to be part of greatness? Then you must step forward to manifest the Divine Ideas into your life experience and not be afraid.

Esther found herself alone to decide what to do. She told Mordecai to gather all the Jews in Susa and ask them to fast for three days. Before taking action we must fast from our doubts and fears. Three is the number of creation, symbolizing the creation a pure and holy place. Then she put on her royal robes and went to the outer chamber of the king. Fortunately the king agreed to see her and asked what she wanted.

Esther did not ask something for herself, but asked the king and Haman to attend a lavish dinner she had just prepared for them. Notice the similarity of Nehemiah's approach. First he fasted and prayed, and then he went to the king with a plan.

"Fools rush in where angels fear to tread." (*Alexander Pope*) Had Nehemiah or Esther rushed in without preparation, they would have scattered the effect of their presentation, lost the power to accomplish their task and even lost their lives. Esther knew Haman was a powerful enemy. She had to lull him into being careless. The king, being so pleased with her invitation, offered to grant any request to Esther, even half his kingdom. This was a temptation from the ego mind. But Esther requested only that they come to a special banquet the next night as well.

Now Haman thought he had won the Queen's favor and was very puffed up. His name means "splendid, magnificent, noise, arrogance, trouble." *(Metaphysical Bible Dictionary)*

During this time Haman had been preparing the gallows for Mordecai. At the second feast Esther sprang the trap. The king again asked Esther what she wanted and she asked for her life and the life of her people. She told him of Haman's edict. She said if the people were to be sold into slavery she would keep her peace, because that would enrich the king's coffers. But this wholesale slaughter would not and the king would also be deprived of his queen.

Shocked, the king stormed out into the garden and Haman jumped onto the couch where Esther sat and grabbed her. The king came back in and seeing Haman ready to assault Esther, ordered him hanged on the gallows being built for Mordecai. The sons of Haman were also hanged. The ring of power was taken from Haman and given to Mordecai. An edict went out from the king that all Jews were allowed to defend themselves and to avenge themselves upon their enemies They did this with such thoroughness that many were claiming to be Jews who were not in order to escape death.

The spread of negative thinking must be completely stopped, hence the killing of Haman's sons. It isn't enough to kill the source idea, but to destroy all subsequent thoughts coming from it or the evil will continue to spread and infect more of subconscious mind.

Mordecai became more and more powerful. His name means *"little man, of Merodach, dedicated to Mars (the Babylonian god of war), contrition."* Charles Fillmore writes that "little man" indicates the humility that always marks the truly great individual. In Esther 10:3 we read, *"For Mordecai the Jew was next in rank to King Ahasuerus, and he was great among the Jews and popular with the multitude of his brethren, for he sought the welfare of his people and spoke peace to all his people."*

Additions to the Book of Esther are in the Apocrypha, the purpose being to add religion to the original translation. So to have the whole text as one book, you would have to leaf in the extra one hundred seven verses into the original story where they would properly fit. But the verses were written after the original book was canonized therefore it could not be added to or rewritten.

The book of Job

This is a tale full of teachings about God and man and their relationship. *"It does not attempt to explain away the mystery of suffering or to justify the ways of God with man. It probes the depths of faith in spite of suffering. Job demands justice and he regards religion and morality as man's claim for happiness." (Oxford RSV Introduction)*

As we begin to read Job 1, it might be helpful to start with *"Once upon a time…"* This is a very old classic teaching story from long before the Hebrew Bible was assembled. In this story Job would not only do the required sacrifices for himself but he would do them for his children in case they forgot to do theirs. Job was steadfast and rigid in his own observances, even distrusting his children to take responsibility to do their own. Job was perfect at doing what he thought was the will of God at the physical level. Many people in mainstream churches and places of worship go through the rituals without thinking or making any choices for themselves, believing they have pleased God or saved their family.

In Job 1:6, *"when the sons of God came to present themselves before the Lord, Satan also came among them. And the Lord said to Satan, 'Whence have you come?' Satan answered the Lord, 'From going to and fro on the earth and from walking up and down it.'"*

This is a great explanation of the appearance of ego mind. It functions at the physical/psychological level only and it affects everyone on earth. It does not bring good or healing. It arrives with the sons (its own lower thoughts), not with God. We bring ego mind with us by allowing it to influence our thinking, be in our affairs and direct us all the time.

God pointed to Job as a blameless man. Satan pointed out that God had surrounded Job with good, so of course he was blameless. Satan wondered if Job would remain blameless if everything were taken from him. God gave Satan permission to test Job, but Satan was not allowed to kill him. The name Job means, *"persecuted, calamitous, afflicted, a coming back; restored to one's senses, converted."* (Metaphysical Bible Dictionary)

In self-righteousness there is fear of evil; the things Job feared came upon him *(Job 3:25)*. Then his three friends came to comfort him and to argue with him. These friends represent the accusations of personal consciousness we level against ourselves.

Ego mind, Satan, began its work against Job. The servants ran to tell Job the bad news. The oxen and asses were stolen, the sheep were burned up, the servants were killed, the Chaldeans took the camels, and the roof of the house fell in on his sons and daughters and they were all killed. Each servant saying, *"…and I alone have escaped to tell you."*

In Job 1:21, Job uttered the famous *"Naked I came from my mother's womb, and naked I shall return; the Lord gave and the Lord has taken away. Blessed be the name of the Lord. In all this Job did not sin or charge God with wrong."*

Eventually we come to realize that all is God including ourselves. There is no blame to be placed, but only the law to be fulfilled in our complete healing and understanding of our true nature.

CHAPTER TWENTY SEVEN

Job Continued

Beginning in Job 2:11, *"Job's three friends heard all of this evil... They made an appointment to come together to console Job."* They represent intellectual reason, but not spiritual understanding.

Eliphaz – Purification that does not measure up to Spiritual Truth.
Bildad – Son of contention, son of strife
Zophar – Chirping, twittering, hopping, small bird
(Metaphysical Bible Dictionary)

The meaning of their names makes it clear they represent the intellect that is not wise but gets its information from memory and outer influences. This is why they could not help Job find a remedy for his afflictions. They would show him how they thought he was wrong, but could not reveal to him the right way. Intellect only points out evil appearances and condemns the sinner. The subsequent chapters are filled with discourses of the friends and Job. They are intellectual arguments about God. Job was questioning why this all happened to him, a righteous man. The friends were sure they understood why it is happening to Job. The ego mind is always sure it knows.

In Job 3, the dam broke and Job finally let it all hang out. He lamented his birth, bewailed his situation, and wondered why he wasn't dead. Why should he be alive if there was no light or joy in his life?

The intellect alone cannot bear the difficulties of life and breaks down in despair.

In Job 4:17 Eliphaz tried to reason with Job, that no one stands before God. Eliphaz described a message he heard from a voice in the night. *"Can a mortal man be righteous before God? Can mortal man be pure before his Maker? Even in his servants he puts no trust, and his angels he charges with error; how much more those who dwell in houses of clay, whose foundation is in the dust, who are crushed like a moth. Between morning and evening they are destroyed; they perish forever without any regarding it."*

In Job 5:17 Eliphaz continued, *"Happy is the man who God reproves; therefore despise not the chastening of the almighty. For he wounds, but he binds up; he smites but his hands heal"* And he ends with *'Hear and know it is for your good.'"*

But Job's life had already been dedicated to righteousness. So this was not helping. He said in Job 6:8, *"O that I might have my request, and that God would grant my desire; and that it would please God to crush me, that he would let loose his hand and cut me off!"*

The human intellect struggles so hard to get free of tribulations that it exhausts itself and wants to just give up. But as Job knew, there was no giving up. We must continue on in our development regardless of the seeming obstacles. We can relieve the intellect of its burdens by using faith and prayer to lift us above the trials.

In Job 7 he continued to remind God of how hard human life was, and even when he lay down to sleep, God terrified him with nightmares. The intellect wants to place blame somewhere else and needs to complain to God of all the earthly woes. Job threatens to be dead so God can't find him to afflict him anymore.

In Job 7:21 he ended with *"Why do you not pardon my transgression and take away my iniquity? For now I shall lie in the earth; you will seek me, but I shall not be."* This is the intellect's way of saying, you'll be sorry when I'm gone.

In Job 8:2 Bildad and Shuhite were fed up with Job's laments and essentially called him a bag of wind. *"…the words of your mouth are a great wind…"* Bildad took a turn arguing from a purely moralistic view. He and Eliphaz were both arguing for divine justice at the moralistic level. They were arguing cause and effect. In all the arguing, it was still on Job's shoulders.

In Job 8:5 they said, "If you will seek God and make supplication to the Almighty, if you are pure and upright, surely then He will rouse himself for you and reward you with a rightful habitation."

In Job 9 he wanted to know how to contend with God. In other words, how would he show God how righteous he was? And who calls God to account for His actions, anyway?

"If one wished to contend with Him, one could not answer Him once in a thousand times. He is wise in heart, and mighty in strength-who has hardened himself against Him, and succeeded?...Lo, He passes by me, and I see him not; He moves on, but I do not perceive him. Behold He snatches away; who can hinder him? Who will say to him, 'What are you doing?'" (Job 9:11)

Job was trying so hard to reconcile the hurt he suffered with a God who created him and would seem to destroy him.

"God gives and God takes away and I can't even say anything about it. Where is the divine justice in this?" We are still in the psychological understanding of God as a punishing parent, a friend who is not a friend, and somehow justifies hurting his creations. In Job 8:3 Bildad answered, *"Does God pervert justice? Does the Almighty pervert the right?"*

This is the eternal struggle within the human sense of right and wrong, and making God subject to right and wrong as we understand it. Or is there some divine justice we do not know about? Many believe that and say, *"It is just God's will,"* or *"God must have something better in mind for you."* And *"God does not give you a cross you cannot bear."* And my grandmother's favorite (when we did not do what she wanted us to) was to throw up her hands and declare, *"My reward is in heaven."*

Actually, these statements have some truth in them when we understand them metaphysically. God's will is for us to exercise free will whether we get ourselves into trouble or not. Humanity seeks to understand without acknowledging that we create our own world of experience. We punish ourselves with the results of our error thinking, many believing it is God punishing us. But God does not punish or give us a cross to bear. We do that to ourselves. God has something better in mind, that we should reflect the divine within us into our life experiences. Our reward is in heaven, the heavenly state of mind that is the kingdom of God within us.

In Job 11:3 Zohar accused Job of iniquity. *"Should your babble silence men, and when you mock, should no one shame you?...Know that God exacts of you less than your guilt!"*

In Job 12 he responded: *"No doubt you are the people (you speak of), and wisdom will die with you. But I have understanding as well as you; I am not inferior to you. Who does not know such things as these? I am a laughing stock to my friends; I who called upon God and he answered me, a just and blameless man, am a laughing stock...The tents of robbers are at peace, and those who provoke God are secure, who bring their god in their hand."*

He was probably referring 'to the carved idols and other such talismans that people carried in their robes and hands. You can be secure even in evil and God will not punish you, but you will punish yourself especially when your god is something physical you created and control.

In Job 13:2 he continued his rebuke of his friends. *"What you know I also know. I am not inferior to you. But I would speak to the Almighty, and I desire to argue my case with God. As for you, you whitewash with lies; worthless physicians are you all. Oh, that you would keep silent and it would be your wisdom!"*

"Behold I have prepared my case; I know that I shall be vindicated." (Job 13:18)

Job had a passionate desire to see God. He would rather hear from God what his iniquities were than listen to his friend's continued sermons. When we become weary with the so-called wisdom of the world, we are refreshed with Truth when listening instead to God.

In Job 14 he continued to rail at God for the frailty of man, and the droughts and the earthquakes, the floods and famines, the falling rocks and the destroyed hopes of man. This is always on humanity's mind. If God is all powerful and in charge, why does God let things happen to people?

In Job 15 Eliphaz went after Job telling him his complaints and utterances did not befit a wise man. *"Your iniquity teaches your mouth... your own mouth condemns you, and not I; your own lips testify against you."* (Job 15:5)

This is an interesting spiritual teaching, but not relevant as a teaching at this point in human development. It is delivered as an insult. At the spiritual level, our words come from the mind that is aligned with Truth. If they do not our own words bless or condemn us. The eventual spiritual development and understanding of this principle is not available to humanity at this stage because the development has not yet progressed that far.

In Job 16:2 he complained of God's hostility. He lashed out at his friends, *"I have heard such things; miserable comforters are you all."*

In Job 18 Bildad fired back: *"How long will you hunt for words? Consider, and then we will speak. Why are we counted as cattle? Why are we stupid in your sight?"*

In Job 19, he answered: *"How long will you torment me, and break me in pieces with words? Ten times you have cast reproach upon me; are you not ashamed to wrong me? And even if it be true that I have erred, my error remains with myself."*

Job 19:25 is familiar to us. The words are used in *The Messiah*. *"I know that my Redeemer (vindicator) lives, and at the last he will stand upon the earth and after my skin has been thus destroyed, then without my flesh I shall see God, whom I shall see on my side, and my eyes shall behold, and not another. My heart faints within me!"*

In Job 20 Zophar described the fate of the wicked in detail, even more so than in the book of Revelation.

In Job 21 Job answered: *"Listen carefully to my words, and let this be your consolation. Bear with me, and I will speak, and after I have spoken, mock on!"*

In Job 22 Eliphaz accused Job of wickedness. *"Can a man be profitable to God? Surely he who is wise is profitable to himself. Is it any pleasure to the Almighty if you are righteous, or is it gain to him if you make your ways blameless? Is it for your fear of him that he reproves you and enters into judgment with you? Is not your wickedness great? There is no end to your iniquities."*

You can get the sense that these are our own inner accusers and critics. We have many of these arguments with ourselves. We put ourselves down, argue and criticize others, and condemn our world.

In Job 23 are some familiar words, *"O that I knew where I might find him, that I might even come to his seat!"* They are in the sacred song entitled, *If With All Your Heart (you truly seek me, you shall ever find me).*

Then in Job 23:4 he went back to envisioning an encounter with God. *"I would lay my case before him and fill my mouth with arguments. I would learn what he would answer me, and understand what he would say to me."*

Humanity always has its mouth full of arguments. It leaves no room to think, to listen, to hear and understand someone else. People often are busy thinking up rebuttals or responses while they are supposedly listening to another.

In Job 6:24 he turned to God for help. *"Teach me, and I will be silent; make me understand how I have erred. How forceful are honest words! But what does reproof from you reprove? Do you think you can reprove words, when the speech of a despairing man is wind...Is there any wrong on my tongue?"*

Job was searching himself for what might be causing his ill fortune. Intellect is always looking for a reason that will make sense of things that happen. What is the cause that brings this effect? What can be blamed?

In Job 27 he maintained his innocence again. *"As God lives, who has taken away my right, and the Almighty who has made my soul bitter; as long as my breath is in me, and the spirit of God is in my nostrils; my lips will not speak falsehood, and my tongue will not utter deceit. Far be it from me to say you are right; till I die I will not put away my integrity from me. I hold fast to my righteousness, and will not let it go; my heart does not reproach me for any of my days."*

In Job 32 *"then came Elihu, the interpreter, or the Holy Spirit, who opens man's eyes to the real righteousness...recognizing that the true inner self of man is spirit.". (Metaphysical Bible Dictionary)*

Elihu was very angry that Job justified himself rather than God. Elihu was angry with himself also saying that he did not speak up because he was younger and assumed the older three would have the answers. But they did not. He said it was the spirit in man, not age that made one wise.

The conversation within the developing individual goes round and round. Job declared his innocence; he rebuked God, then he reasoned out his case, and back around again to declaring his innocence. This is how thoughts and arguments go round and round in the mind like a squirrel on a wheel in a cage. They keep us from falling asleep at night and occupy our idle moments in the daytime. No wisdom or resolution appears.

In Job 38:1, *"Then the Lord answered Job out of the whirlwind. Who is this that darkens counsel by words without knowledge? Gird up your loins like a man, I will question you, and you shall declare to me. Where were you when I laid the foundation of the earth?"*

God expounded on all his creation and wanted to know if Job could do any of this himself. God's words continue all the way through to Job 42, the last chapter in the book of Job.

These are comments from the *Bible Interpreters Dictionary* on Job, and God's utterances at the end of the book. *"Yahweh answers Job's questions but he declines to submit to a cross-examination. Instead he asks the questions, with more than a touch of irony. Here it may be that the poet reveals his purpose: to put man in his proper place in relation to God. Yahweh's evasion of the question of Job's innocence may be the poet's oblique way of saying that no answer is available to man. God cannot be hauled into court or compelled to testify against himself. Ignorant and impotent man cannot presume to tell God how to order the universe."*

No degree of suffering can give mere man, with his finite intelligence, license to question God's justice as Job had done. It is exactly on this point that Job confessed and repented his error; he had spoken without knowledge or understanding.

In Job 42:3b-c, *"Therefore I have uttered what I did not understand, things too wonderful for me, which I did not know."*

Job made no concession, either explicit or implicit, in regard to his innocence and integrity, and Yahweh said nothing to imply that Job had merited his misery. This was an ethical triumph for Job over his friends, who had maintained that he must be guilty of something and would be proved so if God were to speak. Job was only guilty of speaking out of ignorance.

Job complained of the hopelessness of his case in the face of God's arbitrary omnipotence. Now that he actually got a glimpse of God, he realized he had spoken rashly, for God moves on a level beyond human comprehension. The answer that God gave from the whirlwind in Job

38 was as much of an answer as man had ever received, apart from a beatific vision (imparting bliss or joy).

Many times people speak of God in ignorance of what God is. This speaking anchors the state of ignorance in consciousness, especially when the speaker feels absolutely certain of his or her correctness. The speaker must then justify a situation by rebuking God.

In Job 42:10, Job finally "sees" God and he gets it. When he gets it he is restored and so is all that was taken from him. *"And in the land there no women so fair as Job's daughters, and their father gave them inheritance among their brothers…And Job died, an old man, and full of days."*

Again it happens that the daughters are given an inheritance. This was only the third or fourth time daughters were counted in the inheritance distribution. The recognition of the importance of the divine feminine was still barely recognized. Again the phrase was repeated perhaps indicating Job's fulfillment, *"old and full of days."*

CHAPTER TWENTY EIGHT

David and the Psalms

L ove was introduced to humanity in the Psalms. David was the singer of the Hebrew Testament who played the lyre or small harp. Humanity was developing a capacity for the beginnings of love and music. The first focus of love was love of God and God's love for His people, not yet focusing upon love for the individual that dominates the western culture today.

The book of Psalms is a book of hymns, also known as a Psalter, to be used in the temple ceremonies. Over half of them are ascribed to King David. He was a revered singer and was hired as a young man by King Saul to play the harp and sing to lift the king's mood.

The Psalter has some interesting characteristics. The word "Blessed" as used is a Hebrew expression meaning literally *"O How Happy!"* *"Selah"* may mean the place for an instrumental, a response, or the equivalent of *"chorus."* There are notations such as instructions to the choirmaster. There are notations as to the purpose of, or reason for, the hymn. There are words with lost meanings: Shiggaion, Sheminith, Miktam, Maskil, Gittith, Muth-Labben, Alamoth, Mahahath, Mahalath Leanoth. Shushan-Eduth. The last eight are preceded by *"According to"* and may be names of tunes such as *"According to the Hind of the Dawn,"* (Psalm 22.)

"The Book of Psalms reflects many aspects of the religious experience of Israel. Its intrinsic spiritual depth and beauty have made it from earliest

times a treasury of resources for public and private devotion." (Oxford RSV Introduction and footnotes.)

In Psalms 2:2 *"The kings of the earth set themselves, and the rulers take counsel together against the Lord…"* God installs the Christ or "his king" within us and the nations of our thoughts plot to install the ego mind as king. We set up ego driven kings from our own physical/psychological experience and the more we set up, the more they conspire together. Ego mind builds a wall of logic and reason. In the beginning they seem logical and real to us but they are false. The response of spiritual law is immediate and we need to choose thoughts wisely and not foolishly. Either manifests with the same directness. When we ask to be given our true inheritance, our spiritual nature, the false kingdoms of ego mind are destroyed.

Psalm 14 is almost identical to Psalm 53. The Psalmist talks about an evil generation *"They have all gone astray, they are alike, corrupt; there is none that does good, no, not one."* Evil is live spelled backward. Humanity goes through times when all thought is against life, whether war or despair. When we turn our thinking around again, and generate right thinking, *"God is with the generation of the righteous." (Psalms 14:5)*

When in meditation and prayer we turn within, we enter the temple of our own being. Preparation of the consciousness is essential and we find a quiet and composed state of mind. In Psalm 15 is the question that everyone must answer properly for admission into the temple. The keeper at the door asks the question of those wishing to enter. *"O Lord, who shall sojourn in thy tent? Who shall dwell on thy holy hill?"* The rest of the psalm is the required response. The answer describes a state of mind that one must rise to in prayer and meditation in order to enter that holy state which is your inner temple.

"He who walks blamelessly, and does what is right, and speaks truth from his heart; who does not slander with his tongue, and does no evil to his friend, nor takes up a reproach against his neighbor; in whose eyes a reprobate is despised, but who honors those who fear the Lord; who swears to his own hurt and does not change; who does not put out his money at interest, and does not take a bribe against the innocent. He who does these things shall never be moved." Only those who have the required moral qualities may enter.

In Psalm 16:8 is a *"Miktam of David."* This is one of those words listed in the beginning of the chapter. The meaning is no longer known. In this Psalm he is convinced God will not permit him to perish.

"I keep the Lord always before me; because he is at my right hand, I shall not be moved…In thy right hand are pleasures forever more." When they speak of the right hand of God, it holds all the good.

In Psalm 17:8 is a familiar phrase, *"Keep me as the apple of the eye."* We still say we are the apple of someone's eye. In the Psalm it means the pupil, the most precious part.

In Psalm 17:15 it is written, *"As for me, I shall behold thy face in righteousness; when I awake, I shall be satisfied with beholding thy form."* In the sense of awakening from the darkness of ego mind, we awaken to the light, to the Truth. At first we think of God in right-minded ways, seeing through a glass darkly. Then, when awake, we see face to face spiritually and actually behold the form or the Truth. This is quoted in 1 Corinthians 13:12, *"First we see through a glass darkly and then face to face."*

Psalm 18 is also in 2 Samuel 22 where *"David spoke to the Lord in the words of this song after being delivered from his enemies and from Saul."*

"The cords of death encompassed me, the torrents of perdition assailed me… In my distress I called upon the Lord; to my God I cried for help, and from his temple he heard my voice, and my cry to him reached his ears. Then the earth reeled and rocked; the foundations also of the mountains trembled and quaked because he was angry. Smoke went up from his nostrils, and devouring fire from his mouth;-glowing coals flamed forth from him." In verse 19, *"The Lord brought me forth into a broad place; he delivered me, because he delighted in me."*

This Psalm was most likely written when David and his men were trapped on a mountain. Saul's army came up one side and a local militia came up the other side. Just about the time defeat was near and David fell on his knees and counted it all good, a messenger came to Saul and said the Philistines were coming to attack him. So Saul and the militia turned away from David and his men to confront the Philistines and David was saved. It may not be easy to face certain disaster and call it all good, but a change in consciousness from fear to thanksgiving can change everything.

In Psalm 19 are some familiar lines: *"The heavens are telling the glory of God; and the firmament proclaims his handiwork…Let the words of my mouth and the meditation of my heart be acceptable in thy sight, O Lord, my rock and my redeemer."* This is a vision of a higher state of conscious that is just beginning to appear to humanity.

Psalm 20 is a hymn sung at the altar before battle: *"May he grant you your heart's desire, and fulfill all your plans! May we shout for joy over your victory, and in the name of our God set up our banners! May the Lord fulfill all your petitions!"* This is a wonderful affirmative prayer we can use in our own lives. We have many battles in our daily lives and an affirmative morning prayer like this will set us up mentally for a successful day.

In Psalm 22:18 is the familiar *"…they divide my garments among them, and for my raiment they cast lots."* This is the story repeated at the foot of the cross where they divided Jesus' garments and cast lots for his robe. This is a sign of the finality of someone's earthly life. We take our spiritual body with us and only the empty garment is left behind, the physical body.

Psalm 23 is the best known of the psalms. *"The Lord is my Shepherd…"* The words *"the valley of the shadow of death"* are also translated *"the valley of deep darkness."* It is ritually used at funerals, but it indicates hope when we go through valleys of deep darkness and despair in life. It reminds us we are never stuck when something goes wrong. That something is only a shadow. We go through it and emerge out the other side back into the light and into our joy.

Psalm 24 repeats the questions that must be answered by all who entered the temple. One could not enter the temple unless the correct answers are given. *"Who shall ascend the hill of the Lord? And who shall stand in his holy place? He who has clean hands and a pure heart, who does not lift up his soul to what is false, and does not swear deceitfully."* These are important questions to ask as we go into meditation to remind ourselves of what the entrance requires to our inner temple.

Psalm 25:4 *"Make me to know thy ways, O Lord; teach me thy paths. Lead me in thy truth, and teach me, for you are the God of my salvation, for thee I wait all the day long."*

This is a message of patience. We don't find the path of Truth by storming the gates of heaven or loudly demanding God's attention, but by quiet contemplation patiently aligning our minds to receive this blessed knowledge.

Psalm 25:15 reads, *"My eyes are ever toward the Lord, for he will pluck my feet out of the net."* How many times do we become ensnared in our own error thinking? The more we personally struggle the tighter the snare becomes. When we focus on God and turn our thoughts toward Truth, we are untangled and set free.

Psalm 26 is an affirmation that tells us we don't need to argue our point or innocence. We often argue to vindicate ourselves from some untruth spoken about us. It could even be some untruth of which we have accused ourselves through guilt or worry. Most often the more we try to extricate ourselves, the deeper ensnared we become. Even if we win the argument with others or ourselves, the scene continues to play in our thoughts.

The first words are, *"Vindicate me, O Lord..."* It is not our place to vindicate ourselves because we are not guilty. Only the Creator, Who knows our innocence, can relieve the guilt with which we burden ourselves. We affirm *"for I have walked in my integrity, and I have trusted in the Lord without wavering...As for me I walk in my integrity..."* This affirmation of Truth sets us free.

Psalms 42 begins Book II, A Maskil of the Sons of Korah. Psalms 42 and 43 are prayers for healing in preparation for a pilgrimage. They are a lament and cries for help. The following psalms alternate between anguish and blessing, as was the custom in that early culture. Many folks still live that way today, but we try to focus more on the blessings. The anguish of error thinking, which serves no good purpose, diminishes and fades away.

Psalm 50:12, animal sacrifices were offered all throughout the Hebrew Testament, and in other cultures of that time. This psalm makes it clear God does not want animal sacrifices but a sacrifice of thanksgiving. *"If I were hungry I would not tell you; for the world and all that is in it is mine...Offer to God a sacrifice of thanksgiving, (alternate translation, "make your thanksgiving your sacrifice to God")* We are required to sacrifice all that is not for our highest good, all thoughts that are limiting, all that depresses and causes us to think we are not worthy of God's great good. All that is God's is ours, so we will not speak of lack but of plenty.

Psalm 69:1 is David's cry of distress that mirrors how we feel at times: *"Save me, O God! for the waters have come up to my neck. I sink in deep mire, where there is no foothold; I have come into deep waters, and the flood sweeps over me. I am weary with crying. My throat is parched. My eyes grow dim with waiting for my God."* Sometimes we just have to cry out when things get too much to bear. But we do not dwell in self-pity and repeat long litanies of woes over and over. That would only increase our woes.

In Psalm 69:9 is another stressful situation. *"For zeal of thy house has consumed me…"*

Humanity, still developing, can find the zeal of religion or striving to attain the state of mind that is Godlike overwhelming. We can forget that we must connect it with our daily lives. Even then if we swing too far the other way, parading our religion or spiritual practice, it can create another problem. Humanity must keep its focus on its development and not parade its piety with outer trappings such as fasting and sack cloth.

"When I have humbled my soul with fasting, it became a reproach. When I made sackcloth my clothing, I became a byword to them. I am the talk of those who sit in the gate, and the drunkards make songs about me."

Psalm 71:9 is the prayer of old age. *"Do not cast me off in the time of old age; forsake me not when my strength is spent. For my enemies speak concerning me, those who watch for my life consult together and say, 'God has forsaken him; pursue and seize him for there is none to deliver him.'"* Enemy thoughts about weakness and aging that seize upon us and cause our bodies and minds to weaken. In our culture we are encouraged to prepare for the expenses of nursing homes with insurances, planning for our weakness to come upon us. And yet there are those who run marathons in their 80's and 90's.

Jesus said something similar about old age and preparing yourself ahead of time with spiritual understanding and power. In John 21:18, *"Truly, I say to you, When you were young, you girded yourself, and walked where you would; but when you are old, you shall stretch out your hands, and another will gird you, and carry you where you do not wish to go. Follow me."*

The Psalms are concerned with physical life, but the Gospels are about eternal life. Physical old age may come, but eternal life is forever young. It is easy for humanity to become fixed on the physical body and believe it is the ending of life. Age is a matter of mental attitude. Someone said you are only as old as you are behind the eyes. It is a state of mind.

Psalm 72 is a Psalm of Solomon to bless the king. It may have been for a coronation. An almost supernatural aura is given to the king in verses five and six. *"May he be like rain that falls on the mown grass, like showers that water the earth! In his days may righteousness flourish and peace abound, till the moon be no more!"*

At the end of this blessing it says, *"The prayers of David, son of Jesse, are ended."*

Then begins Book III of Psalms.

CHAPTER TWENTY NINE

Psalms Continued

In Psalms Book III, Psalm 73, is a meditation on the justice of God. Like Job, David had difficulty reconciling God's justice with human suffering, and even with his own suffering. *"Cynical and wicked men seem to grow fat in their iniquity, but their prosperity is temporary."*

In Psalms 73:12, *"Behold, these are the wicked; always at ease, they increase in riches. All in vain I have kept my heart clean and washed my hands in innocence. For all the daylong I have been stricken, and chastened every morning. If I had said, 'I will speak thus,' I would have been untrue to the generation of your children. But when I thought how to understand this, it seemed to me a wearisome task, until I went into the sanctuary of God; then I perceived their end. When my soul was embittered, and when I was pricked in heart, I was stupid and ignorant, I was like a beast toward you; you hold my right hand. You still guide me with your counsel."*

The human mind sways back and forth, almost getting to understanding, but not quite. The psalmist kept his heart and hands clean, trying to understand. Even though he went into the sanctuary of God his mind slipped into vengeance – *"then I perceived their end."*

Ego mind creates a prayer that others will be destroyed. Ego mind can sound so logical. It always turns the person away from belief in God. It would have been a shock if they had known that Jesus said, *"Love your enemies!"* The ego mind only says, *"Fear and smash your enemies! In fact, why don't you do it for me God, so I can prove you are no better than I, the ego mind, am!"*

In Psalms 74:18 the psalmist again reminded God of his people that he brought out of Egypt. They wailed that the enemy burned the meeting places and tore down the holy place. *"Remember this, O Lord, how the enemy scoffs, and an impious people reviles your name… Arise O God and plead your cause…the uproar of your adversaries goes on continually."*

Many people are waiting for God to intervene in their lives, to do something, and become upset with God for not showing up to help them. The litany goes on assuming God is a person who is supposed to be listening. The psalmist expected God to strike the evil ones any day, and when He does not strike, there are the pointed reminders to God of his duties to his people. *(Psalm 77)*

> *"Has God forgotten to be gracious?*
> *Are his promises at an end for all time?*
> *Has he in anger shut up his compassion?*
> *Has his steadfast love forever ceased?"*

Still being envisioned as a super-human being type, God was spoken to like a recalcitrant child. Humanity still forms God in its own image with human feelings, emotions, and foibles. It takes a lot of development for humanity to release the anthropomorphic idea of God. It is in the Gospels that God is referred to as Spirit, and we must worship God in spirit and in Truth, as Jesus said.

Psalm 84 is a song that has been set to music in today's world and is sung in many churches. *"How lovely are thy dwellings, O Lord of Hosts. My soul longs and faints for the courts of the Lord. The sparrow has found her a home and the swallow a nest where she may lay her young, at thy altars O Lord of hosts, my King and my God. For a day in thy courts is better than a thousand elsewhere. I would rather be a doorkeeper in the house of my God than to dwell in the tents of wickedness."*

Psalm 90 has an interesting comment on life span. *"The years of our life are threescore and ten, or even by reason of strength fourscore, yet their span is but toil and trouble; they are soon gone, and we fly away."*

For all the times it is mentioned that patriarchs lived to 150 or 600 or 800 years, still 40 to 50 years was considered the life span. This brings up the question, were those huge life spans just symbolic? It was assumed that long life was the reward for good works. Longer life spans were ascribed to the biblical fathers and mothers perhaps to symbolize their importance.

Psalm 91 is about God's protection was also put to modern music. It begins *"He who dwells in the shelter of the Most High."* Humanity is beginning to be aware of the protection that higher mind, higher understanding provides. They don't understand the nature of God as yet, but still see God as wrathful and vengeful. So there is a mixture of images that still need to be sorted out as humanity develops.

Psalm 91:5 is special because it encourages you to always stand under the shield of faith regardless of the appearance or situation. *"You will not fear the terror of the night nor the arrow that flies by day, nor the pestilence that stalks in darkness nor the destruction that wastes at noonday."* Keeping a loving attitude and standing fast in faith keeps us safe from the *"snare of the fowler."* Living in ego mind makes one a target for the arrows of others. Many times there will be arrows of criticism aimed at you, but they will not come near or upset you. Staying in spirit and only looking with the eyes, not the emotions or feelings will dissipate any attack. Harbor no thoughts of retaliation and hold no grudges. Those things open you to attack.

The running affirmation throughout the psalms is that good will prevail and evil will fail. This is not too unlike our affirmations and denials. We affirm that good will be our experience and deny evil any power over us. Evil was attributed to their human enemies of that time. But our internal enemies of negative thinking are no less destructive.

Psalm 96:7 is a liturgy, calling people to worship, and also about God reigning on earth.

"Ascribe to the Lord, O families of the peoples; Ascribe to the Lord glory and strength! Ascribe to the Lord the glory due his name; bring an offering and come into his courts! Worship the Lord in holy array; tremble before him, all the earth!"

There are many rules of worship written in Deuteronomy and other places, but the psalms get into the rhythm and heartbeat of worship. Humanity is beginning to develop something deeper in worship than just rules and proper execution of rituals. Humanity is developing a longing for a very personal relationship with God, longing for a personal response as they sing their songs.

Psalm 101 is a psalm of David, affirming again, *"I will walk with integrity of heart within my house; I will not set before my eyes anything that is base (worthless)."* My house means my mind, my consciousness. The second part has to do with what affects the consciousness. What we choose to look upon and the value we give it, informs its likeness in us and it comes into our experience.

We saw one example of this when Jacob was sorting out his sheep from his father-in-law Laban's sheep. Jacob promised to take only the spotted ones. He carved the bark of sticks into stripes to place over the watering trough so the eyes of the sheep would see the stripes as they were breeding. This produced spotted offspring. Jacob's spotted flocks grew and prospered him.

What we focus our minds upon determines what will manifest in our lives. We don't know if this is true of sheep, but we do know it is true of humanity. Someone said, *"Where our minds go our behinds go."* Where we are focused is our pathway. When we want change, we change our mental focus.

In Psalm 102, illness was still ascribed to God's anger toward the individual. This belief that God inflicted illness and torture still exists with many people today. People believe God is angry with them or has forgotten them. Verses 3 through 10 are a very poetic lament and the agony of every spurned lover. *"My days pass away like smoke, my bones burn like a furnace, my heart is smitten like grass and withered; I forget to eat my bread…I lie awake, I eat ashes like bread, and mingle my tears with my drink, because of your indignation and anger; for you have taken me up and thrown me away."*

In Psalm 103, a psalm of David, there is a different tone. He has discerned love in his relationship to God. This is another important step in the development of humanity. It is a striving to understand the relationship at a higher level. The ancient fear of the thunder and lightning was no longer projected onto a relationship with a deity. The violent language of God's wrath and man's need for obeisance and self-flagellation was being abandoned. These words *"fear the Lord"* are still prevalent, but this was a matter of choice by the translator. Fear of the Lord means reverence, awe, marvel, and wonder.

In Psalm 103:6, far different from Psalm 102, humanity has reached a higher understanding of God.

"The Lord works vindication and justice for all who are oppressed.

"The Lord is merciful and gracious, slow to anger and abounding in steadfast love.

"As far as the east is from the west, so far does he remove our transgressions from us."

"The love of the Lord is from everlasting to everlasting."

Psalms Book IV

"Psalm 107 is a song that may have been sung by groups of pilgrims who came to Jerusalem to celebrate one of the feasts. A song of thanksgiving because the Lord delivered them from trouble." Oxford RSV notes p. 740

Psalm 107 is nearly identical to the story of Jesus calming the Sea of Galilee to save his frightened disciples. Psalms reads *"They cried to the Lord in their distress and he delivered them from their trouble; he made the storm be still and the waves of the sea were hushed. Then they were glad because they had quiet and he brought them to their desired heaven."* When we pray we are delivered from the storms of our own thinking and we discover that the quiet we experience is heaven.

Psalm 110 is a royal song probably composed for a coronation. *"Sit at my right hand, till I make your enemies your footstool. The Lord has sworn and will not change his mind, 'You are a priest forever after the order of Melchizedek.'"*

Melchizedek was the priest, ruler, and king of ancient Salem, now known as Jerusalem. He was said to be without genealogy and we could see him as an early expression of the Christ. We first heard of him when Abraham came back from wars and tithed to Melchizedek. This was the first time tithing was introduced. In the Book of Hebrews the writer speaks more extensively of Melchizedek. The writer points out that the Levites cannot continue their priesthood because they die, but Melchizedek and Jesus Christ do not die but go on for eternity.

Because the name is carried on into the Epistles, it indicates this is a sacred concept, belief or Truth that is carried forward from Genesis, the thread of which leads to Christ consciousness. Even at the beginning of human development the spark of the divine is active. It shows up in this priest, in Joshua, David, Isaiah, Elijah and Elisha. Mortal humanity is anchored in the sacred and the sacred becomes the spiritual foundation for the next stages of development.

In Psalm 116, *"I love the Lord because he has heard my voice and my supplications. Because he inclined his ear to me, therefore I will call on him as long as I live."* There is a growing belief now in answered prayer. Once we experience answered prayer, we are inspired to continue the practice. And the more we practice the more we learn, and more consistent are the results, as attested to by Silent Unity, a worldwide prayer service which has existed for over 125 years.

Psalm 119 is a covenant to study and keep God's laws. *"Blessed are those who keep his testimonies, who seek him with their whole heart, who also do no wrong, but walk in his ways!"* The word blessed means prospered, expanded. Those who seek God's law with their whole heart are prospered. The law does not respond to the casual observer. To receive the blessings one has to be immersed in higher law and faithful to its teachings.

Psalm 119:89 continues to describe this law. *"Forever your word is firmly fixed in the heavens. Your faithfulness endures to all generations; you have established the earth and it stands fast, for all things are your servants. If your law had not been my delight, I should have perished in my affliction. I will never forget your precepts; for by them you have given me life. I am yours, save me… O, how I love your law! It is my meditation all the day… Your word is a lamp to my feet and a light on my path."*

The great Truth coming through here is to love Higher Law, to delight in it, to let it give you new life, and be a light on your path. The law works when we know it, understand it, we love its purity, and pray for wisdom in using it.

Psalm 121 is a short one and very familiar. *"I lift up my eyes to the hills. From whence does my help come? My help comes from the Lord, who made heaven and earth. He will not let your foot be moved, he who keeps you will not slumber. Behold, he who keeps Israel will neither slumber nor sleep. The Lord is your keeper; The Lord is your shade on your right hand. The sun shall not smite you by day nor the moon by night. The Lord will keep you from all evil. The Lord will keep your going out and your coming in from this time forth forever more."* This is a tremendous affirmative prayer of truth that is a reminder of God's unfailing love and support.

From here to Psalm 134 are short liturgies. A most memorable one is 133 *"Behold how good and pleasant it is when brothers dwell in unity!"*

Psalm 136 is a call and response still used in services today in some churches. They are couplets, the second part repeats each time: *"for his steadfast love endures forever."*

Psalm 139 is a declaration of David. This is a fabulous one to copy or keep book marked to relieve doubt or loneliness. It is an affirmation of the Truth of your creation and that you dwell in God forever. *"You know me when I sit down and when I rise up; and you discern my thoughts from afar…whither shall I go from your Spirit? Or whether shall I flee from your presence? If I ascend to heaven, you are there! If I make my bed in Sheol you are there! If I take the wings of the morning and dwell in the uttermost parts of the sea, even there your hand will lead me and your hand right hand will hold me…for you did form my inward parts and you knit me together in my mother's womb…Wonderful are your works! You know me right well…How precious to me are your thoughts, O God! How vast is the sum of them, they are more than sand. (If I would come to the end), when I awake I am still with you."*

ow Psalm 141 has some good advice and a prayer for deliverance from any temptation to speak evil or give in to error thinking. *"Set a guard over my mouth, O Lord, keep watch over the door of my lips. Incline not my heart to evil…"* Jesus taught *"Let your yes be yes and your no be no. All else is evil."* We are prone to rationalize, explain and otherwise defend ourselves leading to the slanting the facts in our favor. There is no good result in this way of thinking.

The rest of the Psalms to 150 are hymns of praise, most of them written by David. Praise and gratitude are an essential part of our consciousness. A most important thing is to maintain an attitude of gratitude and thanksgiving for all the good throughout our lives.

CHAPTER THIRTY

Proverbs, Ecclesiastes, & the Prophets

Humanity became ready to hear wisdom at this point in its development. In prior stages, there was not yet a place or capacity ready to receive it. Humanity had developed enough to encounter ideas of love and commitment to God as in the Psalms. Now the development had reached readiness to understand something of wisdom.

"The Book of Proverbs is a compendium of moral and religious instruction as given to Jewish youth by professional sages in the post-exilic period. It includes much older material from the long tradition of such training in the wisdom deemed necessary for the good life." (RSV p. 769) This is a textbook for wisdom schools. Our schools, colleges and universities of today do not teach students how to live, but more often prepare them to find a career. We have few if any wisdom schools in the modern world. Early universities and yeshivas taught wisdom and literature, mostly to repopulate their faculty. The schools and universities of today have turned to training for jobs and careers, the Master of Business Arts being one of the most coveted.

There are four main parts in this book. Each is a separate work with its own title.

Book One, Proverbs 1:2, is a prologue entitled an Invitation to Wisdom. *"That men may know wisdom and instruction, understand words of insight, receive instruction in wise dealing, righteousness, justice, and equity; that prudence may be given to the simple, knowledge and discretion to the youth—the wise man also may hear and increase learning, and the man of understanding acquire skill, to understand a proverb and a figure, the words of the wise their riddles."*

Book Two beginning with Proverbs 10 is a book of wise sayings. *"A wise child makes a glad father, but a foolish child is a mother's grief. Treasures gained by wickedness do not profit, but righteousness delivers from death. The Lord does not let the righteous go hungry, but he thwarts the cravings of the wicked. A slack hand causes poverty, but the hand of the diligent makes rich."*

These are a just a few of many, many wise sayings. Some of them may sound strange because they come from different cultures and eras. But they are fascinating to read and you will find golden nuggets of wisdom for your life.

Book Three beginning with Proverbs 22 contains a series of exhortations that resemble the instructions of the Egyptian sages. It appears to have been modeled upon the Egyptian Book of Wisdom that may be older than 1000 B.C. entitled *"The Instruction of Amen-em-ope,"*

Since Proverbs is such an old text, other updated versions can add delightful color and often more clarity. There are translations that use different words such as, *"be not evil"* translated to *"be not stupid."* The ego mind would have us be stupid, listen to its fear mongering and live in limitation and death. Below are a few examples of exhortations to living in goodness.

Proverbs 22:1 *"A good name is to be chosen rather than great riches, and favor is better than silver or gold...Train children in the right way, and when old, they will not stray...Drive out the scoffer and strife goes out; quarreling and abuse will cease...Make no friends with those who are given to anger, and do not associate with hotheads."*

Many of these couplets are repeated many times throughout the book and it is worth reading through them, even to study them. Our world could do with a closer look at the wisdom in the Book of Proverbs. Having developed a capacity for love in the Psalms and for wisdom in Proverbs, humanity became ready for a bit of philosophy to balance its experiences and resulting questions.

The Book of Ecclesiastes

Humanity had now begun to develop the budding faculty of reason. In this stage of development it began to ponder the meaning of human existence and what good mankind could find in life. *"Meaningless," says Qohelet (teacher), "everything is meaningless."* How does this pessimistic perspective fit into the rest of the development process? This is a difficult period of development because ego mind arises like a specter causing us to doubt everything and even despair of anything good happening.

From Michael V. Fox, an American biblical scholar and highly regarded authority on biblical wisdom literature writes, *"The boldest, most radical notion in the book is [...] the belief that the individual can and should proceed toward truth by means of his own powers of perception and reasoning; and that he can in this way discover truths previously unknown."* When humanity looks for deeper meaning at the level of intellect it doesn't find it. Everything eventually looks meaningless and empty. The author of Ecclesiastes appears agnostic on the concept of an afterlife. He writes *"All go to one place; all are from the dust, and all turn to dust again. Who knows whether the human spirit goes upward and the spirit of animals goes downward to the earth?"*

According to the Talmud, the point is to state that all is futile under the sun. One should therefore put all one's efforts towards that which is *above* the sun. This is summed up in the second to last verse in *Ecclesiastes 12, "The end of the matter; all has been heard. Fear God, and keep His commandments; for that is the whole duty of everyone for God will bring every deed into judgment, including every secret thing, whether good or evil."*

A great portion of the book concerns itself with death. Qoheleth emphatically affirms human mortality, going so far as to say that the dead in Sheol know nothing. Humanity has begun to face its mortality and the fear of death. Religion was created to stand as a buffer between people and their impending death. People are the only ones of the animal population that know they will eventually die. Animals have survival instinct, but don't face the constant anxious thought of death throughout their lives. Religion created ideas such as heaven and hell, purgatory, Sheol, Gehenna, hell fire, nirvana, etc. There seems to be more hells than heavens, just as we have many more names for negative emotions than for the positive ones, leading to more error thoughts than positive ones.

The Prophets

In the next stage of development the prophetic thoughts within us arise, exhorting us to stay on track with God and goodness. The prophets were the only ones allowed to speak to the kings and other powers that were, to warn and upbraid them for their shortcomings. The whole development of humanity is now coming together preparing for the great step into spirituality. The meanings of their names are the qualities needed for this next stage. As humanity moves through this last step it is still tottering a bit, unsure of how to maintain itself. The qualities all shout at us to hang on until the transition is complete. Eventually the voices die away and we move uncertainly but steadily into our spiritual life. The Course in Miracles says God takes this last step for us when we are ready.

In Malachi the last book of the Hebrew testament we read, *"Bring the full tithes into the storehouse and see if God will not pour out a blessing for you that is so great you will not be able to contain it all."* We bring our entire being into the realm of God ready to experience the blessings of our spiritual nature. The human mind will not be able to contain the blessings that come, but the spiritual mind beginning to unfold within us has unlimited capacity and will welcome them all.

There are four prophetic scrolls: Isaiah, Jeremiah, Ezekiel, and the Book of Twelve. The meanings are from the *Metaphysical Bible Dictionary*

Isaiah: Salvation, Deliverance
Jeremiah: God Enthroned
Ezekiel: God is Powerful, relies on spirit

The scroll of the Book of Twelve contains small prophetic books named after these prophets. These are their names and the Hebrew meaning of each name. The meanings make clear that prophetic thoughts, glimmerings of higher thought, are progressive. They prepare to raise humanity up to its entrance into the spiritual consciousness.

Hosea: Deliverance, Safety, Salvation, Help
Joel: Jehovah is God "The Anonymous Prophet"
Amos: Prophet of Judgment, Burden
Obadiah: Worshipper of Jehovah
Jonah: Highest Prophetic state of mind, a dove.
Micah: Awakening to Truth of being
Nahum: Compassion, Comfort
Habakkuk: Clear Vision, embraces Truth
Zephaniah: Mystery of Jehovah, secret place
Haggai: Joyous, Festive
Zechariah: Whom Jah (Jehovah) has remembered
Malachi: Messenger, Minister of the Lord

A favorite story is that of Jonah and the big fish. Jonah was directed by God to go to the city of Nineveh to preach to it and save it from its wickedness. Jonah's own fears most likely surfaced about this. Would they kill him? Did he speak their language? Why would God want to save a wicked city anyway? So the story goes, Jonah went in the opposite direction to escape God's order. He boarded a ship, which was threatened by a storm and the sailors wanted to know who was out of favor with their god. Jonah confessed and told them to throw him overboard. A big fish swallowed it and he remained in its belly for three days and nights. When Jonah prayed from the belly of the fish, the fish spewed him onto the shore. Again Jonah was instructed to go to Nineveh, which he did and he saved Nineveh. Afterward Jonah was angry and sulked. God asked, do you do well to be angry, Jonah?

This is our story of avoiding what we know we must do. Perhaps it is to make a phone call that we imagine will turn out badly. We find other things to distract us and soon fall into gloom and despair. When we pray from the belly of despair and finally make the call it turns out to be delightful. Even so, we become angry at ourselves for going through all the unnecessary pain, when to simply do it in a timely manner is so easy.

Having been reared in Jerusalem, Isaiah was the one well fitted to become the political and religious counselor of the nation. The experience that prepared him most for his important work was a vision of the majestic and thrice-holy God that he saw in the temple in the death-year of King Uzziah. In *Isaiah 6:1-13* he laments that he has seen the face of God while he is yet unclean or has *"unclean lips."* Seraphim came down and cleansed him of guilt and sin. Then the voice of the Lord asked, *"Who shall I send and who will go for me?"* Isaiah gave the famous answer that rings throughout history, *"Here am I! Send me."*

God sent Isaiah to teach those who *"hear and hear"* but do not understand, *"see and see"* but do not perceive. Isaiah asked how long this would take… *"How long O Lord?"* It ends when all is destroyed but the Holy Seed. All the blockages created by ego mind and error thinking are destroyed. Only spiritual thinking remains through which we truly understand and perceive the Truth of our being.

The fate of the prophets is in Hebrews 11:37. *"They were stoned, they were sawn asunder, were tempted, were slain with the sword: they wandered about in sheepskins and goatskins; being destitute, afflicted, tormented; (of whom the world was not worthy) they wandered in deserts, and in mountains, and in dens and caves of the earth."*

In our struggle to sort out who we really are, the last thing we want is someone constantly in our faces telling us we are wrong or out of favor with God. A self-critical nature will cause the subconscious mind to store that criticism and constantly bring it up to afflict us in terrible ways. The "prophet thoughts" continually point out where we have erred and the ego mind smites them wanting us to believe that we are forever at fault.

Isaiah 2:4 gave his prophecy for world peace and envisioned a time when it would be right for the people to *"beat their swords into plowshares,"* but not while evil people existed. In contrast the prophet Joel, in Joel 4:10, envisioned a time when it would be necessary for good people to *"beat plowshares into swords, and pruning hooks into spears."* This is confusing. Often he who beats his sword into plowshares ends up plowing for those who kept their swords. It is difficult to accept those useful prophetic thoughts while battling the ego mind's constant efforts to confuse.

In Isaiah 7:14 Isaiah counseled King Ahaz who was in a tough spot. Isaiah told him to sit back, be calm, be quiet, and stay out of the revolutions taking place. But Ahaz couldn't resist jumping into the fray. The Syro-Israelite alliance, Assyrian Empire, and Phoenicia, were all literally surrounding Judah. It is called Judah's covenant with death. Isaiah echoed Exodus 14:14 that admonished them to stand still and let

God fight their battles. We struggle endlessly with life situations only to go down in flames, when to stand still would win the day.

As a last ditch stand, Isaiah offered King Ahaz the "Immanuel Sign," or the prophecy of a messianic figure, a child born to a young woman, assumed to be the king's young wife. It didn't work and Ahaz stormed into battle anyway. The Assyrians swept through the land, devastating not only Syria and Israel, but also Judah farther south. King Ahaz symbolizes humanity that is not yet ready to leave the battlefield of ego mind, not yet ready to accept the higher calling.

Deep in consciousness is the Truth of our being. That early implanting of the Immanuel or Christ image by Isaiah remains fertile but dormant. When we are exposed to a spiritual teaching the words come out our mouths, *"this is what I have always believed."* Yes, the Truth is within us and we recognize its emergence into our experience immediately.

In Zephaniah 3:17 is this wonderful blessing as we become willing to turn all over to God. *"The Lord thy God is in the midst of you; a warrior who gives victory; he will rejoice over you with gladness, he will renew you in his love; he will exult over you with singing as on a day of festival!"* This is the Truth of our being emerging more powerfully into consciousness that God is in the very midst of us giving us victory and joy.

Malachi is the last book in the Hebrew Testament. It is time to bring our whole selves, our whole development as humanity, warts and all, into God's storehouse of blessing. We need hide nothing, even the unresolved areas that still plague us. Malachi 3:10 reads, *"Bring the full tithes into the storehouse…thereby put me to the test…I will open the windows of heaven to you and pour out an overflowing blessing."* Humanity was ready for the Gospels and the spiritual teaching of Truth that would lift it into spiritual living, the expression of the divinity within, the Christ.

CHAPTER THIRTY ONE

The New Testament

Prophets and kings of the Hebrew Testament are now dead. The great fathers and mothers now sleep as they say. These people represented the scaffolding that supported the psychological body as it grew to maturity, making humanity ready to build the spiritual body. The development of our spiritual nature begins in the New Testament.

A way to discern developmental progress is by the image of God that people create for themselves. In the Hebrew Testament God was thought of at first as the creator of all, remote and wise. Then God was reduced to a type of human who was temperamental, angry and retaliatory. The god created by the developmentally teenage brain, represented by the kings of the Hebrew Testament, was godly and wise only when things were going humanity's way and seen as a traitor when things did not. God evolves in man's thinking from anthropomorphic to Creative Principle, the Cosmic First Cause. The ultimate mature adult images are of God as a loving creator. Jesus called God "Abba" which affectionately means papa. The Apostle Paul referred to the presence of God within each person as the *"Christ in you."*

In the Hebrew Bible, humanity experienced physical and psychological development. It went through many different levels from the destructive behaviors of adolescent ego wars to learning about love and wisdom in Psalms and Proverbs. The prophets repeatedly pointed the way to God and righteousness. After the book of Malachi, the Hebrew Testament seems to leave humanity on its own to carry on, perhaps continuing to just study the wisdom of the past. But in the Gospels humanity can choose to take the next step into spiritual awareness and a higher way of perceiving life. Jesus referred to it as the kingdom of heaven.

The lessons in the New Testament are about the spiritual Truth of our being, the discovery and the use of spiritual power that is ours to wield. Although the stories in the New Testament are set in physical life circumstances, they are not about the physical life. They are lessons in spiritual growth. Spirit is one presence and one power but it is many faceted in expression, so there are many stories to demonstrate its meaning. The physical and psychological development grows upward like a tree trunk, but the spiritual has infinite branches that fan out in every direction.

The four Gospels contain stories about the life of Jesus, his experiences, teachings and parables. With some exceptions, the same stories and teachings appear in two or more of the Gospels, with small variations in details. But there continues to be a progression of teachings in the Gospels to tell us what the spiritual steps are and how to take them. In the Hebrew Testament humanity was pushed by biology and circumstances. Now we must make the conscious choice to build the spiritual body.

The Apostle Paul said *"It is sown a physical body, it is raised a spiritual body. If there is a physical body, then there is a spiritual body. But it is not the spiritual that is first, but the physical and then the spiritual." (1 Corinthians 15:44)*

There are two birth stories in the Gospels that Christian tradition has combined into the one popular story with which we are most familiar today. The birth stories in Matthew and Luke indicate that the Christ nature is born in us as an infant, because spiritual consciousness in humanity was still in its seedling stage. The story in the Book of Matthew tells us Jesus was born in a house. Only the wealthy lived in houses then. Magi from the east brought him rich gifts of gold, frankincense and myrrh. The Christ is born into the riches of the evolving spiritual consciousness. In the Book of Luke, Jesus was born in a stable and shepherds visited with angels singing all around. The Christ is also born into the humbleness of innocence and heavenly glory.

Every proper name in the New Testament has a Greek meaning. Only two names are duplicated between the Hebrew and New Testaments. They are Saul and Joseph. The name Joseph represents the increasing imaging power of the mind, imagination. Joseph of the Hebrew Testament imagined his future and imagined the interpretation of Pharaoh's dreams. Joseph as betrothed to Mary represented the change form imagining the physical to imagining the spiritual. The name Saul appears in the Epistles and is thought to be of Greek origin having to do with childish name calling rather than a proper name. Considering that Paul probably had difficulties that went back to his childhood, it is likely that other children taunted him as children do calling him a favorite Greek insult, "sauli." Regardless of the origin of his name Saul, he did become known as Paul when he experienced the risen Christ on his journey to Damascus.

There is a powerful cast of characters in the Gospels. First we meet Mary and Joseph, earthly mother and father of Jesus. The angel came immediately into the picture to explain to us that God was the father of this child. We are told that she and Joseph were not yet married and that Mary had not yet known a man, assuring the understanding that physical man was not the father of the infant Jesus. The message is that the physical is not the creator of the spiritual nature. The spiritual nature, the Christ, is God's Divine Idea for humankind and we are all created out of this one perfect pattern.

Jesus, the main character of the four Gospels, was first seen as an infant born in Bethlehem. After a short time an angel came to Mary and Joseph in the night and told them to take the child to Egypt to protect him from King Herod. The biblical writers said it was because Herod ordered all male babies to be slaughtered, but scholars feel that Herod would not likely slaughter babies and cause a terrible uprising in the population of Jerusalem. It is more likely that Mary and Joseph wanted Jesus to be trained by genuine Levite priests and not by the politically appointed priests in the temple in Jerusalem who were not of the priestly tribe of Levi.

At that time there was a huge Jewish temple on Elephantine Island in the Nile that was run by Levite priests. Judging from the ruins still there it was probably larger than the one in Jerusalem. This would account for Jesus' mature understanding of the scriptures at the age of twelve. We read in Luke 2:41 that he conversed about scripture with the rabbis in the temple in Jerusalem and they were amazed at his understanding. In Luke 2:52 it is stated, *"And Jesus increased in wisdom and in stature (years) and in favor with God and man."* This was the last thing written about Jesus until he reappeared at the Jordan River at age 30 to be baptized by his cousin, John the Baptist.

John the Baptist is another opening key figure. John represents the intellect still purifying with physical water baptism. He calls himself *"the one crying in the wilderness."* Our intellect is crying in the wilderness, knowing there is something more but it cannot lead us into the spiritual nature. Jesus stepped into this river of life and asked John to baptize him. As John baptized Jesus with water, the bridge was created for humanity to cross over from their physical/psychological state into spiritual development.

John the Baptist appears in all four Gospels. Dr. Herbert Hunt, in his "A Study of the New Testament," published by the Association of Unity Churches, writes, *"John started a chain reaction in providing the first six disciples…for Jesus' ministry. John brought to a close an old order… and gave place to the new way of 'grace and truth' through Jesus Christ."* The crossing over is also symbolized by some of John's disciples who left him to follow Jesus.

Jesus called the next characters, the twelve disciples, into his ministry and they are listed in a deliberately particular order. They represent twelve powers or principalities within us that are the essential pillars of our spiritual nature. These twelve tribes in the Hebrew Testament were the psychological seeds of these twelve powers. The twelve powers are called into the service of the Christ nature to be spiritualized and to function in a higher way. Simon Peter was called first, representing the power of faith. Without the faith that something can happen we will not be able to move forward. Charles Fillmore wrote, *"…faith quickens spiritual understanding."* Saint Thomas Aquinas wrote *"To one who has faith, no explanation is necessary. To one without faith, no explanation is possible."*

In faith we understand the reality of the unseen, the power of the invisible. Atoms are invisible, powerful, and the foundation of everything in physical form. Someone said the rate and character of vibration of the atoms determines the density of the form. Charles

Fillmore's famous definition of faith is *"Faith is the perceiving power of the mind linked with the power to shape substance."* Substance is explained in Unity's book, The Revealing Word, A Dictionary of Metaphysical Terms. *"It underlies all manifestation and is the spiritual essence, the living energy out of which everything is made."*

"To stir up the capacity of faith, we need to decide to have faith and to be faith-filled. The disciple Peter, who represents faith, discovered that it took practice. He stumbled time and again. When he stepped out of the boat on the Sea of Galilee, he momentarily lost his resolve when he saw how high the waves were. When he began to sink he called out to Jesus to save him. Jesus reached out to Peter, lifted him up, and said, 'Why did you doubt?' Choosing doubt instead of faith happens because doubt is born of fear and is always close at hand." The Divine Design by Carole Lunde, Ch 5.

The second disciple called was Andrew who represents strength. His name in Greek means strong man. *"Just as faith is an intangible, so we are speaking about the kind of strength that is other than our physical and moral fiber. True strength is not in the physical or emotional, but the Spiritual."* The Divine Design by Carole Lunde Ch 6

"Be strong in the Lord, and in the strength of his might," (Ephesians 6:10). Charles Fillmore calls this *"a strengthening affirmation...Be steadfast, strong and steady in thought...never let the thought of weakness enter your consciousness..."* Twelve Powers of Man, p. 38.

The third disciple called was James who represents wisdom or spiritual judgment. This is not the judgment of the ego that lays traps for us of temporary gratification and the illusion of power, or criticizes us to undermine our self-esteem. With wisdom and right discernment we judge what is God-like and what is not. We judge what is according to spiritual principle and what is not, and whether the actions we take reflect that principle. We never employ criticism that tears down, but do those things in loving ways that lift up and affirm God's goodness.

The fourth disciple called was John who represents love. He was described as the one Jesus loved. Notice that John was not the first disciple called but the fourth, because love requires a foundation of the first three, faith, strength and wisdom. That which we call *"love at first sight"* or *"falling in love"* in romantic situations is usually without those three spiritual foundations. The failure of romance can leave one feeling fragmented, disillusioned, alone and disconnected. When we love for the sake of loving without demanding a return from another person, we are always connected with the love of God and never disillusioned. Spiritualized love is the cosmic glue that holds everything together. Charles Fillmore wrote, *"Love is the pure essence of Being that binds together the whole human family...it loves for the sake of loving."*

The fifth disciple called was Philip who represents power. This power is concerned with spiritual mastery. Our words must carry with them the transforming vibration of Spirit that will go forth from us to change our world and manifest our good. Charles Fillmore wrote, *"The mind and body of man have the power of transforming energy from one plane of consciousness to another."* Power is not ours to enslave others or to take something from the world, but to lift us to a spiritual way of thinking and living.

The sixth disciple called was Bartholomew who represents imagination. In the story Bartholomew was behind a tree when Jesus called him. Jesus had to imagine him or intuit his presence. Spiritualized imagination comes into play powerfully in visualizing the unseen and creating our experience. We must be able to *"see"* what is not yet in physical form and not yet visible. At the same time we must be conscious of and able to see the power of Spirit working in our physical life experiences.

The seventh disciple called was Thomas who represents understanding. Spiritualized understanding means discerning the Divine within us and applying it in every day circumstances. Imagination must be connected to understanding because imagination can run wild unless we understand how to align it according to our spiritual evolution. Imagination is not a game we play for amusement, but a power without which we would be spiritually blind and unable to create.

The eighth disciple called was Matthew who represents the power of will. Psychological will is a function of ego mind and is aimed at physical goals. It fails sooner or later as evidenced by efforts to defeat addictions and stay on diets. Bill Wilson recognized the need for a spiritual component to the Twelve Steps of Alcoholics Anonymous. He called it the Higher Power. Spiritualized will becomes the Will of God to bring forth the highest desire of your heart. Our power of will is our forward motion as we lift up our lives to Spirit. Without the will to do something, we do not move forward. *"The will moves to action all the other faculties of mind…the will is the focal point around which action centers." Charles Fillmore Twelve Powers of Man P. 97.*

The ninth disciple called was James, son of Alpheus, who represents order. Order doesn't refer to putting physical things in order or to issue orders. The power of divine order moves upon the unformed to bring forth the new higher order or degree of being. It refers to a higher level of existence, of thought, and spiritual evolution. The Apostle Paul said we are to *"grow up into the head of Christ."* We are to become that new order of being, Christ as us.

The tenth disciple called was Simon the Canaanite who represents zeal or enthusiasm. This is the fire within that will light up or burn up your life, depending upon whether it is employed at the ego level, or it is spiritualized and placed under the command of the Christ nature. It is a fabulous power that gives brightness and joy to life. Jesus said, *"These things I have spoken to you that my joy may be in you and that your joy may be full." (John 15:11)*

The eleventh disciple called was Thaddeus who represents elimination or purity. We have the power to constantly release all waste physically and mentally, purifying ourselves on every level of being. Without this power we would not be able to let go of toxins in the mind and body. Every cell of the body is programmed to eliminate impurities to remain alive and healthy. Without this power the cells would immediately die. The mind also becomes toxic with error thinking and humanity must constantly release the negative thoughts and feelings that accumulate and poison its development.

The twelfth disciple called was Judas who represents life. This power generates the life of the body. The physical life itself is not eternal life, but is a physical force. Physical life is not the carrier of Spirit. As Jesus released his physical life on the cross and arose in Spirit, Judas hanged himself representing the lower vibrational level of life being released back to its atomic level.

Pilate, the Roman governor, was most instrumental in opening the way for the great demonstration of Jesus' resurrection. When Pilate had done his job, he washed his hands of the situation symbolizing the end of his responsibility. Jesus led up to this demonstration of preparing himself by first raising Peter's mother from a faint. Then he raised a child who had just died. He then raised Lazarus who had been dead four days. He was preparing, practicing if you will, to raise himself from the dead and into his next expression in living, visible and invisible. The Great Demonstration is that death has neither reality in God nor power over us. Death is not an ending but a doorway into another plane of existence in ongoing eternal life.

Joseph of Arimathea was described as a ruler of a city, who came to Pilate to ask for the body of Jesus to bury it in his family tomb. Pilate gave his permission but the body was not really his to release. Jesus released it into its atomic state. It was the final act in the story of Jesus' physical life. The next time Jesus appeared, he was in a resurrected state appearing to Mary Magdalene at the tomb, to the disciples in the upper room, on the shore of Galilee and on the road to Emmaus. Actually there were twenty-two incidents of his appearance after his death.

At last we meet Mary Magdalene who appears in the Gospel of Luke 8:2 as a follower among the women, but not named, and in all four of the Gospels at the foot of the cross and at the tomb in the garden. It has been assumed that she was the fallen woman about to be stoned to death and the woman who anointed Jesus' feet at a banquet. But it is not supported in the Gospels that they were all the same person. She was the favored disciple that Jesus first appeared to. He told her to go and tell the others and she carried his message of resurrection forth to the world. The divine feminine, representing the feeling/sensing nature within each of us, is always interfaced with Spirit and carries our awakening into expression.

These characters represent the character-istics of spiritual life that guide us on the path to spiritual transformation. The Hebrew Testament tells us what to do and the New Testament tells us who we are, what we are becoming as spiritual beings, and how that is accomplished.

According to the cast of characters, first step on the path of spirituality is the birthing, then the baptism into spiritual life, building the foundations and pillars of consciousness, and the great demonstration of life over death. Word went out first through Mary Magdalene, then the disciples and also the Apostle Paul so that all may know the Truth that sets us free.

CHAPTER THIRTY TWO

The Gospels

Matthew wrote his Gospel for the Jews hoping to convince them that Jesus was their long awaited Messiah. He began with a genealogy that went back to Abraham, their ancestral father. Luke wrote for the gentiles to bring them to the teachings of Jesus. His genealogy went back to Adam the first son of God linking Jesus with the Source of Creation. The Gospel of Mark is considered to be the oldest Gospel, perhaps written around 80 A.D. He was a pragmatist and did not include a birth story or genealogy. It is believed Matthew and Luke copied much of Mark's work and each added some of their own favorite teachings to their Gospels. The Book of John is the mystical Gospel, a completely different perspective from the first three. *"He takes us behind the scenes to the spiritual and eternal divine nature of this man." Introduction to John in RSV, p. 1286*

Several of the stories are told in more than one Gospel and a few are in all four Gospels signifying their importance to the teachers. The story of Jesus feeding the 5000 is in all four Gospels. Two more almost identical versions of this story use the number 4000, bringing the total repetitions of the story to six. The lessons in life we need the most come to us over and over in slightly different ways until we understand and embody them.

Jesus had much to teach about the power of Spirit and how it is used. He was speaking to humanity newly graduated from the physical and psychological development phases in the Hebrew Testament. In

Matthew 5:33 Jesus spoke of *"men of old"* in order to indicate an older belief and then he said *"but I say to you"* as an updating of this older belief. When he made a statement such as, *"Love your neighbor as yourself,"* it sounded strange to them even though he was quoting Leviticus 19:18. Until then even family members were rarely loved and never neighbors or outsiders.

Jesus had to begin with basics. He used stories with which the people were familiar and for his disciples he used direct teachings which were sometimes a mystery to them. The disciples asked Jesus why he spoke to them (the masses) in parables. In Matthew 13:10 Jesus said, *"To you it has been given to know the secrets of the kingdom of heaven, but to them it has not been given."* He explained that parables were used to teach the masses that did not have the deeper understanding. The direct teachings were for his disciples who were given higher understanding. The disciples were perceivers but the crowds were not yet able to perceive and understand meaning.

A well-known archetypal story is the Good Samaritan. A man was beaten, robbed and left dying by the side of the road. A priest and a Levite passed him by, but a Samaritan stopped to help him. The priest and Levite were filled with prejudices that caused them to pass on the other side of the road. The Samaritan had no such prejudices only compassion. Jesus broke down many of these prejudices and limiting beliefs with his acts and teachings. At that time a prejudice was that women were not to be educated, but he taught them anyway and empowered each one he met. We grow up with many prejudices that were taught to us. We might not even be conscious of them until they are pointed out. They limit us and keep us from developing the awareness of our spiritual nature or, as the Apostle Paul called it, our spiritual body.

Samaritans were not allowed to travel outside of Samaria and so could not worship in the temple in Jerusalem. But Jesus told the Samaritan woman at the well that God is spirit and we were to worship him in spirit...on the mountaintop and in the valleys. God was not just in the temple in Jerusalem, but God was everywhere.

A snapshot of life's journey

The story of the lost son, popularly called the Prodigal Son, is found in the Luke 15:11. It contains the whole process of our adventure into the material world and the return to our spiritual home. It is similar to the archetypal story of the hero's journey, identified by the American scholar Joseph Campbell. This lost son represents the same process of awakening to the spiritual nature.

There was a man who had two sons. The first-born represents the physical nature, static and complaining. This is our static religious nature rooted in the physical. The second-born son always represents the mental nature as we explained while studying the Hebrew Testament. The mental is the part of us that is adventurous, curious and desires to know more about life. He made mistakes that depleted his physical resources. The father represents the giving and forgiving God Principle that never changes, always gives and never takes away.

Both sons had access to the father's wealth regardless of their part in the story. The first-born stayed home. The younger one asked that his inheritance be given to him. He gathered all that he had and set off for a distant country, into materiality and sensation. He spent his inheritance in *"riotous living."* A famine came upon the whole land. In this lower state a famine comes upon our minds, emotions, bodies, relationships, and experiences, using up and depleting everything.

Whenever we squander our spiritual substance for material gain we create famine. We feel empty and starving for sustenance at all levels. The physical world will not give the nourishment we require. The younger son hired himself out to a citizen of that country and was sent to feed pigs. He had sunk to the lowest level, a hireling. He fed pigs. Jews considered pigs to be unclean and inedible. He ate the husks fed to the pigs.

We find ourselves chewing on the empty husks of the physical realm and we will not be nourished. Some chew on the empty rituals of the religion and find no nourishment, some on money and political gain. What are you chewing over and over in your mind, trying to find the satisfaction you crave? We must return to the Source. Before we can return to the Source we just come to ourselves, as it is written that the son *"came to himself."* We have to find the pathway home that is within us. We have to stop chewing on the empty husks of the outer world and turn inward. We return to the Father's house, the spiritual state of mind.

"I will set out and go back to my father." He set his direction. Then he set his mind. *"I will be humble, shorn of all my false pride, be willing to labor at the lowest rank in my father's house."* When his mind and direction were set, he got up out of the pigsty and returned to his father. He *"got up"* into higher consciousness and became teachable. We can't go to the Father in the lower ego state of pride.

"When he was yet a long way off, his father saw him...ran to him... threw his arms around him...kissed him." You don't have to travel huge distances to return home to Spirit. You simply start the journey by setting your foot upon the path and you are met before you go very far. There is no distance in God. God is immediately everywhere present not limited by time and space.

His father gave him a robe representing love, a ring representing wisdom and royalty, sandals representing understanding, and a feast for celebration. These are the gifts we all receive when returning from the ravages of ego mind to the blessings of God Mind.

The older son was jealous and angry, and refused to join the celebration. His father pleaded with him to come in and celebrate, but he preferred to remain outside to complain and feel sorry for himself. Folks often resent someone else's good. People can be short sighted and they don't see the banquet that has been prepared for them from the beginning of time. His father explained that a celebration must take place. *"Your brother was dead and is alive again."* Coming alive again to our true spiritual nature is cause for celebration throughout the universe. When one is lifted up, everyone can join that celebration and be lifted up as well, if they are willing.

Demonstration

Jesus gave demonstrations in the manifestation of prosperity, health, and well-being using the spiritual power within him. They are referred to as miracles. Jesus was the man who demonstrated this spiritual power in order to reveal to us our true nature by revealing his own. Demonstrations of Truth in our lives are the mirrors of spiritual growth. Spiritual teaching is academic unless it can be demonstrated in your life experience. In John 14:12 Jesus said we also are to do the works he did. *"Truly, truly I say to you, he who believes in me will also do the works that I do; and greater works than these will he do, because I go to the Father."*

He began with demonstrating command over the physical world at the wedding in Cana. His mother told him the wine was running out and instructed the servants to do whatever he commanded them. This was the beginning of Jesus' ministry. The divine feminine, represented by Mary, signaled that the wine of physical life had run out and his spiritual power was required to continue the feast. She was in charge of the banquet. The water Jesus commanded to be taken to the head of the feast became wine upon arrival.

The head of the feast upon tasting the wine exclaimed that the best had been saved for last! According to their tradition, the best wine was served first by the eldest and most important person at the banquet. Lesser wines were served according to each man's station in the community. Jesus had no standing at all, but was at the banquet because his mother was there. He was the least in the physical community and became first as the spiritual expression. His mother empowered his ministry and through him we step onto our spiritual path.

The water represents the potential that is transformed into the wine of spiritual life that never runs out, the spiritual that supplants the physical. When we look beyond the details of the story to see the lesson being expressed we find a valuable Truth for our lives. It is time for your spiritual nature to take over and be your focus now. The Apostle Paul said *"...but this one thing I do, forgetting what lies behind and straining forward to what lies ahead, I press on toward the goal for the prize of the upward call of God in Christ Jesus. Let those of us who are mature be thus minded..."* This is what Paul called maturing into the head of Christ.

Jesus demonstrated prosperity many times, but the most popular story is the feeding of the 5000 found in Matthew 14:13, Mark 6:30, Luke 9:10, and John 6:1-14. The similar teaching is the feeding of 4000 found in Matthew 15:32 and Mark 8:19. Because this story is repeated six times, it indicates that it is one of the most popular and important teachings.

When we are meeting an emergency, something is urgently needed. Urgency excites us and we bring sharp focus to bear upon how to demonstrate supply in the face of seeming lack. The magnitude of the need and its immediate resolution is a miracle to the intellect, but is natural to God Mind.

Long before this demonstration, Jesus had built into his consciousness the thought of God as omnipresent supply. He spent all of his life identifying with God Mind, his Father. To call someone "my father" in that culture was to claim to be the spokesperson for him. He had identified himself with God and with this omnipresent supply. *"I am the bread of life."(John 6:35)* We must be working on our prosperity identity all the time, seeing ourselves as one with the Source and speaking it into manifestation in our life experiences.

Practice

Feeding of the 5000 is the step by step process of manifesting abundance. Even though there are slight differences in the six stories, the writers all agree on the steps.

The first thing Jesus did was tell the people to sit down. This means quiet the "thought people" in your mind as much as possible. Andrew and Simon Peter went looking for food and found a young boy carrying his lunch of two fishes and five loaves. They took the loaves and fishes from the boy and brought them to Jesus. Jesus blessed them. Blessing means to affirm and confer prosperity or abundance. Then he broke the loaves and fishes. You take what is at hand. You break the mold or your usual way of seeing things which is limiting, and see instead limitless possibility. Then he gave. When you give your good is multiplied. The food was multiplied over and over so that all were fed. There were twelve baskets left over signifying that there is always an unending return for those who give.

This process is done completely in the mind. When we need prosperity or supply we become still. We change our thinking about what we already have. If you have two dollars in your wallet, envision unlimited abundance by blessing it. Then you give something in complete assurance that there is a return because of your right use of the steps of the law of abundance described below.

The Seven Steps of Demonstrating Abundance

Step 1 - Jesus located the nucleus of supply represented by five barley loaves and two fishes. It did not look like enough to feed 5000 men plus women and children, but it was a beginning. Look for what is around you. What can you begin with, no matter how small?

Step 2 – He established order among the people. He commanded them to sit down in families, ranks, and groups. You must first take command of your thoughts. Tell your thoughts to sit down in order and your mind to be quiet.

Step 3 – Looking up, he gave thanks. We rise above ordinary thinking to Higher Mind and give thanks that we are one with the Source and supply.

Step 4 – He blessed the loaves. Blessing means to prosper. When you bless something, you confer prosperity or expansion upon it. When you bless what is at hand you expand the molecules in it. It has been scientifically proven that atoms and molecules respond to thought. When one looks through a microscope indirectly using mirrors, their configuration does not change. When one looks directly without the mirrors, their configuration changes to match the consciousness of the one looking

Step 5 – He broke the loaves. In his mind he broke the mold, the boundaries, the limitations of size. We look at something small and see only smallness. We must break this perception in our thinking and see or visualize unlimited increase.

Step 6 – He gave the emerging abundance to the disciples to be distributed. All ate and were filled. We must give of the increase to fulfill the law. We are God's distributors of wealth, not the keepers and hoarders.

Step 7 – The twelve disciples gathered up twelve baskets full of the remains of the meal, loaves and fishes both *"so that nothing be lost." (John*

6:12). We gather up and retain the increase in consciousness to fuel our faith, lest we let the lesson fade away.

The disciples requested that Jesus teach them to pray. It would seem that he might have taught them prayer from the beginning as we do in churches. But Jesus wanted them to live in the presence of God and not depend upon an intercessor. He did not want them to memorize a prayer and say it by rote as priests did, creating a barrier between them and God.

The Lord's Prayer as we know it is a series of statements of Truth. It is not begging or beseeching. Jesus' prayer ends with *"deliver us from evil."* Redactors of the Gospels added the extended ending much later. As in English, there is an understood "you" such as *"you give us our daily bread…you deliver us from evil."* When you repeat it with the understood *you,* it is a completely different prayer. It changes from begging for daily bread to affirmation that the bread is already given.

Jesus' Great Demonstration and the centerpiece of Christianity is the crucifixion and resurrection. Life does not end with death. Life never ends. He showed by public demonstration that the death of the body is only a passage from one life experience into the next. The Apostle Paul also came to understand this, saying that if there is a physical body, then there is a spiritual body that is eternal.

Commonly Misunderstood Passages

There are misunderstood passages that point clearly to the need for metaphysical interpretation to understand their meaning. One such passage is in Matthew 13:12. *"To those who have, more will be given… but from those who have nothing, even what they have shall be taken away."* To those who have a prosperity consciousness more will be added. Those who have a poverty consciousness will continue to lose even what they have. Thoughts held predominantly in mind reproduce in our experience after their kind. Those who continually hold thoughts of poverty and fear, direct the power of God within them to produce more poverty in their experience. Likewise prosperity thinking increases prosperity.

In Matthew 15:21 and Mark 7:24 we find two versions of the story of the Syrophoenician or Canaanite Woman and her daughter. It is thought that Jesus called her a dog and refused her request to heal her daughter. Actually she referred to herself as a dog willing to pick up crumbs under the children's table. She had come wailing and crying through the crowd. The disciples tried to hold her back all day but she finally broke through to Jesus. Jesus knew he had to heal the daughter through her mother's consciousness and that could only be done if the mother were calm and quiet. When she said the dogs would gladly eat the crumbs under the table, she became still realizing she could not get the healing for her daughter by emotionally demanding it. It was in that moment of stillness that Jesus told her to go home, her daughter was healed.

We cannot accomplish anything in a state of anguish and emotional upheaval. In Genesis, God came to Adam in the cool of the evening, not in the heat of the day. We can commune with God only in a cool state of mind, not in emotional heat and shouting. In Exodus 14:14 it is written, *"you have only to stand still and God will fight your battles for you."* Lowell Fillmore, son of Charles and Myrtle Fillmore, wrote in his poem The Answer, *"I paused…ceased my anxious human cry, in that still moment…my prayer was answered."*

CHAPTER THIRTY THREE

The Divine Steps

Perception

Spirit is the invisible power and we make it visible by focusing our thoughts upon what we desire to see manifest in our experience. We call upon Spirit within us to look beyond the parables in the Gospels to understand the message. This is the practical level of the perceiving power of metaphysical interpretation.

One well-known story concerns Mary and Martha, friends of Jesus. Martha was busy in the kitchen preparing the Seder and Mary was sitting at the feet of Jesus listening to him. Martha called out to Jesus to send Mary into the kitchen to help her. Jesus' response was that Mary had chosen the better part and he would not take that from her.

The human part of us is like Martha, always busy in the world with physical things. Mary who is absorbed in the spiritual teaching represents our developing spiritual awareness. Our spiritual nature is the better part, the growing part, and the spiritual body we are building for our eternal journey. When we understand this deeper meaning we become aware of how we are living our lives and determine if our focus is only on our physical nature that keeps us limited or if it is on our spiritual nature that is limitless.

Transformation

Healing transforms the appearance of illness into the perfection of heath and wholeness already within each person. Jesus said healing was the law fulfilled. God's will is not sickness or poverty. God's kingdom is health and wholeness inherited by all. There are twenty-three stories of healing in the Gospels and according to the added text to the Gospel of John, many more healings were performed but unwritten. Editors added an ending that declares, *"…if every one of them were written down, I suppose that the world itself could not contain the books that would be written."*

Illness has been with us since the beginning of humanity. Illness was and still is attributed to evil spirits, sins, evil people, or bad luck. Jesus applied a higher law in the healing stories. He saw the perfection in each one and called it forth to manifest in their bodies.

We now know error thinking is the cause of illness. Race mind is filled with the belief in illness which affects the thinking of everyone who is not aware. Hence the majority of the world's population experiences illness. When Jesus healed the man born blind, the bystanders asked who sinned that this man was blind. Was it his parents, his grandparents? Jesus replied only that the law was fulfilled because the man was now whole. This is the higher perception of looking upon the spiritual perfection instead of just the physical appearance and looking for someone or something to blame. The law fulfilled is perfect good health. When we are ill and need healing we look to the perfection of our body temple as our reality. When people asked Jesus for healing, he did not see their ailment or imperfection. He saw the perfect pattern of health within them and called it forth to manifest in their physical experience. He said the things he did we would do also, but first we must understand and learn to bring the higher nature to bear upon the physical appearance.

Physical ailments are symbols of mental conditions prevailing in our consciousness. When the mental conditions are realigned with God Mind, ailments are healed. As we look at the healer and the one who needs healing in these stories, we realize they are both within us. Everyone has the power within them to heal imperfect perceptions and to transform in body and mind.

Living in The Light

In Exodus 34:35 it is written, *"…the people of Israel saw the face of Moses, that the skin of Moses' face shone; and Moses would put the veil upon his face again…"* When Moses went up onto the mountain to talk to God he was filled with the light of God. The illumination of his face frightened the people so he would put on a veil when he came down the mountain to them. But when he went up the mountain again to speak with God he would remove the veil.

The story of the transfiguration of Jesus is in Matthew 17:1, Mark 9:2 and Luke 9:28. He took Peter, James, and John up the mountain with him. They represent faith, love and wisdom. He went into intensive prayer, an exalted state of mind. *"And he was transfigured before them, and his face shone like the sun, and his garments became white as light."*

Luminosity has been noticed in the faces of spiritual teachers such as Harold Sherman, Fenwick Holmes, Charles and Myrtle Fillmore, and depicted in the paintings of saints. It is often shown as a luminous disk above the heads of saints, disciples and Jesus. This luminosity comes from within because the very cells are filled with light and shine forth.

Everything is made of atoms which are filled with energy and when ignited explode into light. Our very bodies are made of energy and light, and will glow when we are in an exalted state. Moses and Jesus came back down from the mountains, to indicate that we are not to live in that exalted state all the time as yet, but to bring the law or the light back down into our present circumstances.

We move on from the Gospels to the Epistles of the Apostle Paul and his scribes. The Apostle Paul was a mystic with an explosive and passionate nature. He started out as a policeman and murderer working for the Sadducees. He hunted down the followers of Jesus and imprisoned them. He was present at the stoning of Stephen, the martyr. On the road to Damascus to hunt down other followers of Jesus, he had a powerful spiritual experience of the risen Christ. After that experience he became an apostle to that which he called Christ Jesus. The scriptures do not say that he ever personally met Jesus even though they lived during the same time period. His experience was not with the physical Jesus but with a powerful appearance before him of the risen Christ.

The stories of Paul's travels and experiences show his efforts to live his spirituality and bring it into his everyday life, and the lives and practices of his people. Paul carried on the teaching in his own unique way. He confronted charlatans and false teachers. He preached to the Greeks from Mars Hill among their many statues of gods. They kept one pedestal empty in case they forgot one. He pointed to that empty pedestal and said that he wanted to talk to them about that god, the invisible God.

Living the spiritual teaching was and is a bumpy road. It is not the smooth heavenly highway some might imagine. In this world of physical life and experiences, the ego mind and outer events are always attempting to distract us from the spiritual path. Jesus was tempted in the Judean desert with the promise of temporal or political power. He declined in favor of spiritual power.

The Apostle Paul attempted to make a connection with James, the brother of Jesus and the Jerusalem church. All doors were closed to him even with the other of Jesus' disciples. Paul was reaching back to connect with the past instead of moving forward on his own path. When we try to return to the past, the things that used to work for us in a certain way no longer do so because we have progressed to a higher place in consciousness. We now use spiritual power instead of ego power. We interact with God Mind instead of personal or ego mind. When one attempts to move back and forth between these two levels of consciousness, everything becomes jumbled and confusing. People try to use spiritual principle for material gain, and material rituals and rules for spiritual gain. Neither works.

We can see that Paul struggled mightily to stay on track with Jesus' teachings and keep his congregations on track as well. Paul traveled constantly, teaching and exhorting listeners to follow the way of Christ. He founded churches and communities as he traveled around Turkey, Greece, and finally Rome, to establish "The Way" now called Christianity. When he would go back to churches he had established he found the people had reverted to their old pagan ways. He would again exhort them to be true to the teaching because he believed Jesus Christ would soon return. Paul could see the whole evolution of consciousness knowing that we were all created to be as Christ and bring the kingdom of heaven on earth. This has been misinterpreted thinking that Jesus would physically return down to earth from the sky in approximately forty-five days. He would be trailing clouds of glory and take the believers up to heaven above like Elijah's chariot of fire. This belief still persists in fundamentalist Christianity today.

Paul declared, *"I press on toward the goal for the prize of the upward call of God in Christ Jesus…"* His movement was forward and upward. And Jesus said, *"No one who sets a hand to the plow and looks back is fit for the Kingdom of God."* Luke 9:62

Revelation, Being the Light

There are indications in the Gospel text that there is something after physical death but no clear description of what that looks like. Jesus said, *"I go to prepare a place for you…"* but nothing further is told to us about it except we would need to expand our spiritual understanding before we could follow him there. In Matthew 22:30 when asked about who would be married to whom after death, Jesus said *"For in the resurrection they neither marry nor are given in marriage, but are like angels in heaven…God is not a god of the dead, but of the living."* He didn't say that we will be angels, but like the angels there will be no earthly bonds as in physical life.

The Book of Revelation contains a vision of that place. St. John the Divine named it the New Jerusalem. He described the appearance of the Divine One as filled with light and glory, the same terms as in the books of Daniel and Ezekiel. John said he rose up higher in spirit. He was carried over all the descriptions of the events of lower mind but never threatened by them. He went directly to the New Jerusalem. So there are actually two stories in the Book of Revelation, the high road and the low road. The low road leads through pain and agony to the refining fire and then to the New Jerusalem. Both roads lead to the New Jerusalem and you can choose the lower road of pain and difficulty or the high road of Spirit and blessing. Everyone evolves toward the upward call of Creation and no one is left out. Only the dross, the darkness of error thinking, is renounced and burned away in the refining fire.

There are great lessons in the letters to the seven churches to keep us tuned up and prepared to build the spiritual body. The first one is to the church at Ephesus. The name Ephesus means seeking satisfaction and the seeking must be raised to the spiritual understanding. The words, *"I have this against you..."* mean that you have something more to look at that is impeding your spiritual progress. This letter speaks of abandoning your first love, your first inspiration. Often we are so focused upon a path of achievement and gaining success that we become disconnected from that first inspiration. Married couples lose sight of the love that brought them together. Business people work so hard they forget the idea and inspiration that was there in the beginning. Repent means to turn around, look at what you left behind and regain it. This is the reminder to *"do the works you did at first."*

The second letter is to the church at Smyrna symbolizing substance, wealth and prosperity through the words *"You are rich."* The message is to be faithful even though difficulties come. *"Those that say they are Jews and are not,"* are the thoughts within our minds that pretend to be positive and spiritual but they are not. These thoughts often show up in the form of opinions and reasonableness from the ego mind. Self-criticism afflicts us, brings us down, and causes us to suffer inwardly regardless of what worldly riches we have.

The third letter is to the church at Pergamum symbolizing personal mind or ego mind. Ego or lower mind is always divided between pros and cons. Many believe in God and Satan at the same time. They fear the evil one and give it equal power with God in their thinking. *"You hold fast to my name"* shouting Jesus! Jesus! but still let the ego mind teach you falsehoods. This divided thinking is a stumbling block to spiritual progress. We cannot believe in God the Absolute and the devil or Satan at the same time. *"The sword of my mouth"* is the Word of Truth that carves away that which is not Truth and reveals that which is Truth.

The fourth letter is to the church at Thyatira, symbolizing the worship of false gods. Humanity still worships false gods often without realizing it. Those false gods are money, success, material things and anything that we are attached to in the outer world. Having those things is not the problem. Worshipping them is the problem. When we let go of these attachments we are given the *"Morning Star,"* a new revelation of Truth. We are set free of the limiting tethers of the material world. The Morning Star is a star of promise and a new day which leads to wisdom and glory.

The fifth letter is to the church at Sardis. It represents material riches but not wealth. *"You have the name of being alive, but you are dead."*

Some use the name Christian without being alive to what it means to be Christ. Claiming to be saved and continuing in the same lower state of mind does not indicate life. We are to awaken to our own Christ Nature and understand what it means to be a new being in Christ.

The sixth letter is to the church at Philadelphia meaning brotherly love. *"To he who conquers I will make him a pillar in the Temple of my God and will write on him the name of my God and the New Jerusalem which comes down from God and my new name."* When we are truly immersed in that great cosmic love called creation, nothing can take that away. In extending your emotional heart, you can be broken. But in extending love as an awareness of your true nature, you cannot be broken. Divine Love is *"An open door that no one can shut."*

The seventh letter is to the church at Laodicea meaning *"lack of feeling."* It says *"you are neither cold nor hot...Luke warm...I spew you out of my mouth! For you say 'I am rich, I have prospered, and I need nothing; not knowing that you are wretched, pitiable, poor, blind and naked."* Only in the riches of Spirit are we truly prospered and eager for our spiritual nature to manifest in every area of our lives. This is the most glorious adventure for which our hearts yearn.

Only the riches of Spirit are as refined gold. Here is the ultimate Truth for us, *"He who conquers I will grant him to sit with me on my throne, as I myself have conquered and sat down with my Father on his throne."* Earlier Jesus said *"I am in the Father, you are in me and I am in you."(John 14:29)*. We are one in God and Christ Jesus. There is no difference and no separation. The people have garnered riches, built huge cathedrals and millions of churches, fought wars over them, but in all that outer effort have never realized the Truth that is within them. Each one of us is Christ, as us, the offspring of the Living God.

A voice called to St. John the Divine and said, *"Come up (higher or here) hither...At once I was in the Spirit..."* And all the revelation rolled out below him. He was shown but was not cast down into the scenes. The book is filled with symbolism because revelations come in visions and not words. And he was taken high above the events below and carried to the New Jerusalem. There was no fear, but only observation. When we become observers of what is happening around us without involving ourselves in the lower mind of pain and difficulty, we become the Christ that blesses and heals.

"I John am he who heard and saw these things. And when I heard and saw them, I fell down to worship at the feet of the angel who showed them to me. But he said to me, 'You must not do that! Worship God!'"

Thus we come to the place of ultimate spiritual experience, truly one with the Creator in all aspects of our being. We are truly in command of the kingdom of our own being. We have gone into the courts of the Lord never again to fall into a lower state of ego mind.

From here when we have done all that is ours to do, God takes the next step for us. This is the mystery that exists for ages and ages. We go from glory to glory because we are God in expression. We are now God's eyes looking back upon the universe to the beginning of time and seeing the whole Creation all at once. And behold it is very good!

Spiritual Evolution

"A whole new world...a new fantastic point of view. No one to tell us no or where to go, or say we're only dreaming. A whole new world..." From Walt Disney's <u>Aladdin</u>

How did we get from a single cell to the multidimensional, self-observing, co-creating godlings that we are? We have gone from imperceptible movement to warp speed, watts to giga watts and we've only just begun.

God shows us that we are in motion through the ability to look back over the history of humankind, the evolution of species, and even our own yesterdays. Where was your life five, ten, or twenty years ago? Have you moved in your thinking, grown up and become wiser? Do you even resemble who you were back then?

We are shown the past, not to dwell upon it, or make it our future, but to perceive movement and growth. How else will we measure our progress? All I have to do when I am feeling stuck is think about where I was forty years ago. It was the dark ages of my life, despairing and lonely. I was floundering. Now I look at my life today and find it is fulfilling and transforming in so many wonderful ways.

Jesus said, *"...ask anything of the Father and He will give it to you..."* Ask to have your perception cleared and expanded. Ask to see more advanced designs for being. Ask to see the next dimension that Jesus was speaking of when the disciples asked where he was going. Always ask to see the next step, and the next. Don't be bashful or think you are arrogant for wanting to know. God's business is your business, as the twelve-year-old Jesus said to his parents. *"Did you not know that I must be about my Father's business?"* You are invited to partake in as much of God's plan for which you have created the capacity to receive.

Years ago the advanced thinking of Gene Roddenberry put us well along the road to thinking beyond our present boundaries. We have the equivalent of the silver screen in our minds and a projector, the faculty called imagination. We can project new images upon the screen of our minds, leaving out what we don't want, and freeing ourselves to progress into the realm of our good desires and beyond.

Marcus Bach describes something like this in his book, "What's Right with The World." He writes, *"It was an awareness, a sensitivity to a cosmic overlife – silent, mystic, an inner journey. A response to something... that is to remain beyond. The totality of God remains forever beyond us, and yet ever available to us."*

Even the most barren of deserts is teeming with life and potential. The Dead Sea isn't really dead. It doesn't have plant or animal life that we can see, but it is rich in mineral life. So rich in fact, that there are many industries around it drawing upon its riches. I was amazed at its beauty when I saw it. The water was so dense with minerals that we couldn't sink into it, but bobbed like corks on the surface. It was the color of a clear green emerald. The surface sparkled like diamonds, a huge field of diamonds. The mud is used for healing, as well as the mineral rich water, life and life giving.

Even a dusty barren land is full of potential. When you think you have run dry of ideas, ask God for more. When you can't see what is ahead, ask for the vision to see. When you need the right vibrational energy to accomplish something, ask God for it. Ask to see, ask to know, and ask to be more! It is there for you as surely as the riches of the desert and the sea.

"The floodgates of my mind had opened. It was as if an unseen intelligence was infiltrating the memory bank of my brain, selecting ideas that had been stored through the years of experience. I organized nothing. I though of nothing. I simply followed the stream of ideas." Barbara Marx Hubbard, *"The Revelation."*

Are there choices we can make in the next dimension of being? What choices can we possibly make for a world we do not yet know? Yet those choices are within us, ours to make. Pierre Teilhard de Chardin in his book "The Phenomenon of Man" said that we are on the leading edge of our own spiritual evolution. We are not pushed by our biology, but beckoned and invited by the Creator, the Omega, the Ultimate Absolute of Creation.

If our Creator/Sustainer has supplied us so richly in this dimension, we will not be abandoned in the next as we continue on. Jesus said he was going *"to prepare a place for us"* in the next experience in living. At that time he said we, as humanity, were not prepared to follow him, but we would be prepared eventually, if we believed in and practiced the things he taught. The Apostle Paul took it a little further when he said, *"Grow up into the head of Christ."* That Christ consciousness within each of us has what it takes to move into the next dimension where we will create an even more godlike expression in living.

We launch ourselves into the next stage of existence. Revelation called it *"the New Jerusalem."* Jesus called it *"many mansions."* The Book of 2 Corinthians 3:18 calls it *"changing from glory into glory."* Language as we know it is limited in its ability to express these higher experiences. A new language is already emerging. We are creating the words, the mental technology, and the spiritual super highway that carries us inward and upward.

We create the divine design of our own being as we go along. God is fascinated to experience the design through us, as us. God conceived creation and man is the manifesting of God in form. Man is the chooser, spearhead, and co-creative partner with God. Man, in Sanskrit, means hand. We are the hand of God stretching forth, creating with God, as God as us, throughout eternity, forever and ever, Amen.

POSTSCRIPT

My Favorite Passages

There are some verses I may not have quoted in the text but I love them for the blessings they conferred upon me just by being written.

John 18:6 expresses the power of the affirmation I AM.

"Then Jesus, knowing all that was to befall him, stepped forward and said to them, 'Whom do you seek?' They answered him, 'Jesus of Nazareth.' Jesus said to them 'I am he." When he said to them perhaps more forcefully than he intended 'I am he' they drew back and fell down to the ground. As they got up he again asked them, 'Whom do you seek?' And they said 'Jesus of Nazareth." And Jesus answered, 'I told you that I am he; so if you seek me, let these men go.'"

According to a great Unity Bible teacher, the late Rev. Ed Rabel, Jesus knew the spiritual power he wielded. When he stepped forward and declared I AM HE, that powerful vibration knocked those seeking him down to the ground. Jesus realized what he had done and gave them a chance to get up. He modified his statement by saying less forcefully, "I told you I am he…" so his plan could continue.

Unity teaches that the affirmation I AM is the most powerful. It is the name of God, our divine nature. When we connect it to a positive, such as "I am prosperous," we manifest prosperity. When we connect it to a negative, such as "I am poor," we manifest poverty in our experience. The I AM comes from God telling Moses, "I AM THAT I AM." When we use that same I AM affirmation we are connecting our divine nature to something. So we learn to say the words "I am" in connection with only the good we want to manifest in our experience.

John 16:33b "Be of good cheer, I have overcome the world." As we rise into our Christ consciousness we, too, overcome our attachment to the world and live free of its limitations!

John 8:32 "You will know the Truth and the Truth will make you free!"

Printed in the United States
By Bookmasters